Practical Mac Learning with R

M000312857

Define, build, and evaluate machine learning models for real-world applications

Brindha Priyadarshini Jeyaraman

Ludvig Renbo Olsen

Monicah Wambugu

Practical Machine Learning with R

Authors: Brindha Priyadarshini Jeyaraman, Ludvig Renbo Olsen, and Monicah Wambugu

Technical Reviewers: Anil Kumar and Rohan Chikorde

Managing Editor: Steffi Monterio and Snehal Tambe

Acquisitions Editors: Koushik Sen

Production Editor: Samita Warang

Editorial Board: Shubhopriya Banerjee, Mayank Bhardwaj, Ewan Buckingham, Mahesh Dhyani, Taabish Khan, Manasa Kumar, Alex Mazonowicz, Pramod Menon, Bridget Neale, Dominic Pereira, Shiny Poojary, Erol Staveley, Ankita Thakur, Nitesh Thakur, and Jonathan Wray

First Published: August 2019

Production Reference: 1300819

ISBN: 978-1-83855-013-4

Published by Packt Publishing Ltd.

Livery Place, 35 Livery Street

Birmingham B3 2PB, UK

Table of Contents

Data Cleaning and Pre-processing   47

Unsupervised Learning

Preface

About

This section briefly introduces the authors, the coverage of this book, the technical skills you'll need to get started, and the hardware and software requirements required to complete all of the included activities and exercises.

About the Book

Practical Machine Learning with R gives you the tools to solve a wide range of business problems - starting by forming a good problem statement, selecting the most appropriate model to solve your problem, and then ensuring that you do not overtrain the model.

About the Authors

Brindha Priyadarshini Jeyaraman is a senior data scientist at AIDA Technologies. She has completed her M.Tech in knowledge engineering with a gold medal from the National University of Singapore. She has more than 10 years of work experience and she is an expert in understanding business problems, and designing and implementing solutions using machine learning. She has worked on several real data science projects in the insurance and finance domain. This book provides a great platform for her to share the knowledge she has gained over the past few years of working in data science and machine learning.

Ludvig Renbo Olsen, BSc in Cognitive Science from Aarhus University, is the author of multiple R packages, such as groupdata2 and cvms. With 4 years of R and python experience, including working as a machine learning researcher at the Danish startup UNSILO, he is passionate about creating tools and tutorials for students and scientists. Guided by Effective Altruism, he intends to positively impact the world through his career.

Monicah Wambugu is the lead data scientist at a financial technology company that offers micro-loans by leveraging on data, machine learning, and analytics to perform alternative credit scoring. She is a graduate student at the School of Information at UC Berkeley Masters in Information Management and Systems. Monicah is particularly interested in how data science and machine learning can be used to design products and applications that respond to the behavioral and socio-economic needs of target audiences.

Description

With huge amounts of data being generated every moment, businesses need applications that apply complex mathematical calculations to data repeatedly and at speed. With machine learning techniques and R, you can easily develop these kinds of applications in an efficient way.

Practical Machine Learning with R begins by helping you grasp the basics of machine learning methods, while also highlighting how and why they work. You will understand how to get these algorithms to work in practice, rather than focusing on mathematical derivations. As you progress from one chapter to another, you will gain hands-on experience of building a machine learning solution in R. Next, using R packages such as rpart, random forest, Multiple Imputation by Chained Equations (MICE) and neuralnet, you will learn to implement algorithms including neural networks, decision trees, and linear and logistic regression. As you progress through the book, you'll delve into various machine learning techniques for both supervised and unsupervised learning approaches. In addition to this, you'll gain insights into partitioning the datasets and mechanisms to evaluate the results from each model and be able to compare them.

By the end of this book, you will have gained expertise in solving your business problems, starting by forming a good problem statement, selecting the most appropriate model to solve your problem, and then ensuring that you do not overtrain it.

Learning Objectives

- Define a problem that can be solved by training a machine learning model
- Obtain, verify and clean data before transforming it into the correct format for use
- Perform exploratory analysis and extract features from data
- Build models for regression, classification and clustering
- Evaluate the performance of a model with the right metrics
- Solve a classification problem using the neuralnet package
- Implement a decision tree using the random forest library

Audience

If you are a data analyst, data scientist, or a business analyst who wants to understand the process of machine learning and apply it to a real dataset using R, this book is just what you need. Data scientists who use Python and want to implement their machine learning solutions using R will also find this book very useful. The book will also enable novice programmers to start their journey in data science. Basic knowledge of any programming language is all you need to get started.

Approach

Practical Machine Learning with R uses a practical and hands-on approach to teach all concepts. You will explore different machine learning algorithms with a project-based approach. By solving problems using concepts taught in the previous chapters, the book demystifies the complexity of machine learning and gives you the confidence to tackle even more challenging problems.

Minimum Hardware Requirements

For the optimal student experience, we recommend the following hardware configuration:

- Processor: Intel Core i5 or equivalent
- Memory: 4GB RAM (8 GB Preferred)
- Storage: 16 GB available space

Software Requirements

You'll also need the following software installed in advance:

- OS: Windows 7 SP1 64-bit, Windows 8.1 64-bit or Windows 10 64-bit, Ubuntu Linux, or a newer version of OS X
- Browser
- R Studio
- R version 3.6 or later
- R libraries as needed (`mice`, `caret`, `rpart`, `groupdata2`, `cvms`, `neuralnet`, `NeuralNetTools`, `rPref`, `mlbench`, `knitr`, `interplot`, `doParallel`, `car`, and so on)

Conventions

Code, database table names, file and folder names, file extensions, pathnames, URLs, user input, and Twitter handles are shown as follows: "The pre-loaded datasets of R can be viewed using the `data()` command"

A block of code is set as follows:

```
# Installing necessary packages
install.packages("mlbench")
install.packages("caret")
# Loading the datasets
data(package = .packages(all.available = TRUE))
```

New terms and important words are shown in bold. Words that you see on the screen, for example, in menus or dialog boxes, appear in the text like this: "The **Help** tab will display all the information about the dataset. "

Installation and Setup

We will be installing R, Rstudio and R packages.

Installing R

1. R can be downloaded from https://www.r-project.org by clicking the **Download CRAN** as shown below:

[Home]

Download

CRAN

Figure 0.1: Screenshot of download link

2. Chose the mirror you would want to download from.

3. Further, based on the operating system that you use; Windows, Linux or (MAC) OS X, select the relevant link:

Figure 0.2: Screenshot of links based on operating system

4. Select **install R for first time**.

5. Download and run the executable.

6. Run the exe file and install in your local directory as shown below:

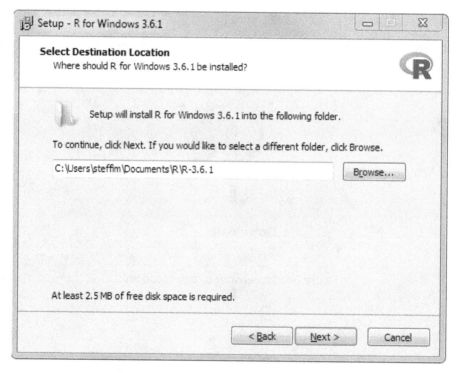

Figure 0.3: Selecting the setup location

Note

The current installation process is for Windows and will be similar for other operating systems.

Installing R Studio

1. Rstudio can be download from https://www.rstudio.com/products/rstudio/download/. Choose the Free version.

2. Based on the **OS** chose the relevant executable from below and download it:

Installers for Supported Platforms

Installers

RStudio 1.2.1335 - Windows 7+ (64-bit)

RStudio 1.2.1335 - Mac OS X 10.12+ (64-bit)

RStudio 1.2.1335 - Ubuntu 14/Debian 8 (64-bit)

RStudio 1.2.1335 - Ubuntu 16 (64-bit)

RStudio 1.2.1335 - Ubuntu 18/Debian 10 (64-bit)

RStudio 1.2.1335 - Fedora 19/RedHat 7 (64-bit)

RStudio 1.2.1335 - Debian 9 (64-bit)

RStudio 1.2.1335 - OpenSUSE 15 (64-bit)

RStudio 1.2.1335 - SLES/OpenSUSE 12 (64-bit)

Figure 0.4: Image caption in sentence case

3. Run the executable and install it, as shown below:

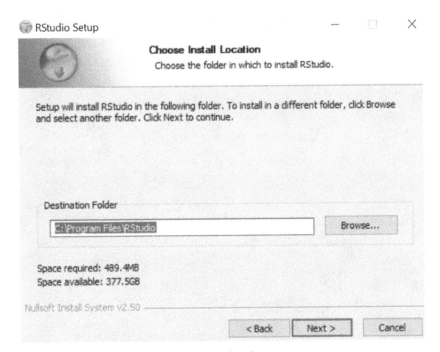

Figure 0.5: Image caption in sentence case

4. After installation, open R Studio in your computer. The following dialog box should be displayed:

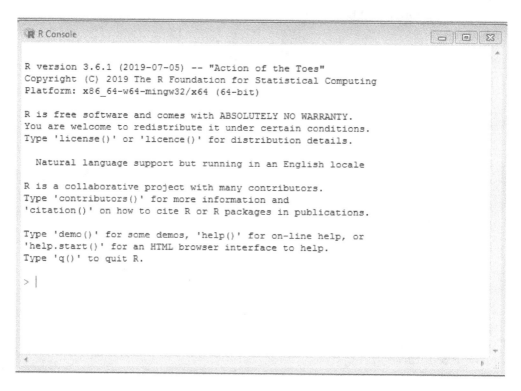

Figure 0.6: R studio dialog box

Installing Libraries

1. Click on packages tab as shown below:

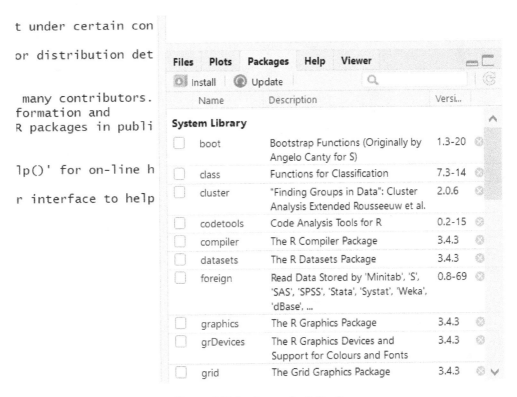

Figure 0.7: Packages in R Studio

2. Select the packages that needs to be installed. The package will be attached on the left as shown below:

```
Type 'q()' to quit R.

> library("MASS", lib.loc="C:/Program Files/R/R-3.4.
3/library")
> |
```

Figure 0.8: Attaching the package MASS

3. Now the function of this library can be used. To install packages that are not displayed in the above, click on the **Install** option:

Figure 0.9: Install option

4. Type the package you would want to install. For instance, select **ggplot2** and click **Install**:

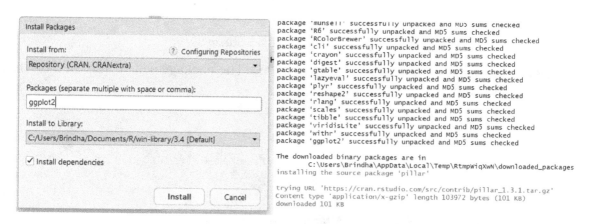

Figure 0.10: Install packages pop-up

The status of the installation of the package can be viewed in the console.

Alternatively, the `install.packages("packagename")` can also be used.

Installing the Code Bundle

Copy the code bundle for the class to the **C:/Code** folder (for Windows).

Additional Resources

The code bundle for this book is hosted on GitHub at: https://github.com/TrainingByPackt/Practical-Machine-Learning-with-R.

We also have other code bundles from our rich catalog of books and videos available at https://github.com/PacktPublishing/. Check them out!

An Introduction to Machine Learning

Learning Objectives

By the end of this chapter, you will be able to:

- Explain the concept of machine learning.

- Outline the process involved in building models in machine learning.

- Identify the various algorithms available in machine learning.

- Identify the applications of machine learning.

- Use the R command to load R packages.

- Perform exploratory data analysis and visualize the datasets.

This chapter explains the concept of machine learning and the series of steps involved in analyzing the data to prepare it for building a machine learning model.

Introduction

Machine learning is a process through which we use data to train models. These models are then used to make predictions on a new set of data that the model hasn't seen before. There are different types of machine learning models, such as supervised learning, unsupervised learning, semi-supervised learning, and reinforcement learning.

The data in a supervised learning model should have labels or an end result. Supervised learning models are broadly classified into classification and regression learning models. In an unsupervised learning process, we may not know the labels or the outcomes beforehand. Clustering is an example of unsupervised learning. Semi-supervised learning models use a combination of supervised and unsupervised learning. In reinforcement learning, an agent learns to navigate an environment with feedback mechanisms that reinforce the goal maximizing actions.

In this chapter, the machine learning process will be demonstrated through examples. The types of machine learning models will be explained and the different evaluation metrics are discussed. We will learn to perform exploratory data analysis and implement a simple linear model in R.

The Machine Learning Process

The **machine learning process** is a sequence of activities performed to deploy a successful model for prediction. A few steps here are iterative and can be repeated based on the outcomes of the previous and the following steps. To train a good model, we must clean our data and understand it well from the business perspective. Using our understanding, we can generate appropriate features. The performance of the model depends on the goodness of the features.

A sample model building process follows these steps:

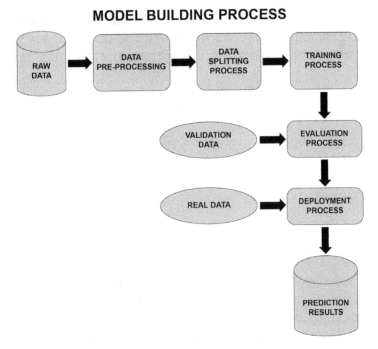

Figure 1.1: The model building process

The model building process consists of obtaining the right data, processing it to derive features, and then choosing the right model. Based on the type of output to be predicted, we need to choose a model. For example, if the output is categorical, a decision tree can be chosen; if the output is numerical, a neural network can be chosen. However, decision trees also can be used for regression and neural networks can be used for classification. Choosing the right data means using data related to the output of our problem. For example, if we are predicting the value of a house, then information such as the location and size are all data that is highly correlated with the predicted value, hence it is of high value. Gathering and deriving good features can make a huge difference.

Raw Data

The **raw data** refers to the unprocessed data that is relevant for the machine learning problem. For instance, if the problem statement is **to predict the value of stocks,** then the data constituting the characteristics of a stock and the company profile data may be relevant to the prediction of the stock value; therefore, this data is known as the raw data.

Data Pre-Processing

The pre-processing step involves:

1. Data cleaning

2. Feature selection

3. Computing new features

The **data cleaning** step refers to activities such as handling missing values in the data, handling incorrect values, and so on. During the **feature selection** process, features that correlate with the output or otherwise are termed important are selected for the purpose of modeling. Additional meaningful features that have high correlation with the output to be predicted can also be derived; this helps to improve the model performance.

The Data Splitting Process

The data can be split into an 80%-20% ratio, where 80% of the data is used to train the model and 20% of the data is used to test the model. The accuracy of the model on the test data is used as an indicator of the performance of the model.

Therefore, data is split as follows:

- **Training data** [80% of the data]: When we split our training data, we must ensure that 80% of the data has sufficient samples for the different scenarios we want to predict. For instance, if we are predicting whether it will rain or not, we usually want the training data to contain 40-60% of rows that represent *will rain* scenarios and 40-60% of rows that represent *will not rain* scenario.

- **Testing data** [20% of the data]: 20% of the data reserved for testing purposes must have a sample for the different cases/classes we are predicting for.

- **Validation data** [new data]: The validation data is any unseen data that is passed to the model for prediction. The measure of error on the validation data is also an indicator of the performance of the model.

The Training Process

The training phase involves the following:

1. Selecting a model

2. Training the model

3. Measuring the performance

4. Tuning the model

A machine learning model is selected for the purpose of training. The performance of the model is measured in the form of precision, recall, a confusion matrix, and so on. The performance is analyzed, and the parameters of the model are tuned to improve the performance.

Evaluation Process

The following are some of the metrics used for the evaluation of a machine learning model:

- **Accuracy**

  Accuracy is defined as the **%** of correct predictions made.

  Accuracy = Number of correct predictions/Total number of predictions

- **Confusion matrix**

  Let's consider a classification problem that has an output value of either *positive* or *negative*. The confusion matrix provides four types of statistics in the form of a matrix for this classification problem.

True Positive	The total number of rows in data that were predicted to be positive and indeed they are actually positive.
False Positive	The total number of positive predictions that were in not positive in reality.
False Negative	The total number of negative predictions that were in real positive.
True Negative	The total number of negative predictions that were indeed negative in reality.

Figure 1.2: Statistics in a classification problem

Let's take an example of patients diagnosed with diabetes. Here, the model has been trained to predict whether a patient has diabetes or not. The actual class means the actual lab result for the person. The predicted class is the predicted result from the trained model.

CONFUSION MATRIX		
Predicted Class	Actual Class	
	Positive [Has Diabetes]	Negative [Does not have Diabetes]
Positive [Has Diabetes]	True Positive [Patient has Diabetes]	False Positive [The patient does not have diabetes, but the model predicted otherwise]
Negative [Does not have Diabetes]	False Negative [Patient has diabetes, but model predicted otherwise]	True Negative [Patient does not have Diabetes]

Figure 1.3: A confusion matrix of diabetes data

- **Precision**

  Precision = True positives/(True positives + False positives)

- **Recall**

  Recall = True positives/(True positives + False negatives)

- **Mean squared error**

  The difference between the original value and the predicted value is known as error. The average of the absolute square of the errors is known as the mean squared error.

- **Mean absolute error**

  The difference between the original value and the predicted value is known as error. The average of the errors is known as the mean absolute error.

- **RMSE**

  Root Mean Squared Error (**RMSE**) is the square root of the mean squared difference between the model predictions and the actual output values.

- **ROC curve**

  The Receiver Operating Characteristic (**ROC**) curve is a visual measure of performance for a classification problem. The curve plots true positive rate to the false positive rate.

- **R-squared**

  This measures the amount of variation in the output variable, which can be explained by the input variables. The greater the value, the more is the variation of output variable by the input variable.

- **Adjusted R-squared**

  This is used for multiple variable regression problems. It is similar to R-squared, but if the input variable added does does not improve the model's predictions, then the value of adjusted R-squared decreases.

Deployment Process

This is also the prediction phase. This is the stage where the model with optimal performance is chosen for deployment. This model will then be used on real data. The performance of the model has to be monitored and the model has to be retrained at regular intervals if required so that the prediction can be made with better accuracy for the future data.

Process Flow for Making Predictions

Imagine that you have to create a machine learning model to predict the value/price of the house by training a machine learning model. The process to do this is as follows:

1. **Raw data**: The input data should contain information about the house, such as its location, size, amenities, number of bedrooms, number of bathrooms, proximity to a train station, and proximity to a bus stop.

2. **Data pre-processing**: During the pre-processing step, we perform cleaning of the raw data; for example, handling missing values, removing outliers, and scaling the data. We then select the features from the raw data that are relevant for our house price prediction, such as location, proximity to a bus stop, and size. We would also create new features such as the **amenity index**, which is a weighted average of all the amenities like nearest supermarket, nearest train station, and nearest food court. This could be a value ranging from 0-1. We can also have a **condition score**, a combination of various factors to signify the move-in condition of the unit. Based on the physical appearance of the house, a subjective score can be given of between 0-1 for factors such as cleanliness, paint on walls, renovations done, and repairs to be done.

3. **Data splitting**: The data will be split into 80% for training and 20% for testing purposes.

4. **Training**: We can select any regression model, such as support vector regression, linear regression, and gradient boosted and implement them using R.

5. **Evaluation**: The models will be evaluated based on metrics such as, mean absolute error (MAE), and RMSE.

6. **Deployment**: The models will be compared with each other using the evaluation metrics. When the values are acceptable to us and the values do not overfit, we would proceed to deploy the model into production. This would require us to develop software to create a workflow for training, retraining, refreshing the models after retraining, and prediction on new data.

The process is now clear. Let's move on to R programming.

Introduction to R

R provides an extensive set of libraries for visualization, data manipulation, statistical analysis, and model building. We will check the installation of R, perform some visualization, and build models in RStudio.

To test if the installation is successful, write this simple command as follows:

```
print("Hi")
```

The output is as follows:

```
"Hi"
```

After installing R, let's write the first R script in RStudio.

Exercise 1: Reading from a CSV File in RStudio

In this exercise, we will set the working directory and then read from an existing CSV file:

1. We can set any directory containing all our code as the working directory so that we need not give the full path to access the data from that folder:

```
# Set the working directory
setwd("C:/R")
```

2. Write an R script to load data into data frames:

```
data = read.csv("mydata.csv")
data
```

The output is as follows:

```
  Col1 Col2 Col3
1   1    2    3
2   4    5    6
3   7    8    9
4   a    b    c
```

Other functions that are used to read files are **read.table()**, **read.csv2()**, **read.delim()**, and **read.delim2()**.

R scripts are simple to write. Let's move on to operations in R.

Exercise 2: Performing Operations on a Dataframe

In this exercise, we will display the values of a column in the dataframe and also add a new column with values into the dataframe using the **rbind()** and **cbind()** functions.

1. Let's print **Col1** values using the **dataframe["ColumnName"]** syntax:

```
data['Col1']
  Col1
```

The output is as follows:

```
1   1
2   4
3   7
4   a
```

2. Create a new column **Col4** using **cbind()** function. This is similar to **rbind()**:

```
cbind(data,Col4=c(1,2,3,4))
```

The output is as follows:

```
  Col1 Col2 Col3 Col4
1   1    2    3    1
2   4    5    6    2
3   7    8    9    3
4   a    b    c    4
```

3. Create a new row in the dataframe using the **rbind()** function:

```
rbind(data,list(1,2,3))
```

The output is as follows:

```
  Col1 Col2 Col3
1   1    2    3
2   4    5    6
3   7    8    9
4   a    b    c
5   1    2    3
```

We have added columns to the dataframe using the **rbind()** and **cbind()** functions. We will move ahead to understanding how exploratory data analysis helps us understand the data better.

Exploratory Data Analysis (EDA)

Exploratory Data Analysis (EDA) is the use of visualization techniques to explore the dataset. We will use the built-in dataset in R to learn to see a few statistics about the data. The datasets used are as follows:

Dataset	Description	Predictor Field
PimaIndiansDiabetes	This data contains diabetes-related information in 9 variables. Has 768 observations.	The diabetes column is an output variable that contains the test result of diabetes.
BostonHousing	This data contains numerical columns of 61 variables. Has 208 observations.	The class column is the output predictor variable.
GermanCredit	This data has variables that characterize the credit worthiness in 62 variables. Has 1000 observations.	The class column is an output predictor variable that takes the values of "good" and "bad."

Figure 1.4: Datasets and their descriptions

View Built-in Datasets in R

To install packages to R, we use the following syntax: **install.packages("Name_of_package")**

The pre-loaded datasets of R can be viewed using the **data()** command:

```
#Installing necessary packages
install.packages("mlbench")
install.packages("caret")
#Loading the datasets
data(package = .packages(all.available = TRUE))
```

The datasets will be displayed in the dataset tab as follows:

Figure 1.5: Dataset tab for viewing all the datasets

We can thus install packages and load the built-in datasets.

Exercise 3: Loading Built-in Datasets

In this exercise, we will load built-in datasets, analyze the contents of the datasets, and read the first and last records from those datasets.

1. We will use the **BostonHousing** and **GermanCredit** datasets shown in the following screenshot:

```
Data sets in package 'broom':

argument_glossary                      Allowed argument names in tidiers
column_glossary                        Allowed column names in tidied tibbles

Data sets in package 'caret':

GermanCredit                           German Credit Data
sacramento                             Sacramento CA Home Prices
absorp (tecator)                       Fat, Water and Protein Content of Meat Samples
bbbDescr (BloodBrain)                  Blood Brain Barrier Data
cars                                   Kelly Blue Book resale data for 2005 model year GM cars
cox2Class (cox2)                       COX-2 Activity Data
cox2Descr (cox2)                       COX-2 Activity Data
cox2IC50 (cox2)                        COX-2 Activity Data
dhfr                                   Dihydrofolate Reductase Inhibitors Data
endpoints (tecator)                    Fat, Water and Protein Content of Meat Samples
fattyAcids (oil)                       Fatty acid composition of commercial oils
logBBB (BloodBrain)                    Blood Brain Barrier Data
mdrrClass (mdrr)                       Multidrug Resistance Reversal (MDRR) Agent Data
mdrrDescr (mdrr)                       Multidrug Resistance Reversal (MDRR) Agent Data
oilType (oil)                          Fatty acid composition of commercial oils
potteryClass (pottery)                 Pottery from Pre-Classical Sites in Italy
scat                                   Morphometric Data on Scat
scat_orig (scat)                       Morphometric Data on Scat
```

Figure 1.6: The GermanCredit dataset

```
Data sets in package 'mitools':

smi                                    Multiple imputations

Data sets in package 'mlbench':

BostonHousing                          Boston Housing Data
BostonHousing2                         Boston Housing Data
BreastCancer                           Wisconsin Breast Cancer Database
DNA                                    Primate splice-junction gene sequences (DNA)
Glass                                  Glass Identification Database
HouseVotes84                           United States Congressional Voting Records 1984
Ionosphere                             Johns Hopkins University Ionosphere database
LetterRecognition                      Letter Image Recognition Data
Ozone                                  Los Angeles ozone pollution data, 1976
PimaIndiansDiabetes                    Pima Indians Diabetes Database
PimaIndiansDiabetes2                   Pima Indians Diabetes Database
Satellite                              Landsat Multi-Spectral Scanner Image Data
Servo                                  Servo Data
Shuttle                                Shuttle Dataset (Statlog version)
Sonar                                  Sonar, Mines vs. Rocks
Soybean                                Soybean Database
Vehicle                                Vehicle Silhouettes
Vowel                                  Vowel Recognition (Deterding data)
Zoo                                    Zoo Data

Console   Terminal
```

Figure 1.7: The BostonHousing dataset

2. Check the installed packages using the following code:

```
data(package = .packages(all.available = TRUE))
```

3. Choose **File | New File | R Script**:

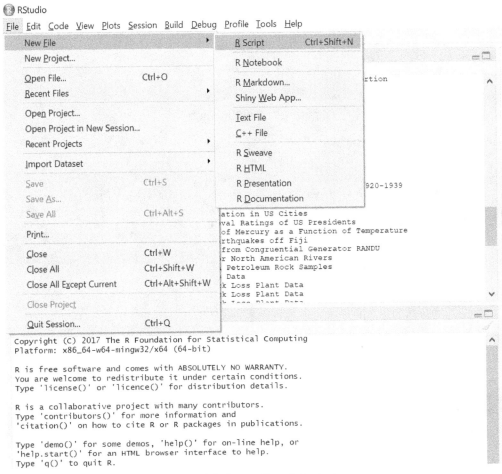

Figure 1.8: A new R script window

4. Save the file into the local directory by clicking *Ctrl* + S on windows.

5. Load the **mlbench** library and the **BostonHousing** dataset:

```
library(mlbench)
#Loading the Data
data(BostonHousing)
```

6. The first five rows in the data can be viewed using the **head()** function, as follows:

```
#Print the first 5 lines in the dataset
head(BostonHousing)
```

7. Click the **Run** option as shown:

Figure 1.9: The Run option

The output will be as follows:

```
      crim zn indus chas   nox    rm  age    dis rad tax ptratio
1 0.00632 18  2.31    0 0.538 6.575 65.2 4.0900   1 296    15.3
2 0.02731  0  7.07    0 0.469 6.421 78.9 4.9671   2 242    17.8
3 0.02729  0  7.07    0 0.469 7.185 61.1 4.9671   2 242    17.8
4 0.03237  0  2.18    0 0.458 6.998 45.8 6.0622   3 222    18.7
5 0.06905  0  2.18    0 0.458 7.147 54.2 6.0622   3 222    18.7
6 0.02985  0  2.18    0 0.458 6.430 58.7 6.0622   3 222    18.7
      b lstat medv
1 396.90  4.98 24.0
2 396.90  9.14 21.6
3 392.83  4.03 34.7
4 394.63  2.94 33.4
5 396.90  5.33 36.2
6 394.12  5.21 28.7
```

Figure 1.10: The first rows of Boston Housing dataset

8. The description of the dataset can be viewed using **<<Dataset>>**. In place of **<<Dataset>>**, mention the name of the dataset:

```
# Display information about Boston Housing dataset
?BostonHousing
```

The **Help** tab will display all the information about the dataset. The description of the columns is available here:

BostonHousing {mlbench}   R Documentation

Boston Housing Data

Description

Housing data for 506 census tracts of Boston from the 1970 census. The dataframe BostonHousing contains the original data by Harrison and Rubinfeld (1979), the dataframe BostonHousing2 the corrected version with additional spatial information (see references below).

Usage

```
data(BostonHousing)
data(BostonHousing2)
```

Format

The original data are 506 observations on 14 variables, medv being the target variable:

crim   per capita crime rate by town
zn   proportion of residential land zoned for lots over 25,000 sq.ft
indus   proportion of non-retail business acres per town
chas   Charles River dummy variable (= 1 if tract bounds river; 0 otherwise)

Figure 1.11: More information about the Boston Housing dataset

9. The first n rows and last m rows in the data can be viewed as follows:

```
#Print the first 10 rows in the dataset
head(BostonHousing,10)
```

The output is as follows:

```
        crim    zn indus chas    nox    rm    age      dis rad tax
1   0.00632 18.0   2.31     0 0.538 6.575   65.2 4.0900    1 296
2   0.02731  0.0   7.07     0 0.469 6.421   78.9 4.9671    2 242
3   0.02729  0.0   7.07     0 0.469 7.185   61.1 4.9671    2 242
4   0.03237  0.0   2.18     0 0.458 6.998   45.8 6.0622    3 222
5   0.06905  0.0   2.18     0 0.458 7.147   54.2 6.0622    3 222
6   0.02985  0.0   2.18     0 0.458 6.430   58.7 6.0622    3 222
7   0.08829 12.5   7.87     0 0.524 6.012   66.6 5.5605    5 311
8   0.14455 12.5   7.87     0 0.524 6.172   96.1 5.9505    5 311
9   0.21124 12.5   7.87     0 0.524 5.631 100.0 6.0821    5 311
10 0.17004 12.5   7.87     0 0.524 6.004   85.9 6.5921    5 311
   ptratio        b lstat medv
1     15.3 396.90  4.98 24.0
2     17.8 396.90  9.14 21.6
3     17.8 392.83  4.03 34.7
4     18.7 394.63  2.94 33.4
5     18.7 396.90  5.33 36.2
6     18.7 394.12  5.21 28.7
7     15.2 395.60 12.43 22.9
8     15.2 396.90 19.15 27.1
9     15.2 386.63 29.93 16.5
10    15.2 386.71 17.10 18.9
```

Figure 1.12: The first 10 rows of the Boston Housing dataset

10. Print the last rows:

```
#Print the last rows in the dataset
tail(BostonHousing)
```

The output is as follows:

```
        crim zn indus chas    nox    rm  age      dis rad tax
501 0.22438  0  9.69     0 0.585 6.027 79.7 2.4982    6 391
502 0.06263  0 11.93     0 0.573 6.593 69.1 2.4786    1 273
503 0.04527  0 11.93     0 0.573 6.120 76.7 2.2875    1 273
504 0.06076  0 11.93     0 0.573 6.976 91.0 2.1675    1 273
505 0.10959  0 11.93     0 0.573 6.794 89.3 2.3889    1 273
506 0.04741  0 11.93     0 0.573 6.030 80.8 2.5050    1 273
    ptratio        b lstat medv
501    19.2 396.90 14.33 16.8
502    21.0 391.99  9.67 22.4
503    21.0 396.90  9.08 20.6
504    21.0 396.90  5.64 23.9
505    21.0 393.45  6.48 22.0
506    21.0 396.90  7.88 11.9
```

Figure 1.13: The last rows of the Boston Housing dataset

11. Print the last 7 rows:

```
#Print the last 7 rows in the dataset
tail(BostonHousing,7)
```

The output is as follows:

```
        crim zn indus chas    nox   rm  age     dis rad tax
500 0.17783  0  9.69     0 0.585 5.569 73.5 2.3999   6 391
501 0.22438  0  9.69     0 0.585 6.027 79.7 2.4982   6 391
502 0.06263  0 11.93     0 0.573 6.593 69.1 2.4786   1 273
503 0.04527  0 11.93     0 0.573 6.120 76.7 2.2875   1 273
504 0.06076  0 11.93     0 0.573 6.976 91.0 2.1675   1 273
505 0.10959  0 11.93     0 0.573 6.794 89.3 2.3889   1 273
506 0.04741  0 11.93     0 0.573 6.030 80.8 2.5050   1 273
    ptratio      b lstat medv
500    19.2 395.77 15.10 17.5
501    19.2 396.90 14.33 16.8
502    21.0 391.99  9.67 22.4
503    21.0 396.90  9.08 20.6
504    21.0 396.90  5.64 23.9
505    21.0 393.45  6.48 22.0
506    21.0 396.90  7.88 11.9
```

Figure 1.14: The last seven rows of the Boston Housing dataset

Thus, we have loaded a built-in dataset and read the first and last lines from the loaded dataset. We have also checked the total number of rows and columns in the dataset by cross-checking it with the information in the description provided.

Selectively running lines of code:

We can select lines of code within the script and click the **Run** option to run only those lines of code and not run the entire script:

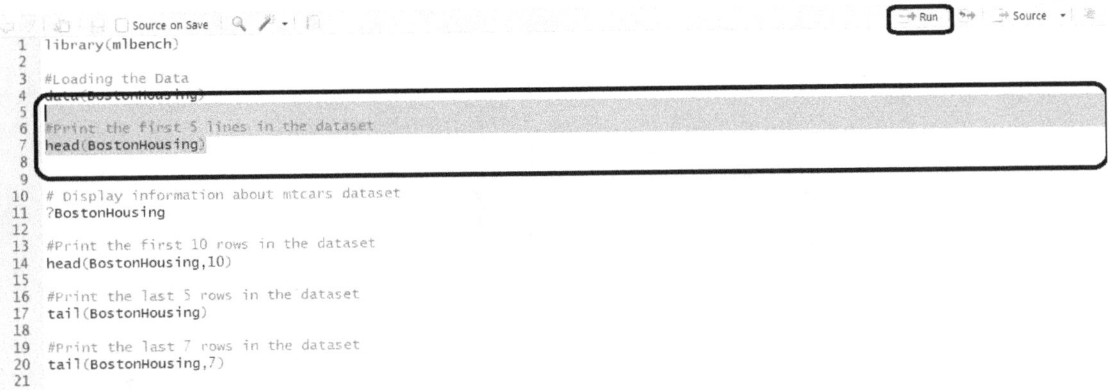

Figure 1.15: Selectively running the code

Now, we will move to viewing a summary of the data.

Exercise 4: Viewing Summaries of Data

To perform EDA, we need to know the data columns and data structure. In this exercise, we will cover the important functions that will help us explore data by finding the number of rows and columns in the data, the structure of the data, and the summary of the data.

1. The columns names of the dataset can be viewed using the **names()** function:

```
# Display column names of GermanCredit
library(caret)


data(GermanCredit)


# Display column names of GermanCredit
names(GermanCredit)
```

A section of the output is as follows:

```
 [1] "Duration"
 [2] "Amount"
 [3] "InstallmentRatePercentage"
 [4] "ResidenceDuration"
 [5] "Age"
 [6] "NumberExistingCredits"
 [7] "NumberPeopleMaintenance"
 [8] "Telephone"
 [9] "ForeignWorker"
[10] "Class"
[11] "CheckingAccountStatus.lt.0"
[12] "CheckingAccountStatus.0.to.200"
[13] "CheckingAccountStatus.gt.200"
[14] "CheckingAccountStatus.none"
[15] "CreditHistory.NoCredit.AllPaid"
[16] "CreditHistory.ThisBank.AllPaid"
[17] "CreditHistory.PaidDuly"
[18] "CreditHistory.Delay"
[19] "CreditHistory.Critical"
[20] "Purpose.NewCar"
```

Figure 1.16: A section of names in the GermanCredit dataset

2. The total number of rows in the data can be displayed using **nrow**:

```
# Display number of rows of GermanCredit
nrow(GermanCredit)
```

The output is as follows:

```
[1] 1000
```

3. The total number of columns in the data can be displayed using **ncol**:

```
# Display number of columns of GermanCredit
ncol(GermanCredit)
```

The output is as follows:

```
[1] 62
```

4. To know the structure of the data, use the **str** function:

```
# Display structure of GermanCredit
str(GermanCredit)
```

A section of the output is as follows:

```
'data.frame':   1000 obs. of  62 variables:
 $ Duration                      : int  6 48 12 42 24 36 24 36 12 30 ...
 $ Amount                        : int  1169 5951 2096 7882 4870 9055 2835 6948 3059 5234 ...
 $ InstallmentRatePercentage     : int  4 2 2 2 3 2 3 2 2 4 ...
 $ ResidenceDuration             : int  4 2 3 4 4 4 4 2 4 2 ...
 $ Age                           : int  67 22 49 45 53 35 53 35 61 28 ...
 $ NumberExistingCredits         : int  2 1 1 1 2 1 1 1 1 2 ...
 $ NumberPeopleMaintenance       : int  1 1 2 2 2 2 1 1 1 1 ...
 $ Telephone                     : num  0 1 1 1 1 0 1 0 1 1 ...
 $ ForeignWorker                 : num  1 1 1 1 1 1 1 1 1 1 ...
 $ Class                         : Factor w/ 2 levels "Bad","Good": 2 1 2 2 1 2 2 2 2 1 ...
 $ CheckingAccountStatus.lt.0    : num  1 0 0 1 1 0 0 0 0 0 ...
 $ CheckingAccountStatus.0.to.200: num  0 1 0 0 0 0 0 1 0 1 ...
 $ CheckingAccountStatus.gt.200  : num  0 0 0 0 0 0 0 0 0 0 ...
 $ CheckingAccountStatus.none    : num  0 0 1 0 0 1 1 0 1 0 ...
 $ CreditHistory.NoCredit.AllPaid: num  0 0 0 0 0 0 0 0 0 0 ...
 $ CreditHistory.ThisBank.AllPaid: num  0 0 0 0 0 0 0 0 0 0 ...
 $ CreditHistory.PaidDuly        : num  0 1 0 1 0 1 1 1 1 0 ...
 $ CreditHistory.Delay           : num  0 0 0 0 1 0 0 0 0 0 ...
 $ CreditHistory.Critical        : num  1 0 1 0 0 0 0 0 0 1 ...
 $ Purpose.NewCar                : num  0 0 0 0 1 0 0 0 0 1 ...
```

Figure 1.17: A section of names in the GermanCredit dataset

The column name **Telephone** is of numeric data type. Few data values are also displayed alongside it to explain the column values.

5. The summary of the data can be obtained by the **summary** function:

```
# Display the summary of GermanCredit
summary(GermanCredit)
```

A section of the output is as follows:

```
   Duration           Amount        InstallmentRatePercentage ResidenceDuration       Age         NumberExistingCredits NumberPeopleMaintenance
Min.   : 4.0    Min.   :  250    Min.   :1.000              Min.   :1.000    Min.   :19.00    Min.   :1.000        Min.   :1.000
1st Qu.:12.0    1st Qu.: 1366    1st Qu.:2.000              1st Qu.:2.000    1st Qu.:27.00    1st Qu.:1.000        1st Qu.:1.000
Median :18.0    Median : 2320    Median :3.000              Median :3.000    Median :33.00    Median :1.000        Median :1.000
Mean   :20.9    Mean   : 3271    Mean   :2.973              Mean   :2.845    Mean   :35.55    Mean   :1.407        Mean   :1.155
3rd Qu.:24.0    3rd Qu.: 3972    3rd Qu.:4.000              3rd Qu.:4.000    3rd Qu.:42.00    3rd Qu.:2.000        3rd Qu.:1.000
Max.   :72.0    Max.   :18424    Max.   :4.000              Max.   :4.000    Max.   :75.00    Max.   :4.000        Max.   :2.000
   Telephone      Foreignworker       Class      CheckingAccountStatus.lt.0 CheckingAccountStatus.0.to.200 CheckingAccountStatus.gt.200
Min.   :0.000    Min.   :0.000    Bad :300    Min.   :0.000              Min.   :0.000                 Min.   :0.000
1st Qu.:0.000    1st Qu.:1.000    Good:700    1st Qu.:0.000              1st Qu.:0.000                 1st Qu.:0.000
Median :1.000    Median :1.000               Median :0.000              Median :0.000                 Median :0.000
Mean   :0.596    Mean   :0.963               Mean   :0.274              Mean   :0.269                 Mean   :0.063
3rd Qu.:1.000    3rd Qu.:1.000               3rd Qu.:1.000              3rd Qu.:1.000                 3rd Qu.:0.000
Max.   :1.000    Max.   :1.000               Max.   :1.000              Max.   :1.000                 Max.   :1.000
CheckingAccountStatus.none CreditHistory.NoCredit.AllPaid CreditHistory.ThisBank.AllPaid CreditHistory.PaidDuly CreditHistory.Delay
Min.   :0.000              Min.   :0.00                   Min.   :0.000                  Min.   :0.00           Min.   :0.000
1st Qu.:0.000              1st Qu.:0.00                   1st Qu.:0.000                  1st Qu.:0.00           1st Qu.:0.000
Median :0.000              Median :0.00                   Median :0.000                  Median :1.00           Median :0.000
Mean   :0.394              Mean   :0.04                   Mean   :0.049                  Mean   :0.53           Mean   :0.088
3rd Qu.:1.000              3rd Qu.:0.00                   3rd Qu.:0.000                  3rd Qu.:1.00           3rd Qu.:0.000
Max.   :1.000              Max.   :1.00                   Max.   :1.000                  Max.   :1.00           Max.   :1.000
CreditHistory.Critical Purpose.NewCar   Purpose.UsedCar   Purpose.Furniture.Equipment Purpose.Radio.Television Purpose.DomesticAppliance
Min.   :0.000          Min.   :0.000    Min.   :0.000     Min.   :0.000               Min.   :0.00             Min.   :0.000
1st Qu.:0.000          1st Qu.:0.000    1st Qu.:0.000     1st Qu.:0.000               1st Qu.:0.00             1st Qu.:0.000
Median :0.000          Median :0.000    Median :0.000     Median :0.000               Median :0.00             Median :0.000
Mean   :0.293          Mean   :0.234    Mean   :0.103     Mean   :0.181               Mean   :0.28             Mean   :0.012
3rd Qu.:1.000          3rd Qu.:0.000    3rd Qu.:0.000     3rd Qu.:0.000               3rd Qu.:1.00             3rd Qu.:0.000
Max.   :1.000          Max.   :1.000    Max.   :1.000     Max.   :1.000               Max.   :1.00             Max.   :1.000
```

Figure 1.18: A section of the summary of the GermanCredit dataset

The summary provides information such as minimum value, 1st quantile, median, mean, 3rd quantile, and maximum value. The description of these values is as follows:

Information	Description
Minimum value	This is the smallest value amongst all the data values
1st Quantile	This is the value below which 25% of the data lies
Mean	This is the average of all the data values
3rd Quantile	This is the data point below which 75% of the data lies
Maximum value	This is the maximum value amongst all the data value.

Figure 1.19: Summary parameters

6. To view the summary of only one column, the particular column can be passed to the **summary** function:

```
# Display the summary of column 'Amount'
summary(GermanCredit$Amount)
```

The output is as follows:

```
 Min. 1st Qu.  Median    Mean 3rd Qu.    Max.
  250    1366    2320    3271    3972   18424
```

We've had a glimpse of the data. Now, let's visualize it.

Visualizing the Data

Data can be difficult to interpret. In this section, we will interpret it using graphs and other visualizing tools.

Histograms: A histogram displays the total count for each value of the column. We can view a histogram using the **hist()** function in R. The function requires the column name to be passed as the first parameter and the color of the bars displayed on the histogram as the second parameter. The name of the x axis is automatically given by the function as the column name:

```
#Histogram for InstallmentRatePercentage column

hist(GermanCredit$InstallmentRatePercentage,col="red")
```

The output is as follows:

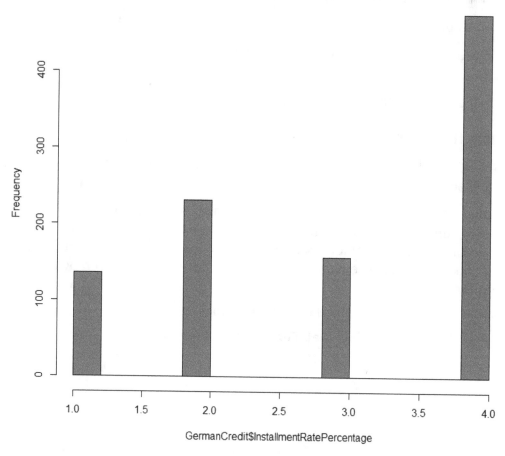

Figure 1.20: An example histogram

Bar plots: Bar plots in the **ggplot** package are another way to visualize the count for a column of data. The **aes()** function allows color coding of the values. In the upcoming example, the number of gears is plotted against the count. We have color-coded the gear values using the **aes()** function. Now, the **factor()** function is used to display only the unique values on the axis. For instance, the data contains 3, 4, and 5, and so you will see only these values on the *x axis*.

```
# Bar Plots
ggplot(GermanCredit, aes(factor(ResidenceDuration),fill=
factor(ResidenceDuration))) +geom_bar()
```

The output is as follows:

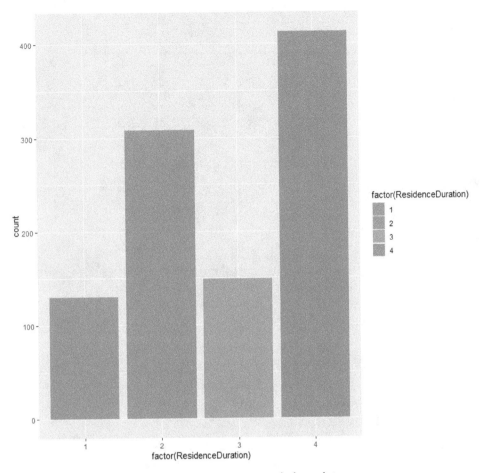

Figure 1.21: An example bar plot

Scatter plots: This requires **ggplot**, which we installed in the previous exercises. We plot **Age** on the x axis, **Duration** on the y axis, and **Class** in the form of color.

```
install.packages("ggplot2",dependencies = TRUE)

#Scatter Plot

library(ggplot2)

qplot(Age, Duration, data = GermanCredit, colour =factor(Class))
```

The output is as follows:

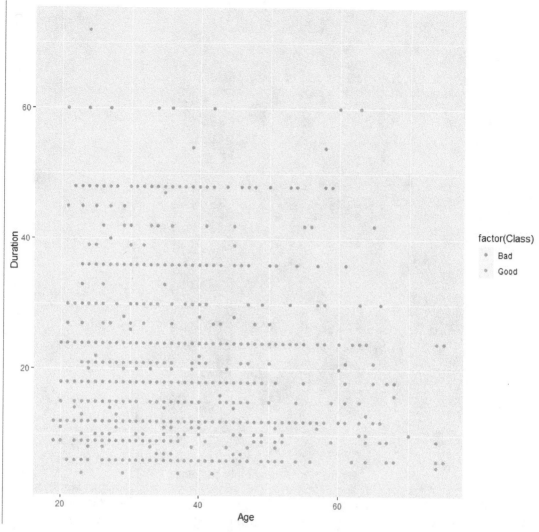

Figure 1.22: An example scatter plot

We can also view the third column by adding the **facet** parameter, as shown here:

```
#Scatter Plot
library(ggplot2)
qplot(Age,Duration,data=GermanCredit,facets=Class~.,colour=factor(Class))
```

The output is as follows:

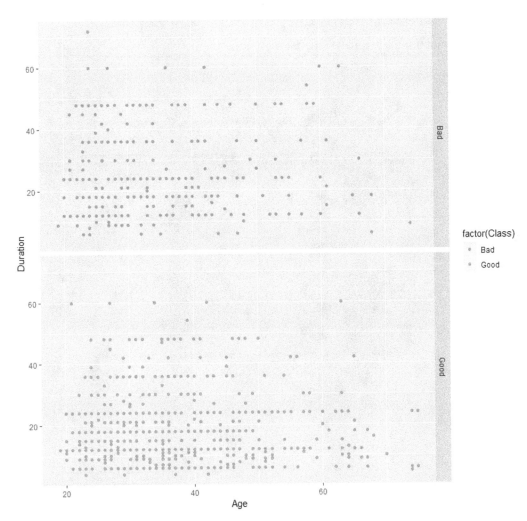

Figure 1.23: An example scatter plot facet

Box Plots: We can view data distribution using a box plot. It shows the *minimum, maximum*, 1st quartile, and *3rd* quartile. In R, we can plot it using the **boxplot()** function. The dataframe is provided to the **data** parameter. **NumberExistingCredits** is the *y* axis and **InstallmentRatePercentage** is the *x* axis. The name of the plot can be provided in **main**. The names for the *x* axis and *y* axis are given in **xlab** and **ylab**, respectively. The color of the boxes can be set using the **col** parameter. An example is as follows:

```
# Boxplot of InstallmentRatePercentage by Car NumberExistingCredits
boxplot(InstallmentRatePercentage~NumberExistingCredits,
```

```
          data=GermanCredit, main="Sample Box Plot",
          xlab="InstallmentRatePercentage",
          ylab="NumberExistingCredits",
          col="red")
```

The output is as follows:

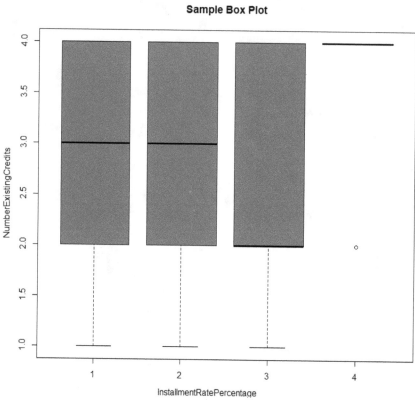

Figure 1.24: An example box plot

Correlation: The correlation plot is used to identify the correlation between two features. The correlation value can range from -1 to 1. Values between (0.5, 1) and (-0.5, -1) mean strong positive correlation and strong negative correlation, respectively. The **corrplot()** function can plot the correlation of all the features with each other in a simple map. It is also known as a correlation heatmap:

```
#Plot a correlation plot
GermanCredit_Subset=GermanCredit[,1:9]
install.packages("corrplot")
```

```
library(corrplot)

correlations = cor(GermanCredit_Subset)

print(correlations)
```

The output is as follows:

```
                              Duration      Amount
Duration                    1.00000000  0.62498420
Amount                      0.62498420  1.00000000
InstallmentRatePercentage   0.07474882 -0.27131570
ResidenceDuration           0.03406720  0.02892632
Age                        -0.03613637  0.03271642
NumberExistingCredits      -0.01128360  0.02079455
NumberPeopleMaintenance    -0.02383448  0.01714215
Telephone                  -0.16471821 -0.27699511
ForeignWorker               0.13819629  0.05005001
                           InstallmentRatePercentage ResidenceDuration
Duration                                  0.07474882        0.03406720
Amount                                   -0.27131570        0.02892632
InstallmentRatePercentage                 1.00000000        0.04930237
ResidenceDuration                         0.04930237        1.00000000
Age                                       0.05826568        0.26641918
NumberExistingCredits                     0.02166874        0.08962523
NumberPeopleMaintenance                  -0.07120694        0.04264343
Telephone                                -0.01441288       -0.09535937
ForeignWorker                             0.09002443        0.05409740
                                  Age NumberExistingCredits
Duration                 -0.036136374           -0.011283597
Amount                    0.032716417            0.020794552
InstallmentRatePercentage 0.058265684            0.021668743
ResidenceDuration         0.266419184            0.089625233
Age                       1.000000000            0.149253582
NumberExistingCredits     0.149253582            1.000000000
NumberPeopleMaintenance   0.118200833            0.109666700
Telephone                -0.145258701           -0.065553213
ForeignWorker             0.006151396            0.009716975
                         NumberPeopleMaintenance   Telephone
Duration                            -0.02383448 -0.16471821
Amount                               0.01714215 -0.27699511
InstallmentRatePercentage           -0.07120694 -0.01441288
ResidenceDuration                    0.04264343 -0.09535937
Age                                  0.11820083 -0.14525870
NumberExistingCredits                0.10966670 -0.06555321
NumberPeopleMaintenance              1.00000000  0.01475344
Telephone                            0.01475344  1.00000000
ForeignWorker                       -0.07707085 -0.10740091
                          ForeignWorker
Duration                    0.138196285
Amount                      0.050050007
InstallmentRatePercentage   0.090024429
ResidenceDuration           0.054097396
Age                         0.006151396
NumberExistingCredits       0.009716975
NumberPeopleMaintenance    -0.077070853
Telephone                  -0.107400909
ForeignWorker               1.000000000
```

Figure 1.25: A section of the output for correlations

The plot for correlations is as follows:

```
corrplot(correlations, method="color")
```

The output is as follows:

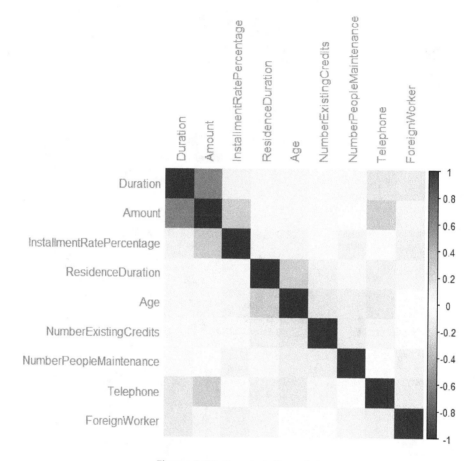

Figure 1.26: A correlation plot

Density plot: The density plot can be used to view the distribution of the data. In this example, we are looking at the distribution of weight in the GermanCredit dataset:

```
#Density Plot
densityData <- density(GermanCredit$Duration)
plot(densityData, main="Kernel Density of Weight")
polygon(densityData, col="yellow", border="green")
```

The output is as follows:

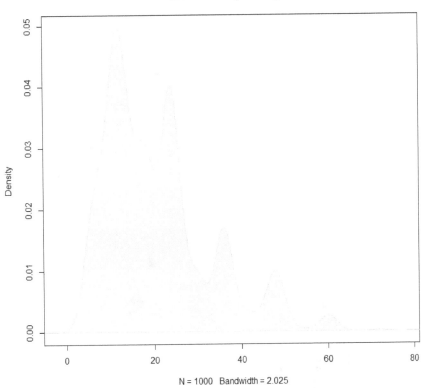

Figure 1.27: An example density plot

We have learned about different plots. It's time to use them with a dataset.

Activity 1: Finding the Distribution of Diabetic Patients in the PimaIndiansDiabetes Dataset

In this activity, we will load the PimaIndiansDiabetes dataset and find the age group of people with diabetes. The dataset can be found at https://github.com/TrainingByPackt/Practical-Machine-Learning-with-R/blob/master/Data/PimaIndiansDiabetes.csv.

The expected output should contain a bar plot of the count of positive and negative data present in the dataset with respect to age, as follows:

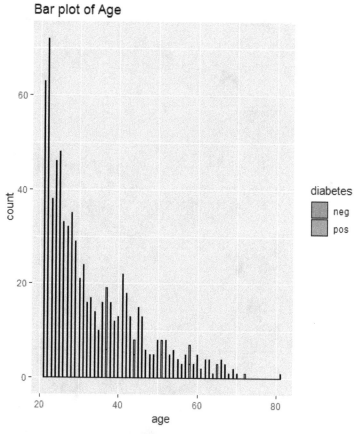

Figure 1.28: Bar plot for diabetes

These are the steps that will help you solve the activity:

1. Load the dataset.

2. Create a **PimaIndiansDiabetesData** variable for further use.

3. View the first five rows using **head()**.

4. Display the different unique values for the **diabetes** column.

> **Note**
>
> The solution for this activity can be found on page 312.

Activity 2: Grouping the PimaIndiansDiabetes Data

During this activity, we will be viewing the summary of the PimaIndiansDiabetes dataset and grouping them to derive insights from the data.

These are the steps that will help you solve the activity:

1. Print the structure of the dataset. [Hint: use **str()**]

2. Print the summary of the dataset. [Hint: use **summary()**]

3. Display the statistics of the dataset grouped by **diabetes** column. [Hint: use **describeBy(data,groupby)**]

The output will show the descriptive statistics of the value of **diabetes** grouped by the **pregnant** value.

```
#Descriptive statistics grouped by pregnant values

Descriptive statistics by group

group: neg
    vars   n  mean    sd median trimmed    mad min max range skew kurtosis    se
X1     1 500 68.18 18.06     70   69.97  11.86   0 122   122 -1.8      5.58
0.81
---------------------------------------------------------------------------------
-------------------

group: pos
    vars   n  mean    sd median trimmed    mad min max range  skew
kurtosis   se
X1     1 268 70.82 21.49     74   73.99  11.86   0 114   114 -1.92      4.53
1.31
```

The output will show the descriptive statistics of the value of **diabetes** grouped by the **pressure** value.

```
#Descriptive statistics grouped by pressure values
Descriptive statistics by group
group: neg
```

	vars	n	mean	sd	median	trimmed	mad	min	max	range	skew	kurtosis	se
X1	1	500	3.3	3.02	2	2.88	2.97	0	13	13	1.11	0.65	0.13


```
group: pos
```

	vars	n	mean	sd	median	trimmed	mad	min	max	range	skew	kurtosis	se
X1	1	268	4.87	3.74	4	4.6	4.45	0	17	17	0.5	-0.47	0.23

> **Note**
>
> The solution for this activity can be found on page 314.

Activity 3: Performing EDA on the PimaIndiansDiabetes Dataset

During this activity, we will be plotting the correlation among the fields in the PimaIndiansDiabetes dataset so that we can find which of the fields have a correlation with each other. Also, we will create a box plot to view the distribution of the data so that we know the range of the data, and which data points are outliers. The dataset can be found at https://github.com/TrainingByPackt/Practical-Machine-Learning-with-R/blob/master/Data/PimaIndiansDiabetes.csv.

These are the steps that will help you solve the activity:

1. Load the **PimaIndiansDiabetes** dataset.

2. View the correlation among the features of the **PimaIndiansDiabetes** dataset.

3. Round it to the second nearest digit.

4. Plot the correlation.

5. Create a box plot to view the data distribution for the **pregnant** column and color by **diabetes**.

Once you complete the activity, you should obtain a boxplot of data distribution for the pregnant column, which is as follows:

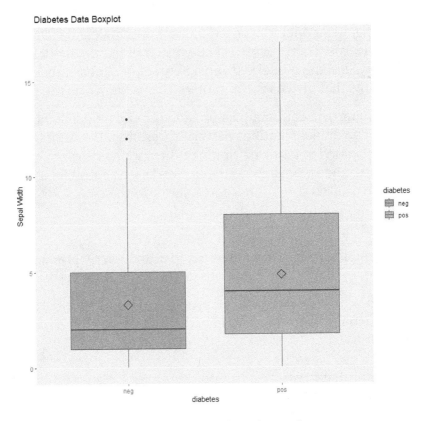

Figure 1.29: A box plot using ggplot

> **Note**
> The solution for this activity can be found on page 316.

We have learned how to perform correlation among all the columns in a dataset and how to plot a box plot for individual fields and then color it by certain categorical values.

Machine Learning Models

There are various algorithms that can be applied to numerous kinds of business problems. Broadly, the algorithms fall under supervised and unsupervised learning.

In supervised learning, the model is exposed to a set of samples with known outcomes/labels from which it learns. This process is known as training the model. After the learning/training process, the model is given a new set of data samples, based on which it performs predictions that give us the outcome. This is known as the prediction phase.

In unsupervised learning, the data samples provided to the model do not contain outcomes or labels. The model identifies patterns present in the samples and highlights the most commonly occurring patterns. Some of the approaches are clustering (hierarchical, k-means, and so on) and neural networks (self-organizing maps). This approach can also be used to detect unusual behavior in the data.

Types of Prediction

The prediction techniques are broadly categorized into numeric prediction and categoric prediction.

Numeric prediction: When the output to be predicted is a number, it is called numeric prediction. As shown in the following example, the output is 5, 3.8, 7.6, which are numeric in nature:

Feature 1	Feature 2	Feature 3	Output Value
2	5	6	5
3	2	4	3.8
4	1	2	7.6

Figure 1.30: Numeric prediction data

Categorical prediction: When the output to be predicted is a category (non-numeric), it is known as categorical prediction. It is mostly defined as a classification problem. The following data shows an example of categorical value prediction for the outputs A and G.

Feature 1	Feature 2	Feature 3	Output Value
2	5	6	A
3	2	4	G
4	1	2	A

Figure 1.31: Categorical prediction data

It is important to identify the nature of the output variable because the model should be chosen based on the type of output variable. In certain cases, the data is transformed into another type to cater to the requirements of the particular algorithm. We will now go through a list of machine learning algorithms in the following section and will discuss in detail the type of predictions they can be used for.

Supervised Learning

Supervised learning is broadly classified as follows:

- **Linear regression**: This is a technique whereby the input variable and the output field are related by a linear equation, $Y=aX+b$. It can be implemented using the `lm()` function in R. This is used for predicting numerical values, for instance, predicting the revenue of a company for the next year.

- **Logistic regression**: This technique is used for a classification problem where the output is categorical in nature. For instance, will it rain tomorrow? The answer would be **Y** or **N**. This technique fits a function that is a closest fit of the data and is also a linear combination of the input variables. The `glm()` function in R is used for implementing it.

- **Decision trees**: A decision tree is a tree with multiple nodes and branches, where each node represents a feature and the branches from the node represent a condition for the feature value. The tree can have multiple branches, signifying multiple conditions. The leaf node of the tree is the outcome. If the outcome is continuous, it is known as a regression tree.

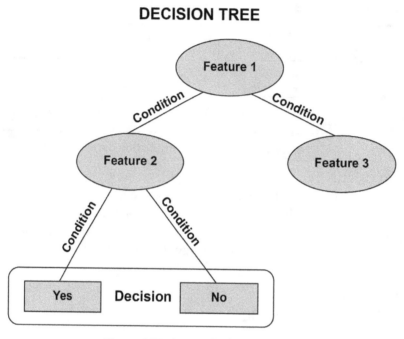

Figure 1.32: A sample decision tree

- **Support vector machines**: This approach maps inputs to a higher dimensional space using a kernel function. The data is separated by hyperplanes in this higher dimensional space. The support vector machine identifies the most optimal hyperspace with a large separation. It can be used for classification problems such as categorical prediction, as well as numeric prediction. It is also known as support vector regression.

- **Naïve Bayes**: It is a probabilistic model that uses the Bayes' theorem to perform classification.

- **Random forest**: This can be used for performing classification and regression problems. It is an ensemble approach, which involves training multiple decision trees and combining the results to give the prediction.

- **Neural networks**: A neural network is inspired by the a human brain. It consists of interconnected neurons or nodes. It uses a backpropagation algorithm for learning. It can be used for categorical, as well as numeric, predictions.

Unsupervised Learning

For unsupervised learning, hierarchical clustering and k-means clustering are used.

- **Hierarchical clustering**: The goal of a clustering process is to identify groups within the data. Each group must have data points that are very similar to each other. Also, two groups must be very different from each other in terms of their characteristics. Hierarchical clustering forms a dendrogram, a tree-like structure. There are two types of hierarchical clustering. Agglomerative clustering forms a tree-like structure in a bottom-up manner, whereas divisive hierarchical clustering forms a tree-like structure in a top-down manner.

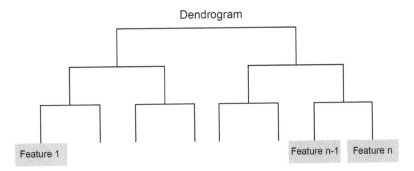

Figure 1.33: A dendrogram

- **K-means clustering**: In k-means clustering, the data is grouped into k clusters. The data is grouped based on the similarity score between the data points. Here, k is a predefined value. The choice of the value determines the quality of the cluster.

Applications of Machine Learning

The following are a few practical applications of machine learning:

- **Recommendation systems**: You can find a number of recommendations occurring on e-commerce websites. For instance, Amazon has several algorithms recommending products to its users. Predicting the user's next purchase or displaying products similar to the products purchased by the user are some scenarios where machine learning algorithms are used.

- **Forecasting sales**: In many product-based companies, the sales could be predicted for the next month/quarter/year. This can help them to better plan their resources and stocks.

- **Fraud detection**: Credit card fraud can be detected by using the transaction data. Classifiers can classify the fraudulent transactions, or outlier/anomaly detection can detect the anomalies in the transaction data.

- **Sentiment analysis**: Textual data is available in abundance. Sentiment analysis on textual data can be done using machine learning. For example, the user's sentiments can be identified as positive or negative, based on reviews of a certain product crawled from the internet. Logistic regression or Naïve Bayes can be used to identify the category using a bag of words representing the sentiments.

- **Stock prediction**: The stock price is predicted based on the characteristics of the stock in the past. Historical data containing the opening price, closing price, high, and low can be used.

Regression

In this section, we will cover linear regression with single and multiple variables. Let's implement a linear regression model in R. We will predict the median value of an owner-occupied house in the Boston Housing dataset.

The Boston Housing dataset contains the following fields:

Field	Explanation
crim	per capita crime rate by town
zn	proportion of residential land zoned for lots over 25,000 sq.ft
indus	proportion of non-retail business acres per town
chas	Charles River dummy variable (= 1 if tract bounds river; 0 otherwise)
nox	nitric oxides concentration (parts per 10 million)
rm	average number of rooms per dwelling
age	proportion of owner-occupied units built prior to 1940
dis	weighted distances to five Boston employment centres
rad	index of accessibility to radial highways
tax	full-value property-tax rate per USD 10,000
ptratio	pupil-teacher ratio by town
b	$1000(B - 0.63)^2$ where B is the proportion of blacks by town
lstat	percentage of lower status of the population
medv	median value of owner-occupied homes in USD 1000's

Figure 1.34: Boston Housing dataset fields

Here is a model for the **indus** field.

```
#Build a simple linear regression
model1 <- lm(medv~indus, data = BostonHousing)
#summary(model1)
AIC(model1)
```

The output is as follows:

```
[1] 3551.601
```

Build a model considering the **age** and **dis** fields:

```
model2 = lm(medv ~ age + dis, BostonHousing)
summary(model2)
AIC(model2)
Call:
lm(formula = medv ~ age + dis, data = BostonHousing)
Residuals:
    Min      1Q  Median      3Q     Max
-15.661  -5.145  -1.900   2.173  31.114
Coefficients:
              Estimate Std. Error t value Pr(>|t|)
(Intercept)   33.3982     2.2991  14.526  < 2e-16 ***
age           -0.1409     0.0203  -6.941  1.2e-11 ***
dis           -0.3170     0.2714  -1.168    0.243
---
Signif. codes:  0 '***' 0.001 '**' 0.01 '*' 0.05 '.' 0.1 ' ' 1
Residual standard error: 8.524 on 503 degrees of freedom
Multiple R-squared:  0.1444,    Adjusted R-squared:  0.141
F-statistic: 42.45 on 2 and 503 DF,  p-value: < 2.2e-16
```

The output is as follows:

```
[1] 3609.558
```

AIC is the Akaike information criterion, denoting that the lower the value, the better the model performance. Therefore, the performance of **model1** is superior to that of **model2**.

In a linear regression, it is important to find the distance between the actual output values and the predicted values. To calculate RMSE, we will find the square root of the mean of the squared error using **sqrt(sum(error^2)/n)**.

We have learned to build various regression models with single or multiple fields in the preceding example.

Another type of supervised learning is classification. In the next exercise we will build a simple linear classifier, to see how similar that process is to the fitting of linear regression models. After that, you will dive into building more regression models in the activities.

Exercise 5: Building a Linear Classifier in R

In this exercise, we will build a linear classifier for the **GermanCredit** dataset using a linear discriminant analysis model.

The German Credit dataset contains the credit-worthiness of a customer (whether the customer is 'good' or 'bad' based on their credit history), account details, and so on. The dataset can be found at https://github.com/TrainingByPackt/Practical-Machine-Learning-with-R/blob/master/Data/GermanCredit.csv.

1. Load the dataset:

    ```
    # load the package
    library(caret)
    data(GermanCredit)
    #OR
    #GermanCredit <-read.csv("GermanCredit.csv")
    ```

2. Subset the dataset:

    ```
    #Subset the data
    GermanCredit_Subset=GermanCredit[,1:10]
    ```

3. Find the fit model:

    ```
    # fit model
    fit <- lda(Class~., data=GermanCredit_Subset)
    ```

4. Summarize the fit:

```
# summarize the fit
summary(fit)
```

The output is as follows:

```
        Length Class   Mode
prior    2      -none- numeric
counts   2      -none- numeric
means    18     -none- numeric
scaling  9      -none- numeric
lev      2      -none- character
svd      1      -none- numeric
N        1      -none- numeric
call     3      -none- call
terms    3      terms  call
xlevels  0      -none- list
```

5. Make predictions.

```
# make predictions
predictions <- predict(fit, GermanCredit_Subset[,1:10],allow.new.
levels=TRUE)$class
```

6. Calculate the accuracy of the model:

```
# summarize accuracy
accuracy <- mean(predictions == GermanCredit_Subset$Class)
```

7. Print accuracy:

```
accuracy
```

The output is as follows:

```
[1] 0.71
```

In this exercise, we have trained a linear classifier to predict the credit rating of customers with an accuracy of 71%. In *chapter 4, Introduction to neuralnet and Evaluation Methods*, we will try to beat that accuracy, and investigate whether 71% is actually a good accuracy for the given dataset.

Activity 4: Building Linear Models for the GermanCredit Dataset

In this activity, we will implement a linear regression model on the GermanCredit dataset. The dataset can be found at https://github.com/TrainingByPackt/Practical-Machine-Learning-with-R/blob/master/Data/GermanCredit.csv.

These are the steps that will help you solve the activity:

1. Load the dataset.

2. Subset the data.

3. Fit a linear model for predicting **Duration** using **lm()**.

4. Summarize the results.

5. Use **predict()** to predict the output variable in the subset.

6. Calculate Root Mean Squared Error.

Expected output: In this activity, we expect an RMSE value of 76.3849.

> **Note**
>
> The solution for this activity can be found on page 319.

In this activity, we have learned to build a linear model, make predictions on new data, and evaluate performance using RMSE.

Activity 5: Using Multiple Variables for a Regression Model for the Boston Housing Dataset

In this activity, we will build a regression model and explore multiple variables from the dataset.

Refer to the example of linear regression performed with one variable and use multiple variables in this activity.

The dataset can be found at https://github.com/TrainingByPackt/Practical-Machine-Learning-with-R/blob/master/Data/BostonHousing.csv.

These are the steps that will help you solve the activity:

1. Load the dataset.

2. Build a regression model using multiple variables.

3. View the summary of the built regression model.

4. Plot the regression model using the **plot()** function.

The final graph for the regression model will look as follows:

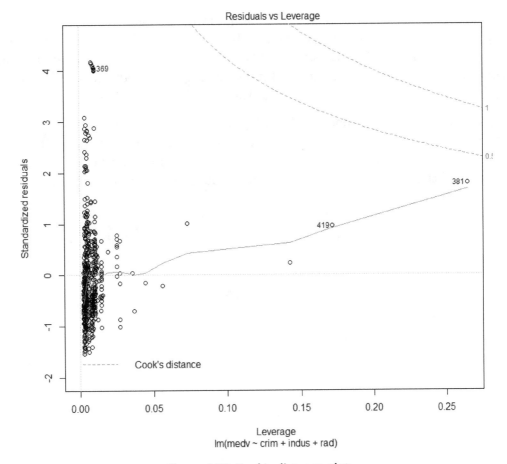

Figure 1.35: Cook's distance plot

Note

The solution for this activity can be found on page 320.

We have now explored the datasets with one or more variables.

Summary

In this chapter, we learned about the machine learning process. The various steps are iterative in nature and ensure that the data is processed in a systematic manner. We explored the various evaluation metrics for evaluating a trained model. We also covered two types of variables: categorical and numeric.

We covered the different ways to view the summary of the data. We also delved into the various plots available in R for visualizing the data and for performing EDA. We looked at the German Credit, Boston Housing, and Diabetes datasets and performed some visualization on these datasets to understand them better. We also learned how to plot correlations for the features in the data and the ways to interpret them.

We looked into the common machine learning models used by data scientists. We also came to understand some of the types of models that can be used for numeric prediction and categorical prediction. Furthermore, we implemented a classifier in R and interpreted the results. We explored built-in datasets for building linear regression and classifier models.

Data Cleaning and Pre-processing

Learning Objectives

By the end of this chapter, you will be able to:

- Perform the sort, rank, filter, subset, normalize, scale, and join operations in an R data frame.

- Identify and handle outliers, missing values, and duplicates gracefully using the MICE and rpart packages.

- Perform undersampling and oversampling on a dataset.

- Apply the concepts of ROSE and SMOTE to handle unbalanced data.

This chapter covers the important concepts of handling data and making the data ready for analysis.

Introduction

Data cleaning and preparation takes about 70% of the effort in the entire process of a machine learning project. This step is essential because the quality of the data determines the accuracy of the prediction model. A clean dataset should contain good samples of the scenarios that we want to predict, and this will give us good prediction results. Also, the data should be balanced, which means that every category we want to predict should have similar number of samples. For example, if we want to predict whether it will rain or not on any particular day, and if the sample data size is 100, the data could contain 40 samples for It will rain and 60 samples for It will not rain today, or vice versa. However, if the ratio is 20:80 or 30:70, it is an unbalanced dataset, and this will not yield good results for the minority class.

In the following section, we will look at the essential operations performed on data frames in R. These operations will help us to manipulate and analyze the data. The datasets we will be utilizing in this chapter are as follows:

Dataset	Description	Output Variable
PimaIndiansDiabetes2	This dataset contains 9 variables related to diabetes. It has 768 observations. The dataset contains missing data.	The "diabetes" column is the output variable. It contains the result of a diabetes test.
German Credit Data	This dataset has 62 variables that characterize the creditworthiness of loan applicants. It has 1000 observations.	The "Class" column is the output variable with values "Good" and "Bad".
Mushrooms	This dataset contains hypothetical information in 22 variables. It has 23 observations.	The "Class" column is the output variable with values "edible" or "poisonous".
Mtcars [Motor Trend Car Road Tests]	This dataset has 11 variables that contain the details of fuel consumption. It has 32 observations.	The class mpg(miles per gallon) is the output predictor.

Figure 2.1: Datasets

We will begin with advanced operations on R data frames.

Advanced Operations on Data Frames

In the previous chapter, we performed a number of operations on data frames, including **rbind()**. There are many more operations that can be performed on data frames, which are very useful while preparing the data for the model. The following exercises will describe these operations in detail and illustrate them through their corresponding implementation in R:

- **The order function**: The **order** function is used to sort a data frame. We can specify ascending or descending order using the "-" symbol.

- **The sort function:** The **sort** function can also be used to sort the data. The order can be specified as **"decreasing=TRUE"** or **"decreasing"="FALSE"**.

- **The rank function:** The **rank** function is used to rank the values in the data in a numerical manner.

Sorting, ordering, and ranking are operations that act as techniques to identify outliers. Outliers are values that are either too big or too small and do not fit in the value range. As datasets are often messy, fixing datasets is usually a challenge. It helps to sort through multiple records and decide the next suitable candidate. Hence, these operations form the basis of pre-processing in R.

Exercise 6: Sorting the Data Frame

In this exercise, we will be organizing the data using the **order()**, **sort()**, and **rank()** functions. We will be using the built-in **PimaIndiansDiabetes** dataset:

1. Load the library and dataset:

```
library(mlbench)
library(caret)
data(PimaIndiansDiabetes)
```

2. Sort the dataset by **glucose** values using the **order()** function:

```
# sort by glucose
sorted_data <- PimaIndiansDiabetes[order(glucose),]
# View the output
head(sorted_data)
```

The output is as follows:

	pregnant	glucose	pressure	triceps	insulin	mass	pedigree	age	diabetes
76	1	0	48	20	0	24.7	0.140	22	neg
183	1	0	74	20	23	27.7	0.299	21	neg
343	1	0	68	35	0	32.0	0.389	22	neg
350	5	0	80	32	0	41.0	0.346	37	pos
503	6	0	68	41	0	39.0	0.727	41	pos
63	5	44	62	0	0	25.0	0.587	36	neg

Figure 2.2: The first rows of the data sorted by glucose

3. Sort the dataset by **glucose** and **pressure** values using the **order()** function:

```
# sort by  glucose and  pressure
sorted_data <- PimaIndiansDiabetes[order( glucose,  pressure),]
head(sorted_data)
```

The output is as follows:

	pregnant	glucose	pressure	triceps	insulin	mass	pedigree	age	diabetes
76	1	0	48	20	0	24.7	0.140	22	neg
343	1	0	68	35	0	32.0	0.389	22	neg
503	6	0	68	41	0	39.0	0.727	41	pos
183	1	0	74	20	23	27.7	0.299	21	neg
350	5	0	80	32	0	41.0	0.346	37	pos
63	5	44	62	0	0	25.0	0.587	36	neg

Figure 2.3: The first rows of data sorted by glucose and pressure

4. Sort the dataset by **glucose** values and in descending order by **pressure** values using the **order()** function:

```
#sort in ascending order by glucose and descending order by pressure
sorted_data <- PimaIndiansDiabetes[order( glucose, - pressure),]
head(sorted_data)
```

The output is as follows:

	pregnant	glucose	pressure	triceps	insulin	mass	pedigree	age	diabetes
350	5	0	80	32	0	41.0	0.346	37	pos
183	1	0	74	20	23	27.7	0.299	21	neg
343	1	0	68	35	0	32.0	0.389	22	neg
503	6	0	68	41	0	39.0	0.727	41	pos
76	1	0	48	20	0	24.7	0.140	22	neg
63	5	44	62	0	0	25.0	0.587	36	neg

Figure 2.4: The first rows of data sorted by glucose and pressure in descending order

5. Sort the dataset by **glucose** using the **sort()** function:

```
#Using the sort function to sort glucose
sort(glucose)
```

The output is as follows:

```
sort(glucose)
  [1]    0    0    0    0    0   44   56   57   57   61   62   65   67   68   68   68   71   71
 [19]   71   71   72   73   73   73   74   74   74   74   75   75   76   76   77   77   78   78
 [37]   78   78   79   79   79   80   80   80   80   80   80   81   81   81   81   81   81   82
 [55]   82   82   83   83   83   83   83   83   84   84   84   84   84   84   84   84   84   84
 [73]   85   85   85   85   85   85   85   86   86   86   87   87   87   87   87   87   87   88
 [91]   88   88   88   88   88   88   88   88   89   89   89   89   89   89   90   90   90   90
[109]   90   90   90   90   90   90   90   91   91   91   91   91   91   91   91   91   92   92
[127]   92   92   92   92   92   92   92   93   93   93   93   93   93   93   94   94   94   94
[145]   94   94   94   95   95   95   95   95   95   95   95   95   95   95   95   95   96   96
[163]   96   96   96   96   96   96   97   97   97   97   97   97   97   97   97   98   98   98
```

Figure 2.5: A section of sorted glucose values

6. Sort the dataset by **glucose** in descending order using the **sort()** function:

```
#Sort in descending order
sort(glucose, decreasing = TRUE)
```

The output is as follows:

```
sort(glucose, decreasing = TRUE)
  [1] 199 198 197 197 197 197 196 196 196 195 195 194 194 194 193 193 191 190 189 189 189 189 188 188 187 187 187 187 186 184 184 184 183 183 183 182
 [37] 181 181 181 181 181 180 180 180 180 180 179 179 179 179 179 178 177 176 176 175 175 174 174 173 173 173 173 173 172 171 171 171 170 170 169
 [73] 168 168 168 168 167 167 167 166 166 166 165 165 165 165 164 164 164 163 163 163 162 162 162 162 162 162 161 161 161 160 159 159 158 158 158 158
[109] 158 158 158 158 157 157 156 156 156 155 155 155 155 155 154 154 154 154 154 153 153 152 152 152 152 151 151 151 151 151 151 151 150 150 150 149
[145] 148 148 148 148 147 147 147 147 147 147 147 146 146 146 146 146 146 146 146 145 145 145 145 145 144 144 144 144 144 144 144 143 143 143 143
[181] 143 143 142 142 142 142 141 141 141 141 141 140 140 140 140 139 139 139 139 139 139 139 139 138 138 138 138 138 138 137 137 137 137 137 137
[217] 137 137 136 136 136 136 136 136 136 136 135 135 135 135 134 134 134 134 134 134 133 133 133 133 133 132 132 132 132 132 131 131 131 131 131 130
[253] 130 130 130 130 130 129 129 129 129 129 129 129 129 129 129 129 128 128 128 128 128 128 128 128 128 128 128 127 127 127 127 127
[289] 126 126 126 126 126 126 126 126 126 125 125 125 125 125 125 125 125 125 125 125 125 125 124 124 124 124 124 124 124 124 124 124 123 123
[325] 123 123 123 123 123 123 123 122 122 122 122 122 122 122 122 122 122 122 121 121 121 121 121 121 120 120 120 120 120 120 120 120 120 120
```

Figure 2.6: A section of glucose values in descending order

7. Sort the dataset according to rank of values of **glucose**:

```
#Using the rank function to rank the values of glucose
rank(glucose)
```

The output is as follows:

```
rank(glucose)
  [1] 622.5  76.0 735.0 101.5 554.5 377.0  36.5 368.5 764.5 464.5 317.5 694.5 567.5 748.5 688.0 206.0 394.5 284.0 241.0 368.5 476.0 189.0 761.0 403.0
 [25] 589.5 464.5 617.0 173.0 602.0 386.0 308.5 660.5  94.0 129.0 431.5 241.0 561.0 230.0 110.0 327.5 725.0 530.0 271.5 701.0 665.5 725.0 609.0  18.5
 [49] 241.0 258.0 241.0 219.0  94.0 714.5 627.0  23.0 742.5 206.0 609.0 258.0  67.5 530.0   6.0 579.0 358.0 189.0 308.5 308.5 154.0 609.0 206.0 567.5
 [73] 476.0 503.5  40.0   3.0  11.0 154.0 520.0 341.0 350.0  26.5  59.5 219.0 554.5 317.5 271.5 206.0 546.5 284.0  44.5 442.0  50.5 535.5 584.0 596.0
 [97] 129.0  18.5 137.0 431.5 678.0 631.5 464.5  50.5  76.0 476.0 164.5 596.0  59.5 154.0 701.0 649.0 101.5  31.5 667.0 609.0 452.0  36.5 173.0 189.0
[121] 673.5 327.5 284.0 525.0 350.0  94.0 414.0 394.5 386.0 258.0 706.5 431.5 698.5  67.5 164.5 464.5 206.0 137.0 503.5 258.0 491.0 271.5 296.0 296.0
[145] 643.5 230.0   8.5 271.5 617.0 110.0 546.5 358.0 653.0 639.5 745.5 636.5 189.0 308.5  94.0 678.0 631.5 230.0 358.0 206.0 520.0 248.5 622.5 414.0
[169] 317.5 327.5 230.0 535.5  86.0  40.0  29.5 720.0  76.0 503.5 589.5 514.0  86.0 403.0   3.0  23.0 579.0 756.0 730.0 491.0 308.5 567.5 327.5 442.0
[193] 665.5 540.5  76.0 660.5 258.0 284.0 308.5 622.5 350.0 561.0 296.0 189.0 241.0 327.5 761.0 673.5 164.5 738.0  50.5 617.0 720.0 574.0 341.0 631.5
[217] 308.5 464.5  76.0 341.0 716.0 660.5 403.0 584.0 206.0  86.0 219.0 673.5 764.5 386.0 584.0 535.5  40.0 431.5  26.5 701.0 730.0 720.0 681.0 248.5
```

Figure 2.7: A section of the ranked values of glucose

Through these given examples, we have learned how to sort using **order()**, **sort()**, and **rank()**.

Join Operations

The join operations are extremely useful while handling data present in multiple tables. We can merge two datasets/data frames using a common column using the join operation. For instance, if one data frame contains credit card transaction information, and the other data frame contains the credit card customer information, and the two have to be merged based on customer ID, then we must use join operations to perform the merge. In this chapter, we will focus on the inner join, the outer join, the left join, and the right join in detail.

Inner join: The inner join gives us only the data where the fields in both the data frames have been merged by an exact match.

The syntax is as follows:

```
merge(df1, df2, by="fields used to merge")
```

Note that in the preceding code line, the following abbreviations are used:

df1 <- dataframe1

df2 <- dataframe2

The code to perform an inner join is as follows:

```
# Inner Join
data1 <- head(PimaIndiansDiabetes)
data2 <- head(PimaIndiansDiabetes)
merge(data1, data2, by='glucose')
```

The output is as follows:

```
> merge(data1, data2, by='glucose')
  glucose pregnant.x pressure.x triceps.x insulin.x mass.x pedigree.x age.x diabetes.x pregnant.y pressure.y triceps.y
1      85          1         66        29         0   26.6      0.351    31        neg          1         66        29
2      89          1         66        23        94   28.1      0.167    21        neg          1         66        23
3     116          5         74         0         0   25.6      0.201    30        neg          5         74         0
4     137          0         40        35       168   43.1      2.288    33        pos          0         40        35
5     148          6         72        35         0   33.6      0.627    50        pos          6         72        35
6     183          8         64         0         0   23.3      0.672    32        pos          8         64         0
  insulin.y mass.y pedigree.y age.y diabetes.y
1         0   26.6      0.351    31        neg
2        94   28.1      0.167    21        neg
3         0   25.6      0.201    30        neg
4       168   43.1      2.288    33        pos
5         0   33.6      0.627    50        pos
6         0   23.3      0.672    32        pos
> |
```

Figure 2.8: An inner join

Outer join: The outer join will join based on the exact match, but it will also keep the data that is not matched.

The syntax is as follows:

```
merge(df1, df2, by="common_key_column", all=TRUE)
```

The code to perform outer join is as follows:

```
#Outer Join
data1 <- head(PimaIndiansDiabetes)
data2 <- tail(PimaIndiansDiabetes)
merge(data1, data2, by='glucose', all=TRUE)
```

The output is as follows:

```
> merge(data1, data2, by='glucose',all=TRUE)
   glucose pregnant.x pressure.x triceps.x insulin.x mass.x pedigree.x age.x diabetes.x pregnant.y pressure.y triceps.y
1       85          1         66        29         0   26.6      0.351    31        neg         NA         NA        NA
2       89          1         66        23        94   28.1      0.167    21        neg          9         62         0
3       93         NA         NA        NA        NA     NA         NA    NA       <NA>          1         70        31
4      101         NA         NA        NA        NA     NA         NA    NA       <NA>         10         76        48
5      116          5         74         0         0   25.6      0.201    30        neg         NA         NA        NA
6      121         NA         NA        NA        NA     NA         NA    NA       <NA>          5         72        23
7      122         NA         NA        NA        NA     NA         NA    NA       <NA>          2         70        27
8      126         NA         NA        NA        NA     NA         NA    NA       <NA>          1         60         0
9      137          0         40        35       168   43.1      2.288    33        pos         NA         NA        NA
10     148          6         72        35         0   33.6      0.627    50        pos         NA         NA        NA
11     183          8         64         0         0   23.3      0.672    32        pos         NA         NA        NA
   insulin.y mass.y pedigree.y age.y diabetes.y
1         NA     NA         NA    NA       <NA>
2          0   22.5      0.142    33        neg
3          0   30.4      0.315    23        neg
4        180   32.9      0.171    63        neg
5         NA     NA         NA    NA       <NA>
6        112   26.2      0.245    30        neg
7          0   36.8      0.340    27        neg
8          0   30.1      0.349    47        pos
9         NA     NA         NA    NA       <NA>
10        NA     NA         NA    NA       <NA>
11        NA     NA         NA    NA       <NA>
> |
```

Figure 2.9: An outer join

Left outer join: The left outer join will join based on exact matches, but it will also keep the data from **df1** (which is not matched).

The syntax is as follows:

```
merge(df1, df2, by="common_key_column", all.x=TRUE)
```

The code to perform a left outer join is as follows:

```
#Left Join
data1 <- head(PimaIndiansDiabetes)
data2 <- tail(PimaIndiansDiabetes)
merge(data1, data2, by='glucose',all.x=TRUE)
```

The output is as follows:

```
> merge(data1, data2, by='glucose',all.x=TRUE)
  glucose pregnant.x pressure.x triceps.x insulin.x mass.x pedigree.x age.x diabetes.x pregnant.y pressure.y triceps.y
1      85          1         66        29         0   26.6      0.351    31        neg         NA         NA        NA
2      89          1         66        23        94   28.1      0.167    21        neg          9         62         0
3     116          5         74         0         0   25.6      0.201    30        neg         NA         NA        NA
4     137          0         40        35       168   43.1      2.288    33        pos         NA         NA        NA
5     148          6         72        35         0   33.6      0.627    50        pos         NA         NA        NA
6     183          8         64         0         0   23.3      0.672    32        pos         NA         NA        NA
  insulin.y mass.y pedigree.y age.y diabetes.y
1        NA     NA         NA    NA       <NA>
2         0   22.5      0.142    33        neg
3        NA     NA         NA    NA       <NA>
4        NA     NA         NA    NA       <NA>
5        NA     NA         NA    NA       <NA>
6        NA     NA         NA    NA       <NA>
> |
```

Figure 2.10: A left outer join

Right outer join: The right outer join will join based on exact matches, but it will also keep the data from **df2** (that which isn't matched).

The syntax is as follows:

```
merge(df1, df2, by="common_key_column", all.y=TRUE)
```

The code to perform a right outer join is as follows:

```
#Right Join
data1 <- head(PimaIndiansDiabetes)
data2 <- tail(PimaIndiansDiabetes)


merge(data1, data2, by='glucose',all.y=TRUE)
```

The output is as illustrated:

```
> merge(data1, data2, by='glucose',all.y=TRUE)
  glucose pregnant.x pressure.x triceps.x insulin.x mass.x pedigree.x age.x diabetes.x pregnant.y pressure.y triceps.y
1      89          1         66        23        94   28.1      0.167    21        neg          9         62         0
2      93         NA         NA        NA        NA     NA         NA    NA       <NA>          1         70        31
3     101         NA         NA        NA        NA     NA         NA    NA       <NA>         10         76        48
4     121         NA         NA        NA        NA     NA         NA    NA       <NA>          5         72        23
5     122         NA         NA        NA        NA     NA         NA    NA       <NA>          2         70        27
6     126         NA         NA        NA        NA     NA         NA    NA       <NA>          1         60         0
  insulin.y mass.y pedigree.y age.y diabetes.y
1         0   22.5      0.142    33        neg
2         0   30.4      0.315    23        neg
3       180   32.9      0.171    63        neg
4       112   26.2      0.245    30        neg
5         0   36.8      0.340    27        neg
6         0   30.1      0.349    47        pos
> |
```

Figure 2.11: A right outer join

Pre-Processing of Data Frames

Pre-processing is done on data frames to improve the quality of the dataset. At times, values are spread over a long range, and it becomes essential to align the values to a common scale without altering the ranges of values.

Standardizing is a pre-processing technique that converts data values, such that they can now be compared to each other. For instance, if the age is in the range of 1-100 and salary is in the range of 2000-60000, the two fields cannot be directly compared because the range of values they take are different. Therefore, we will transform the values such that the mean is 0 and standard deviation is 1. Standardization can be performed using:

- **Scale**: Each value in the variable is divided by standard deviation to bring them to a scale where the value 1 corresponds to one standard deviation of the original variable.

- **Normalize**: Squeezing the data into the range of 0-1 is called normalization.

- **Center**: The mean of the column is subtracted from each value in the column, so the new mean of the column becomes 0.

When values have different scales, they contribute differently to the analysis. It is good to scale features where we need to compute distance, like in k-nearest neighbors, Principal Component Analysis (PCA), gradient descent, and tree-based models.

The **preProcess()** function in R can take 16 arguments. In the upcoming exercise, we will look at the **method** argument. The **method()** argument is a vector that mentions the type of processing. The processing types we will look at in detail are **center**, **scale**, and **pca**.

Exercise 7: Centering Variables

In this exercise, we will perform the *center* pre-processing operation on the Pima Indians diabetes dataset:

1. Attach the packages:

```
#Attach the packages
library(mlbench)
library(caret)

# load the dataset PimaIndiansDiabetes
data(PimaIndiansDiabetes)
```

2. View the summary of the dataset:

```
# view data
summary(PimaIndiansDiabetes[,1:2])
```

The output is as follows:

```
pregnant               glucose
Min.    : 0.000    Min.    : 0.0
1st Qu.: 1.000    1st Qu.: 99.0
Median : 3.000    Median :117.0
Mean    : 3.845    Mean    :120.9
3rd Qu.: 6.000    3rd Qu.:140.2
Max.    :17.000    Max.    :199.0
```

3. Perform the **center** operation:

```
params <- preProcess(PimaIndiansDiabetes[,1:2],
                        method=c("center"))
print(params)
```

The output is as follows:

```
Created from 768 samples and 2 variables

Pre-processing:
  - centered (2)
  - ignored (0)
```

4. Transform using the previous method:

```
# transform the dataset using the parameters
new_dataset <- predict(params, PimaIndiansDiabetes[,1:2])
```

The **predict()** function will take the centered values (params) and transform the variables according to these **param** values.

5. Summarize the transformed dataset:

```
# summarize the transformed dataset
summary(new_dataset)
```

The output is as follows:

```
pregnant                 glucose
Min.    :-3.8451    Min.    :-120.895
1st Qu.:-2.8451    1st Qu.: -21.895
Median :-0.8451    Median :  -3.895
Mean    : 0.0000    Mean    :   0.000
3rd Qu.: 2.1549    3rd Qu.:  19.355
Max.    :13.1549    Max.    :  78.105
```

The new values are found by subtracting the original values by the mean value and hence the mean value is now zero. In the next exercise, we will normalize the value using the **range** operation.

Exercise 8: Normalizing the Variables

In this exercise, we will perform the **range** operation during pre-processing on the **PimaIndiansDiabetes** dataset:

1. Attach the caret and mlbench packages

    ```
    #Attach the caret and mlbench packages
    library(mlbench)
    library(caret)


    # load the dataset PimaIndiansDiabetes
    data(PimaIndiansDiabetes)
    ```

2. View the summary of the dataset:

    ```
    # view the data
    summary(PimaIndiansDiabetes[,1:2])
    ```

3. The output is as follows:

    ```
    pregnant                 glucose
    Min.    :-3.8451    Min.    :-120.895
    1st Qu.:-2.8451    1st Qu.: -21.895
    Median :-0.8451    Median :  -3.895
    Mean    : 0.0000    Mean    :   0.000
    3rd Qu.: 2.1549    3rd Qu.:  19.355
    Max.    :13.1549    Max.    :  78.105
    ```

4. Transform the dataset using **range**:

```
# To normalise we will create a range
params <- preProcess(PimaIndiansDiabetes [,1:2], method=c("range"))
print(params)
```

The output is as follows:

```
Created from 768 samples and 2 variables

Pre-processing:
  - ignored (0)
  - re-scaling to [0, 1] (2)
```

5. Use **predict()** to create the new pre-processed dataset:

```
# Transform the dataset using the parameters
new_dataset <- predict(params, PimaIndiansDiabetes [,1:2])
```

6. View the summary of the transformed dataset:

```
# summarize the transformed dataset
summary(new_dataset)
```

The output is as follows:

```
    pregnant              glucose
Min.    :0.00000    Min.    :0.0000
1st Qu.:0.05882    1st Qu.:0.4975
Median :0.17647    Median :0.5879
Mean    :0.22618    Mean    :0.6075
3rd Qu.:0.35294    3rd Qu.:0.7048
Max.    :1.00000    Max.    :1.0000
```

We have successfully normalized the values, and the values now lie between 0 and 1.

Exercise 9: Scaling the Variables

In this exercise, we will perform the **scale** operation during pre-processing of the **PimaIndiansDiabetes** dataset:

1. Load the dataset:

```
data(PimaIndiansDiabetes)
```

2. View the **summary** of the dataset:

```
summary(PimaIndiansDiabetes[,1:2])
```

The output is as follows:

```
   pregnant          glucose
Min.   : 0.000   Min.   :  0.0
1st Qu.: 1.000   1st Qu.: 99.0
Median : 3.000   Median :117.0
Mean   : 3.845   Mean   :120.9
3rd Qu.: 6.000   3rd Qu.:140.2
Max.   :17.000   Max.   :199.0
```

3. Transform the dataset using **scale**:

```
# to scale we will use scale keyword
params <- preProcess(PimaIndiansDiabetes[,1:2], method=c("scale"))
print(params)
```

The output is as follows:

```
Created from 768 samples and 2 variables

Pre-processing:
  - ignored (0)
  - scaled (2)
```

4. Use **predict()** to create the new pre-processed dataset:

```
#Scale the data
new_dataset <- predict(params, PimaIndiansDiabetes[,1:2])
```

5. View the summary of the transformed dataset:

```
# summarize the transformed dataset
summary(new_dataset)
```

The output is as follows:

```
   pregnant          glucose
Min.   :0.0000   Min.   :0.000
1st Qu.:0.2968   1st Qu.:3.096
Median :0.8903   Median :3.659
Mean   :1.1411   Mean   :3.781
3rd Qu.:1.7806   3rd Qu.:4.387
Max.   :5.0451   Max.   :6.224
```

Thus, we have learned to perform the **scale** operation.

Activity 6: Centering and Scaling the Variables

In this activity, we will perform the **center** and **scale** operations during pre-processing on the **PimaIndiansDiabetes** dataset.

The dataset can be found at https://github.com/TrainingByPackt/Practical-Machine-Learning-with-R/blob/master/Data/PimaIndiansDiabetes.csv.

These are the steps that will help you solve the activity:

1. Load the dataset.

2. View the **summary** of the dataset.

3. Find the parameters for centering and scaling with **preProcess()**.

4. Use **predict()** to transform the dataset.

5. View the summary of the transformed dataset.

The summary of the new dataset will be as follows:

```
          pregnant                glucose
Min.    :-1.1411    Min.    :-3.7812
1st Qu.:-0.8443    1st Qu.:-0.6848
Median :-0.2508    Median :-0.1218
Mean    : 0.0000    Mean    : 0.0000
3rd Qu.: 0.6395    3rd Qu.: 0.6054
Max.    : 3.9040    Max.    : 2.4429
```

> **Note**
>
> The solution for this activity can be found on page 326.

Extracting the Principle Components

We will extract the principle components from the variables/columns in the dataset. These components are combinations of the features in the dataset. These features are created such that they contain maximum information and maximum variance. The the first feature will have maximum covariance, and the covariance will reduce in the successive features.

In the next exercise, generate the principle components for the **PimaIndiansDiabetes** dataset.

Exercise 10: Extracting the Principle Components

In this exercise, we will perform pre-processing just as we did in the previous exercises, and we'll use **center**, **scale**, and **pca** to do this. We will follow the same approach as in *Exercise 8, Normalizing the Data.*

1. Load the dataset:

   ```
   # load the dataset
   data(PimaIndiansDiabetes)
   ```

2. Set the params:

   ```
   params <- preProcess(PimaIndiansDiabetes, method=c("center", "scale",
                                                      "pca"))
   ```

3. Perform PCA from the parameters:

   ```
   # perform pca on the dataset using the parameters
   new_dataset <- predict(params, PimaIndiansDiabetes)
   ```

4. View the new dataset:

   ```
   # view the new dataset
   summary(new_dataset)
   ```

   The output is as follows:

   ```
    diabetes        PC1              PC2               PC3               PC4
   neg:500    Min.   :-5.7234   Min.   :-2.5884   Min.   :-3.0881   Min.   :-3.3193
   pos:268    1st Qu.:-0.8836   1st Qu.:-1.0341   1st Qu.:-0.6399   1st Qu.:-0.5607
              Median : 0.1187   Median :-0.2817   Median :-0.1248   Median :-0.1216
              Mean   : 0.0000   Mean   : 0.0000   Mean   : 0.0000   Mean   : 0.0000
              3rd Qu.: 0.9679   3rd Qu.: 0.9630   3rd Qu.: 0.5221   3rd Qu.: 0.4842
              Max.   : 5.1249   Max.   : 3.6624   Max.   : 4.9516   Max.   : 4.5255
         PC5               PC6              PC7                PC8
    Min.   :-2.53987   Min.   :-3.2331   Min.   :-3.35229   Min.   :-3.07473
    1st Qu.:-0.57205   1st Qu.:-0.4797   1st Qu.:-0.29719   1st Qu.:-0.36180
    Median :-0.06336   Median :-0.0770   Median : 0.04523   Median :-0.01823
    Mean   : 0.00000   Mean   : 0.0000   Mean   : 0.00000   Mean   : 0.00000
    3rd Qu.: 0.56452   3rd Qu.: 0.3787   3rd Qu.: 0.38323   3rd Qu.: 0.38259
    Max.   : 2.64228   Max.   : 4.6103   Max.   : 1.77314   Max.   : 3.53473
   ```

   Figure 2.12: Our data frame after the center, scale and PCA operations

We note that there are seven principle components for the **PimaIndiansDiabetes** dataset.

5. Compare **new_dataset** with the original using the `glimpse` function of the `dplyr()` package:

```
library(dplyr)
glimpse(PimaIndiansDiabetes)
```

The output is as follows:

```
Observations: 768
Variables: 9
$ pregnant <dbl> 6, 1, 8, 1, 0, 5, 3, 10, 2, ...
$ glucose  <dbl> 148, 85, 183, 89, 137, 116, ...
$ pressure <dbl> 72, 66, 64, 66, 40, 74, 50, ...
$ triceps  <dbl> 35, 29, 0, 23, 35, 0, 32, 0,...
$ insulin  <dbl> 0, 0, 0, 94, 168, 0, 88, 0, ...
$ mass     <dbl> 33.6, 26.6, 23.3, 28.1, 43.1...
$ pedigree <dbl> 0.627, 0.351, 0.672, 0.167, ...
$ age      <dbl> 50, 31, 32, 21, 33, 30, 26, ...
$ diabetes <fct> pos, neg, pos, neg, pos, neg...
```

6. The glimpse of the **new_dataset** is as follows:

```
glimpse(new_dataset)
```

The output is as follows:

```
Observations: 768
Variables: 9
$ diabetes <fct> pos, neg, pos, neg, pos, neg...
$ PC1       <dbl> -1.0678069, 1.1209528, 0.396...
$ PC2       <dbl> 1.2340908, -0.7333737, 1.594...
$ PC3       <dbl> 0.09586737, -0.71247385, 1.7...
$ PC4       <dbl> 0.49666654, 0.28487058, -0.0...
$ PC5       <dbl> -0.10991328, -0.38925352, 0....
$ PC6       <dbl> 0.35694989, -0.40606472, -0....
$ PC7       <dbl> -0.85826202, -0.75654101, 1....
$ PC8       <dbl> 0.97366903, 0.35398386, 1.06...
```

Since the value will have maximum variance, they are good for modeling.

Subsetting Data

The subsetting of data means that the data can be filtered based on certain criteria, or such that some columns can be selected from a dataset. The syntax for subsetting is as follows:

- The syntax to select columns is `dataframe[c('col1','col2','col3')]`.

- If the columns are toward the start or end of the data frame, another syntax is `dataframe[,col1:col n]`, where `col1` is the index of the first column and `col n` is the index of the column until which you would like to select the data.

- The syntax to select a range of columns is `dataset[c(indexn:indexm)]`.

- The syntax to subset a data frame is `subset[dataframe,condn1 & cond2,select=c(col1,col2))`.

Often, it happens that we need only a section of data and not the entire data, subsetting enables us to use a section of the data frame for analysis, ensuring quicker analysis.

Exercise 11: Subsetting a Data Frame

In this exercise, we will subset a data frame using data operations:

1. Load the dataset:

```
library(mlbench)

data("PimaIndiansDiabetes")
```

2. Select the **age**, **glucose**, and **pressure** columns from the **PimaIndiansDiabetes** dataset:

```
Subsetting Data
# select variables age, glucose, pressure
myvars <- c("age", "glucose", "pressure")
newdata <- PimaIndiansDiabetes[myvars]
head(newdata)
```

The output is as follows:

```
  age glucose pressure
1  50     148       72
2  31      85       66
3  32     183       64
4  21      89       66
5  33     137       40
6  30     116       74
```

3. Select the first three columns in the **PimaIndiansDiabetes** dataset:

```
# another method
newdata <- PimaIndiansDiabetes[, 1:3]
head(newdata)
```

The output is as follows:

```
  pregnant glucose pressure
1        6     148       72
2        1      85       66
3        8     183       64
4        1      89       66
5        0     137       40
6        5     116       74
```

4. Select the first column, and columns 5 through 9:

```
# select 1st and 5th through 9th variables
newdata <- PimaIndiansDiabetes[c(1,5:9)]
head(newdata)
```

The output is as follows:

```
  pregnant insulin mass pedigree age diabetes
1        6       0 33.6    0.627  50      pos
2        1       0 26.6    0.351  31      neg
3        8       0 23.3    0.672  32      pos
4        1      94 28.1    0.167  21      neg
5        0     168 43.1    2.288  33      pos
6        5       0 25.6    0.201  30      neg
```

5. Select the **insulin** and **age** columns that satisfy the *insulin*>= 10, *age* <30 conditions:

```
# using subset function
newdata <- subset(PimaIndiansDiabetes,
                  insulin >= 20 & age < 30,
                  select=c(insulin, age))
head(newdata)
```

The output is as follows:

```
   insulin age
4       94  21
7       88  26
21     235  27
28     140  22
32     245  28
33      54  22
```

Thus, we have selected the required part of the data frame in each of these cases.

Data Transposes

Let's transpose the **PimaIndiansDiabetes** data frame; that is, convert the columns to rows and rows to columns. Use the **t(dataframe)** syntax as follows:

```
#Transpose Data
t_PimaIndiansDiabetes<-head(t(PimaIndiansDiabetes))
head(PimaIndiansDiabetes)
```

The first five rows of the original dataset are as follows:

```
  pregnant glucose pressure triceps insulin mass pedigree age diabetes
1        6     148       72      35       0 33.6    0.627  50      pos
2        1      85       66      29       0 26.6    0.351  31      neg
3        8     183       64       0       0 23.3    0.672  32      pos
4        1      89       66      23      94 28.1    0.167  21      neg
5        0     137       40      35     168 43.1    2.288  33      pos
6        5     116       74       0       0 25.6    0.201  30      neg
```

Figure 2.13: The original data

The transposed dataset is as follows:

```
head(t_PimaIndiansDiabetes)
```

The output is as follows:

	1	2	3	4	5	6	7	8
pregnant	" 6"	" 1"	" 8"	" 1"	" 0"	" 5"	" 3"	"10"
	9	10	11	12	13	14	15	16
pregnant	" 2"	" 8"	" 4"	"10"	"10"	" 1"	" 5"	" 7"
	17	18	19	20	21	22	23	24
pregnant	" 0"	" 7"	" 1"	" 1"	" 3"	" 8"	" 7"	" 9"
	25	26	27	28	29	30	31	32
pregnant	"11"	"10"	" 7"	" 1"	"13"	" 5"	" 5"	" 3"
	33	34	35	36	37	38	39	40
pregnant	" 3"	" 6"	"10"	" 4"	"11"	" 9"	" 2"	" 4"
	41	42	43	44	45	46	47	48
pregnant	" 3"	" 7"	" 7"	" 9"	" 7"	" 0"	" 1"	" 2"
	49	50	51	52	53	54	55	56
pregnant	" 7"	" 7"	" 1"	" 1"	" 5"	" 8"	" 7"	" 1"
	57	58	59	60	61	62	63	64
pregnant	" 7"	" 0"	" 0"	" 0"	" 2"	" 8"	" 5"	" 2"
	65	66	67	68	69	70	71	72
pregnant	" 7"	" 5"	" 0"	" 2"	" 1"	" 4"	" 2"	" 5"
	73	74	75	76	77	78	79	80
pregnant	"13"	" 4"	" 1"	" 1"	" 7"	" 5"	" 0"	" 2"

Figure 2.14: The transposed dataset

Often, it is essential to transpose a dataset, before we use it for analysis.

Identifying the Input and Output Variables

For any dataset, we should identify the input variables and the output variables. For the iris dataset, the input variables are the following:

1. SepalLength

2. SepalWidth

3. PetalLength

4. PetalWidth

The output variable, or the field to be predicted, is **Species**.

Identifying the Category of Prediction

Based on the category of prediction, we will perform different pre-processing steps. The category of prediction could be any of these:

- **Categorical Prediction**: In this type of prediction, the output to be predicted will have class values such as *yes*, *no*, or given categories.

- **Numeric Prediction**: In a numeric prediction, the output that will be predicted is a numeric value, such as predicting the cost of a house.

Handling Missing Values, Duplicates, and Outliers

In any dataset, we might have missing values, duplicate values, or outliers. We need to ensure that these are handled appropriately so that the data used by the model is clean.

Handling Missing Values

Missing values in a data frame can affect the model during the training process. Therefore, they need to be identified and handled during the pre-processing stage. They are represented as NA in a data frame. Using the example that follows, we will see how to identify a missing value in a dataset.

Using the `is.na()`, `complete.cases()`, and `md.pattern()` functions, we will identify the missing values.

The `is.na()` function, as the name suggests, returns TRUE for those elements marked NA or, for numeric or complex vectors, `NaN` (Not a Number) , and FALSE. The `complete.cases()` function returns TRUE if the value is missing and `md.pattern()` gives a summary of the missing values.

Exercise 12: Identifying the Missing Values

In the following example, we are adding rows with missing values to the `PimaIndiansDiabetes` dataset. We will be converting the columns of this dataset into numeric values. Using the `is.na()`, `complete.cases()`, and `md.pattern()` functions from the `MICE` library, we will identify the missing values.

1. Add the missing values:

```
library(mlbench)
data("PimaIndiansDiabetes")

#Adding NA values
PimaIndiansDiabetes_new <- rbind(
   PimaIndiansDiabetes,c(1, 212,NA,NA,3,44,0.45,23,"neg"))
```

```
PimaIndiansDiabetes_new <- rbind(
  PimaIndiansDiabetes_new,c(1, 212,NA,NA,3,44,0.45,23,"pos"))
```

2. Convert the characters to numeric:

```
#Convert character to numeric
PimaIndiansDiabetes_new$pregnant=as.numeric(
  PimaIndiansDiabetes_new$pregnant)
PimaIndiansDiabetes_new$glucose=as.numeric(
  PimaIndiansDiabetes_new$glucose)
PimaIndiansDiabetes_new$pressure=as.numeric(
  PimaIndiansDiabetes_new$pressure)
PimaIndiansDiabetes_new$triceps=as.numeric(
  PimaIndiansDiabetes_new$triceps)
PimaIndiansDiabetes_new$insulin=as.numeric(
  PimaIndiansDiabetes_new$insulin)
PimaIndiansDiabetes_new$mass=as.numeric(
  PimaIndiansDiabetes_new$mass)
PimaIndiansDiabetes_new$pedigree=as.numeric(
  PimaIndiansDiabetes_new$pedigree)
PimaIndiansDiabetes_new$age=as.numeric(
  PimaIndiansDiabetes_new$age)
PimaIndiansDiabetes_new$diabetes=as.numeric(
  PimaIndiansDiabetes_new$diabetes)
```

3. Identify the missing values using the ! (not) logical operator. Using the ! operator we will find the values that are not complete cases:

```
#Identifying missing values
#List the rows containing missing values
PimaIndiansDiabetes_new[
  !complete.cases(
    PimaIndiansDiabetes_new),]
```

The output is as follows:

	pregnant	glucose	pressure	triceps	insulin	mass	pedigree	age	diabetes
769	1	212	NA	NA	3	44	0.45	23	1
770	1	212	NA	NA	3	44	0.45	23	2

Figure 2.15: The identified missing values

4. Use the **is.na()** function to find NA values:

```
is.na(PimaIndiansDiabetes_new)
```

The output is as follows:

758	FALSE	FALSE	FALSE	FALSE	FALSE	FALSE	FALSE	FALSE	FALSE
759	FALSE	FALSE	FALSE	FALSE	FALSE	FALSE	FALSE	FALSE	FALSE
760	FALSE	FALSE	FALSE	FALSE	FALSE	FALSE	FALSE	FALSE	FALSE
761	FALSE	FALSE	FALSE	FALSE	FALSE	FALSE	FALSE	FALSE	FALSE
762	FALSE	FALSE	FALSE	FALSE	FALSE	FALSE	FALSE	FALSE	FALSE
763	FALSE	FALSE	FALSE	FALSE	FALSE	FALSE	FALSE	FALSE	FALSE
764	FALSE	FALSE	FALSE	FALSE	FALSE	FALSE	FALSE	FALSE	FALSE
765	FALSE	FALSE	FALSE	FALSE	FALSE	FALSE	FALSE	FALSE	FALSE
766	FALSE	FALSE	FALSE	FALSE	FALSE	FALSE	FALSE	FALSE	FALSE
767	FALSE	FALSE	FALSE	FALSE	FALSE	FALSE	FALSE	FALSE	FALSE
768	FALSE	FALSE	FALSE	FALSE	FALSE	FALSE	FALSE	FALSE	FALSE
769	FALSE	FALSE	TRUE	TRUE	FALSE	FALSE	FALSE	FALSE	FALSE
770	FALSE	FALSE	TRUE	TRUE	FALSE	FALSE	FALSE	FALSE	FALSE

Figure 2.16: The section of output showing the NA values as TRUE

5. Finding the last values using the **tail()** function is done as follows:

```
tail(is.na(PimaIndiansDiabetes_new) )
```

The output is as follows:

	pregnant	glucose	pressure	triceps	insulin	mass	pedigree	age	diabetes
765	FALSE	FALSE	FALSE	FALSE	FALSE	FALSE	FALSE	FALSE	FALSE
766	FALSE	FALSE	FALSE	FALSE	FALSE	FALSE	FALSE	FALSE	FALSE
767	FALSE	FALSE	FALSE	FALSE	FALSE	FALSE	FALSE	FALSE	FALSE
768	FALSE	FALSE	FALSE	FALSE	FALSE	FALSE	FALSE	FALSE	FALSE
769	FALSE	FALSE	TRUE	TRUE	FALSE	FALSE	FALSE	FALSE	FALSE
770	FALSE	FALSE	TRUE	TRUE	FALSE	FALSE	FALSE	FALSE	FALSE

Figure 2.17: Identifying the missing values

6. Find the missing data using the **md.pattern()** function:

```
library(mice)
md.pattern(PimaIndiansDiabetes_new)
```

The output is as follows:

	pregnant	glucose	insulin	mass	pedigree	age	diabetes	pressure	triceps	
768	1	1	1	1	1	1	1	1	1	0
2	1	1	1	1	1	1	1	0	0	2
	0	0	0	0	0	0	0	2	2	4

Figure 2.18: The output from MICE

Now that we have identified the missing values, it's time to handle them gracefully.

Techniques for Handling Missing Values

When we encounter a missing value, we can handle it in a couple of ways. Some of the techniques include deleting or replacing them using mean or median.

In the following section, these techniques will be illustrated in detail with examples:

- **Delete missing values**: Deleting the row with the missing value will remove the bad data from the dataset:

```
#Remove rows containing missing values
newdata <- na.omit(PimaIndiansDiabetes_new)
is.na(newdata)
```

The **is.na()** function will return **FALSE** if it is not an **NA** value for the data.

- **Impute missing values using the MICE package**: Another approach is imputation, where the missing value is replaced with the mean, median, or mode of the field.

In the next exercise, we will learn how to impute using the **MICE** package.

Exercise 13: Imputing Using the MICE Package

The exercise will give us an overview of the **MICE** package. This exercise is a continuation of the previous exercise, and we will impute the missing values in this exercise using the **complete()** method.

1. Find the NA values:

```
#View the NA
tail(PimaIndiansDiabetes_new)
```

The output is as follows:

	pregnant	glucose	pressure	triceps	insulin	mass	pedigree	age	diabetes
765	2	122	70	27	0	36.8	0.340	27	1
766	5	121	72	23	112	26.2	0.245	30	1
767	1	126	60	0	0	30.1	0.349	47	2
768	1	93	70	31	0	30.4	0.315	23	1
769	1	212	NA	NA	3	44.0	0.450	23	1
770	1	212	NA	NA	3	44.0	0.450	23	2

Figure 2.19: The NA values in the dataset

2. Import the **MICE** package:

```
library(mice)
```

3. Impute the data using **MICE**:

```
impute_step1 = mice(PimaIndiansDiabetes_new)
imputed_data = complete(impute_step1)
```

The output is as follows:

```
iter imp variable
 1    1  pressure  triceps
 1    2  pressure  triceps
 1    3  pressure  triceps
 1    4  pressure  triceps
 1    5  pressure  triceps
 2    1  pressure  triceps
 2    2  pressure  triceps
 2    3  pressure  triceps
 2    4  pressure  triceps
 2    5  pressure  triceps
 3    1  pressure  triceps
 3    2  pressure  triceps
 3    3  pressure  triceps
 3    4  pressure  triceps
 3    5  pressure  triceps
 4    1  pressure  triceps
 4    2  pressure  triceps
 4    3  pressure  triceps
 4    4  pressure  triceps
 4    5  pressure  triceps
 5    1  pressure  triceps
 5    2  pressure  triceps
 5    3  pressure  triceps
 5    4  pressure  triceps
 5    5  pressure  triceps
```

Figure 2.20: Imputed data

4. View the imputed values:

    ```
    #View the imputed values
    tail(imputed_data)
    ```

    The output is as follows:

	pregnant	glucose	pressure	triceps	insulin	mass	pedigree	age	diabetes
765	2	122	70	27	0	36.8	0.340	27	1
766	5	121	72	23	112	26.2	0.245	30	1
767	1	126	60	0	0	30.1	0.349	47	2
768	1	93	70	31	0	30.4	0.315	23	1
769	1	212	84	0	3	44.0	0.450	23	1
770	1	212	52	36	3	44.0	0.450	23	2

Figure 2.21: Imputed values

Thus, we have imputed the NA values using MICE.

Exercise 14: Performing Predictive Mean Matching

The abbreviation pmm is short for predictive mean matching. It will predict the value to be written into the missing field. A sample is as follows:

```
mice(Dataset, m=1,maxit=30,meth='pmm',seed=50)
```

In the preceding line of code, the following are used:

m = The number of imputed datasets

meth = The imputation method used. Other methods can also be used.

maxit = The number of iterations for each imputation

In this exercise, we will predict the missing value using pmm.

1. Find the NA values:

    ```
    tail(PimaIndiansDiabetes_new)
    ```

    The output is as follows:

	pregnant	glucose	pressure	triceps	insulin	mass	pedigree	age	diabetes
765	2	122	70	27	0	36.8	0.340	27	1
766	5	121	72	23	112	26.2	0.245	30	1
767	1	126	60	0	0	30.1	0.349	47	2
768	1	93	70	31	0	30.4	0.315	23	1
769	1	212	NA	NA	3	44.0	0.450	23	1
770	1	212	NA	NA	3	44.0	0.450	23	2

Figure 2.22: NA values in the PimaIndiansDiabetes dataset

2. Impute the values using MICE and add **pmm** as the method:

```
impute_step1 <- mice(PimaIndiansDiabetes_new,
   m=5,maxit=30,meth='pmm',seed=50)
```

The output is as follows:

```
iter imp variable
 1    1   pressure  triceps
 1    2   pressure  triceps
 1    3   pressure  triceps
 1    4   pressure  triceps
 1    5   pressure  triceps
 2    1   pressure  triceps
 2    2   pressure  triceps
 2    3   pressure  triceps
 2    4   pressure  triceps
 2    5   pressure  triceps
 3    1   pressure  triceps
```

Figure 2.23: A section of output after imputation

3. Find the summary:

```
summary(impute_step1)
```

The output is as follows:

```
Class: mids
Number of multiple imputations:  5
Imputation methods:
pregnant  glucose pressure  triceps   insulin      mass pedigree      age
   ""        ""    "pmm"     "pmm"       ""         ""      ""          ""
diabetes
   ""

PredictorMatrix:
         pregnant glucose pressure triceps insulin mass pedigree age diabetes
pregnant      0       1        1       1       1     1     1      1      1
glucose       1       0        1       1       1     1     1      1      1
pressure      1       1        0       1       1     1     1      1      1
triceps       1       1        1       0       1     1     1      1      1
insulin       1       1        1       1       0     1     1      1      1
mass          1       1        1       1       1     0     1      1      1
```

Figure 2.24: Imputed summary

4. Use the **complete()** function on the imputed data:

```
completedData <- complete(impute_step1,1)
tail(completedData)
```

The output is as follows:

	pregnant	glucose	pressure	triceps	insulin	mass	pedigree	age	diabetes
765	2	122	70	27	0	36.8	0.340	27	1
766	5	121	72	23	112	26.2	0.245	30	1
767	1	126	60	0	0	30.1	0.349	47	2
768	1	93	70	31	0	30.4	0.315	23	1
769	1	212	74	22	3	44.0	0.450	23	1
770	1	212	84	11	3	44.0	0.450	23	2

Figure 2.25: The last values imputed

Thus, we have imputed values using **pmm**.

Handling Duplicates

Duplicate data means rows that repeat themselves in the dataset. These duplicate data rows need to be removed, as they will reduce the quality of the data. If our training data contains duplicates, the duplicates can overtrain a model and bias it to predict those samples well. Thus, the model does not learn the other samples (non-duplicates) as well.

Exercise 15: Identifying Duplicates

There are functions in R that can be used to identify the duplicates in the data frame. We will identify duplicates using the **duplicated()** function.

1. Add a duplicate value:

```
#Adding duplicate values
PimaIndiansDiabetes_new <- rbind(
    PimaIndiansDiabetes,c(1, 93,70,31,0,30.4,0.315,23,"pos"))
PimaIndiansDiabetes_new <- rbind(
    PimaIndiansDiabetes_new,c(1, 93,70,31,0,30.4,0.315,23,"pos"))
PimaIndiansDiabetes_new <- rbind(
    PimaIndiansDiabetes_new,c(1, 93,70,31,0,30.4,0.315,23,"pos"))
```

2. Identify duplicates using the **duplicated()** function:

```
#Identify Duplicates
duplicated(PimaIndiansDiabetes_new)
```

The output is as follows:

```
[697] FALSE FALSE FALSE FALSE FALSE FALSE FALSE FALSE FALSE FALSE FALSE FALSE
[709] FALSE FALSE FALSE FALSE FALSE FALSE FALSE FALSE FALSE FALSE FALSE FALSE
[721] FALSE FALSE FALSE FALSE FALSE FALSE FALSE FALSE FALSE FALSE FALSE FALSE
[733] FALSE FALSE FALSE FALSE FALSE FALSE FALSE FALSE FALSE FALSE FALSE FALSE
[745] FALSE FALSE FALSE FALSE FALSE FALSE FALSE FALSE FALSE FALSE FALSE FALSE
[757] FALSE FALSE FALSE FALSE FALSE FALSE FALSE FALSE FALSE FALSE FALSE FALSE
[769] FALSE  TRUE  TRUE
```

Figure 2.26: A section of the output for duplicate values

3. Display the duplicate values:

```
#Display the duplicates
PimaIndiansDiabetes_new[duplicated(PimaIndiansDiabetes_new),]
```

The output is as follows:

```
    pregnant glucose pressure triceps insulin mass pedigree age diabetes
770        1      93       70      31       0 30.4    0.315  23      pos
771        1      93       70      31       0 30.4    0.315  23      pos
```

Figure 2.27: A section of the output for duplicate values

4. Find the value that has been duplicated:

```
#Display the unique values of the list of duplicates
unique(PimaIndiansDiabetes_new[duplicated(PimaIndiansDiabetes_new),])
```

The output is as follows:

```
    pregnant glucose pressure triceps insulin mass pedigree age diabetes
770        1      93       70      31       0 30.4    0.315  23      pos
```

Figure 2.28: A section of the output for duplicate values

5. Identify the unique values:

```
#Display the unique values
unique(PimaIndiansDiabetes_new)
```

The output is as follows:

763	9	89	62	0	0	22.5	0.142	33	neg
764	10	101	76	48	180	32.9	0.171	63	neg
765	2	122	70	27	0	36.8	0.34	27	neg
766	5	121	72	23	112	26.2	0.245	30	neg
767	1	126	60	0	0	30.1	0.349	47	pos
768	1	93	70	31	0	30.4	0.315	23	neg
769	1	93	70	31	0	30.4	0.315	23	pos

Figure 2.29: A section of output

Thus, the **unique()** and **duplicated()** functions can be used to eliminate duplicate values.

Techniques Used to Handle Duplicate Values

A technique to handle duplicate values is to remove duplicate rows:

```
#Remove duplicates

unique_data <- iris[!duplicated(iris),]
```

In the next section, we will handle outliers.

Handling Outliers

Any datapoint with a value that is very different from the other data points is an outlier. Outliers can affect the training process negatively and therefore they need to be handled gracefully. In the following section, we will illustrate via examples both the process of detecting an outlier and the techniques used to handle them.

Exercise 16: Identifying Outlier Values

The **outlier** package can detect the outlier values. Using the **opposite=TRUE** parameter will fetch the outliers from the other side of dataset. The outlier values can be verified using a boxplot.

1. Attach the **outlier** package:

    ```
    library(outliers)
    ```

2. Detect outliers:

    ```
    #Detect outliers
    outlier(PimaIndiansDiabetes[,1:4])
    ```

    The output is as follows:

pregnant	glucose	pressure	triceps
17	0	0	99

Detect outliers from the other end:

```
#This detects outliers from the other side
outlier(PimaIndiansDiabetes[,1:4],opposite=TRUE)
```

The output is as follows:

```
pregnant  glucose pressure  triceps
       0      199      122        0
```

3. Plot the outliers using box plots. Using a boxplot, we can view the range of the data and the outliers:

```
#View the outliers
boxplot(PimaIndiansDiabetes[,1:4])
```

The output is as follows:

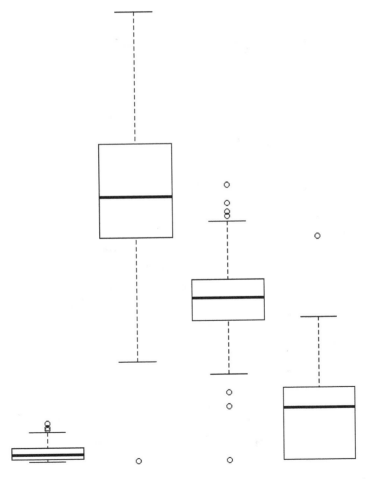

Figure 2.30: A boxplot to identify the outliers

A boxplot can be used to view the distribution of the data where the extreme values and the range of values can be viewed in the plot. For instance, the sepal width field has outliers (circles) with values of 4 and 2, and most of the data contains a sepal width of 3. The black line within each box is the median value.

Techniques Used to Handle Outliers

The following are some of the techniques used to handle outliers:

- Removing the outliers (as covered in the previous section)

- Imputing the missing values with mean, median, or mode (as covered in the previous section)

- Predicting the values for the outlier fields using the other values in the dataset

Exercise 17: Predicting Values to Handle Outliers

In this exercise, we will be predicting values to handle outliers. The rpart package can be used to predict the values, as shown in this exercise:

1. We will first add the outliers:

```
#Add rows with missing values
iris_new <- rbind(iris, c(1, 2,NA,NA,"setosa"))
iris_new <- rbind(iris_new, c(NA,NA,3,4,"setosa"))
iris_new <- rbind(iris_new, c(4,2,3,4,NA))
```

2. Since we have NA values, we will convert the characters to numeric values:

```
#Convert character to numeric
iris_new$Sepal.Length <- as.numeric(iris_new$Sepal.Length)
iris_new$Sepal.Width <- as.numeric(iris_new$Sepal.Width)
iris_new$Petal.Length <- as.numeric(iris_new$Petal.Length)
iris_new$Petal.Width <- as.numeric(iris_new$Petal.Width)
```

3. Attach the **rpart** package:

```
install.packages(rpart)
library(rpart)
```

4. Use the **rpart** function on **Species** in the **iris** dataset:

```
class_mod <- rpart(Species ~ . - Sepal.Length, data=iris_new[!
is.na(iris_new$Species), ], method="class", na.action=na.omit)
# since Species is a factor
```

5. Use the **rpart** function on **Petal.Length** in the **iris** dataset:

```
anova_mod <- rpart(Petal.Length ~ . - Sepal.Length, data=iris_new[!
is.na(iris_new$Petal.Length), ], method="anova", na.action=na.omit)
# since Petal.Length is numeric.
```

6. Use the **predict()** function to find the categoric and numeric predicted values:

```
categoric_pred <- predict(class_mod, iris_new[is.na(iris_new$Species), ])
numeric_pred <- predict(anova_mod, iris_new[is.na(iris_new$Petal.Length),
])
```

7. View the values:

```
categoric_pred
```

The output is as follows:

```
      setosa versicolor virginica
153        0 0.02173913 0.9782609
```

8. View the value for numeric prediction:

```
numeric_pred
```

The output is as follows:

```
151
1.462
```

This shows that in row 153, the species is predicted to be virginica with 97.8 percent probability.

In row 151, the petal length is predicted to be 1.462.

Handling Missing Data

To preprocess data, the syntax is **preProcess(dataframe, method="medianImpute")**, and the syntax for predicting is **predict(preProcess(),newdata=dataframe)**. The **medianImpute** method will replace the values with the median value.

Exercise 18: Handling Missing Values

In this exercise, we will use the **caret** package to impute the missing values in the iris dataset. This package will work on only numeric data, so the first four columns can be selected in the dataset.

These are the steps that will solve the exercise:

1. Attach the **caret** package:

    ```
    library(caret)
    ```

2. Print the rows with **NA** values:

    ```
    #print the rows with NA
    tail(iris_new[,1:4])
    ```

    The output is as follows:

    ```
        Sepal.Length Sepal.Width Petal.Length Petal.Width
    147          6.3         2.5          5.0         1.9
    148          6.5         3.0          5.2         2.0
    149          6.2         3.4          5.4         2.3
    150          5.9         3.0          5.1         1.8
    151          1.0         2.0           NA          NA
    152           NA          NA          3.0         4.0
    ```

3. Use the **preProcess()** method of the **caret** package to impute the values:

    ```
    #Impute
    iris_caret <- predict(preProcess(iris_new[,1:4],method =
    'medianImpute'),newdata = iris_new[,1:4])
    ```

4. Use **predict()** to generate the imputed data:

    ```
    #View the imputed values
    tail(iris_caret)
    ```

    The output is as follows:

    ```
        Sepal.Length Sepal.Width Petal.Length Petal.Width
    147          6.3         2.5          5.0         1.9
    148          6.5         3.0          5.2         2.0
    149          6.2         3.4          5.4         2.3
    150          5.9         3.0          5.1         1.8
    151          1.0         2.0          4.3         1.3
    152          5.8         3.0          3.0         4.0
    ```

Thus, we have replaced the NA values with data using prediction.

Activity 7: Identifying Outliers

In this activity, identify the outliers for the **mtcars** dataset. Also, display the outliers and plot a boxplot to verify it. The data can be found at https://github.com/TrainingByPackt/Practical-Machine-Learning-with-R/blob/master/Data/mtcars.csv.

These are the steps that will help you solve the activity:

1. Load the **mtcars** dataset.

2. Detect outliers using the **outlier()** function.

3. Detect outliers using the **outlier()** function using the **opposite=TRUE** option.

4. Plot a boxplot.

The output will display the outliers using a boxplot, as illustrated:

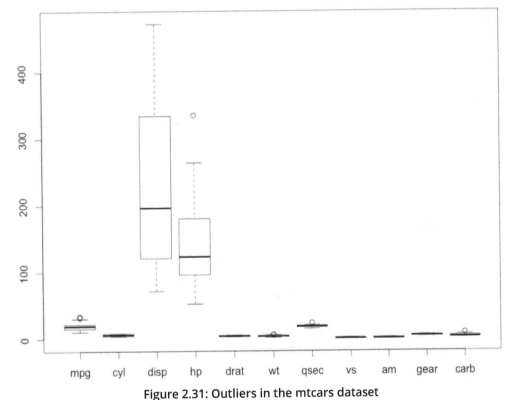

Figure 2.31: Outliers in the mtcars dataset

Note

The solution for this activity can be found on page 327.

Pre-Processing Categorical Data

A variable that contains distinct categories is called a categorical variable. For instance, the variable animal could have the classes cat, dog, and fish, and the variable married could have the classes yes and no. Pre-processing of a categorical field is essential because the model may not understand non-numeric literals. Therefore, these will be converted to numeric values.

Categorical data can be pre-processed in the following manner. The character values are converted to numeric values, which can be assigned by us:

```
#Categorical Variable

iris_new$Species <- factor(iris_new$Species, levels =
c('setosa','versicolor','virginica'), labels = c(1,2,3))

iris_new$Species
```

The output is as follows:

	pregnant	glucose	pressure	triceps	insulin	mass	pedigree	age	diabetes
1	6	148	72	35	0	33.6	0.627	50	pos
2	1	85	66	29	0	26.6	0.351	31	neg
3	8	183	64	0	0	23.3	0.672	32	pos
4	1	89	66	23	94	28.1	0.167	21	neg
5	0	137	40	35	168	43.1	2.288	33	pos
6	5	116	74	0	0	25.6	0.201	30	neg

Figure 2.32: Converting non-literal to numeric values

In the previous example, we saw how to convert a character factor to a numeric factor.

Handling Imbalanced Datasets

In many business scenarios, the data can be imbalanced. For example, if we are identifying credit card fraud, out of 100 transactions, only 5 transactions are likely to be fraudulent. Therefore, the data contains 95 samples of good transactions and 5 samples for fraudulent transactions. So, if we use the data directly, the good sample will overpower the model compared to the fraudulent sample, and the model might not learn to predict credit card fraud with high accuracy. Hence, we can employ the following techniques to prevent this problem:

- Oversampling
- Undersampling
- SMOTE
- ROSE

We will use the **PimaIndiansDiabetes** dataset, which is a set of patients with diabetes, and the output field is either **neg** or **pos**:

```
head(PimaIndiansDiabetes)
```

The output is as follows:

```
'data.frame':   768 obs. of  9 variables:
 $ pregnant: num  6 1 8 1 0 5 3 10 2 8 ...
 $ glucose : num  148 85 183 89 137 116 78 115 197 125 ...
 $ pressure: num  72 66 64 66 40 74 50 0 70 96 ...
 $ triceps : num  35 29 0 23 35 0 32 0 45 0 ...
 $ insulin : num  0 0 0 94 168 0 88 0 543 0 ...
 $ mass    : num  33.6 26.6 23.3 28.1 43.1 25.6 31 35.3 30.5 0 ...
 $ pedigree: num  0.627 0.351 0.672 0.167 2.288 ...
 $ age     : num  50 31 32 21 33 30 26 29 53 54 ...
 $ diabetes: Factor w/ 2 levels "neg","pos": 2 1 2 1 2 1 2 1 2 2 ...
```

Figure 2.33: First five records of PimaIndiansDiabetes

Observe the variables in the **PimaIndiansDiabetes** dataset.

```
str(PimaIndiansDiabetes)
```

The output is as follows:

```
Stochastic Gradient Boosting

1000 samples
  10 predictor
   2 classes: 'Class1', 'Class2'

No pre-processing
Resampling: Cross-Validated (10 fold, repeated 5 times)
Summary of sample sizes: 899, 899, 900, 900, 901, 901, ...
Addtional sampling using SMOTE

Resampling results across tuning parameters:

  interaction.depth  n.trees  ROC        Sens       Spec
  1                   50      0.9652074  0.9138803  0.8644444
  1                  100      0.9741817  0.9273211  0.8935556
  1                  150      0.9764500  0.9369963  0.8931111
  2                   50      0.9735849  0.9240098  0.8908889
  2                  100      0.9775766  0.9339219  0.8895556
  2                  150      0.9782565  0.9376679  0.9006667
  3                   50      0.9754686  0.9330379  0.8948889
  3                  100      0.9786717  0.9418388  0.8997778
  3                  150      0.9788557  0.9431624  0.8933333

Tuning parameter 'shrinkage' was held constant at a value of 0.1
Tuning
 parameter 'n.minobsinnode' was held constant at a value of 10
ROC was used to select the optimal model using the largest value.
The final values used for the model were n.trees = 150, interaction.depth = 3, shrinkage =
 0.1 and n.minobsinnode = 10.
```

Figure 2.34: Variables in PimaIndiansDiabetes dataset

Get a summary of the **diabetes** variable:

```
summary(PimaIndiansDiabetes$diabetes)
```

The output is as follows:

```
neg pos
500 268
```

The **diabetes** field has imbalanced samples, where the number of **pos** is low that is, 268, and the number of **neg** samples are high in number, that is, 500.

The imbalance in the preceding example should be addressed, because it can affect the performance of the machine learning model.

Undersampling

This is a technique where a few samples from the larger class are removed to decrease the count so that the ratio is balanced. The disadvantage is that we will likely lose information in our model as the samples are picked randomly. For instance, we will randomly pick 268 out of 500 samples for the neg class.

Exercise 19: Undersampling a Dataset

In this exercise, we will consider the diabetes field of the **PimaIndianDiabetes** dataset and downsample it.

1. View the summary of the **diabetes** field to see the class count:

   ```
   summary(PimaIndiansDiabetes$diabetes)
   ```

   The output is as follows:

   ```
   neg pos
   500 268
   ```

2. Use **downSample()** to undersample the data:

   ```
   set.seed(9560)
   undersampling <- downSample(
       x = PimaIndiansDiabetes[,-ncol(PimaIndiansDiabetes)],
       y = PimaIndiansDiabetes$diabetes)
   table(undersampling$Class)
   ```

   The output is as follows:

   ```
   neg pos
   268 268
   ```

In this example, we saw how the class with more data was undersampled to reduce the count of data.

Oversampling

This is a technique where the samples with a lower count are repeated/duplicated to increase the count so that the ratio is balanced. The disadvantage is that we are more likely to overfit our model, and we do not have unique data for training and testing. The duplicated samples are randomly picked. For instance, we can randomly pick and duplicate to increase **pos** samples from 268 to 500.

Exercise 20: Oversampling

The goal of this exercise is to perform oversampling for the data that contains minorities. The minority of the positive class having a count of 268 is oversampled to match the majority that had a count of 500.

1. Set a seed value so that we can repeat the experiments and have the sample results:

   ```
   set.seed(9560)
   ```

2. Perform oversampling using **upSample()**:

   ```
   oversampling <- upSample(
       x = PimaIndiansDiabetes[,-ncol(PimaIndiansDiabetes)],
       y = PimaIndiansDiabetes$diabetes)
   table(oversampling$Class)
   ```

   The output is as follows:

   ```
   neg pos
   500 500
   ```

Through the preceding example, we learned how to use **upSample()** to oversample the **pos** minority class for the diabetes column.

ROSE

The **Random Oversampling Examples** (**ROSE**) technique uses synthetic samples generated for the minority class, and is another technique that is used for binary imbalanced classification problems. It uses a smoothed bootstrap approach to create artificial samples in the data, thereby balancing it. ROSE creates artificial samples for the minority class.

Exercise 21: Oversampling using ROSE

In this exercise, we will learn to generate synthetic samples for the minority class to balance the dataset by oversampling using random examples in ROSE.

1. Attach the packages:

    ```
    library(caret)
    library(ROSE)
    ```

2. Set the seed value:

    ```
    set.seed(2)
    ```

3. Create an imbalanced dataset:

    ```
    imbalance_data <- twoClassSim(1000, intercept = -15, linearVars = 5)
    ```

4. View the count of the classes in this imbalanced dataset:

    ```
    table(imbalance_data$Class)
    ```

    The output is as follows:

    ```
    Class1 Class2
       908     92
    ```

5. Use **ROSE** to balance the minority class, which is **Class2**, to increase the sample for this class:

    ```
    balanced_data <- ROSE(Class ~ .,
                      data = imbalance_data, seed=3)$data table(balanced_
    data$Class)
    ```

    The output is as follows:

    ```
    Class1 Class2
       480    520
    ```

Through the preceding example, we learned to implement the ROSE method to perform oversampling.

SMOTE

Synthetic Minority Oversampling Technique (**SMOTE**) is used to handle imbalanced binary classes. In this technique, the minority class is oversampled and the majority class is undersampled.

Exercise 22: Implementing the SMOTE Technique

In this exercise, we will implement the SMOTE concept. Here are the steps to complete the exercise:

1. Set the seed:

   ```
   set.seed(2)
   ```

2. Create the imbalanced data:

   ```
   imbalance_data <- twoClassSim(1000, intercept = -15, linearVars = 5)
   ```

3. View the summary of the **Class** column:

   ```
   table(imbalance_data$Class)
   ```

   The output is as follows:

   ```
   Class1 Class2
      903     97
   ```

4. Use the **repeatedcv** method to get the **ctrl** values:

   ```
   ctrl <- trainControl(method = "repeatedcv",
                        number = 10,
                        repeats = 5,
                        summaryFunction = twoClassSummary,
                        classProbs = TRUE)
   ```

5. Set the sampling as **smote**:

   ```
   ctrl$sampling <- "smote"
   ```

6. Set the **smote_fit** values:

   ```
   smote_fit <- train(Class ~ .,
                      data = imbalance_data,
                      method = "gbm",
                      verbose = FALSE,
                      metric = "ROC",
                      trControl = ctrl)
   ```

7. Print the **smote_fit** values:

   ```
   smote_fit
   ```

The output is as follows:

```
Stochastic Gradient Boosting

1000 samples
  10 predictor
   2 classes: 'Class1', 'Class2'

No pre-processing
Resampling: Cross-Validated (10 fold, repeated 5 times)
Summary of sample sizes: 899, 899, 900, 900, 901, 901, ...
Addtional sampling using SMOTE

Resampling results across tuning parameters:

  interaction.depth  n.trees  ROC        Sens       Spec
  1                   50      0.9652074  0.9138803  0.8644444
  1                  100      0.9741817  0.9273211  0.8935556
  1                  150      0.9764500  0.9369963  0.8931111
  2                   50      0.9735849  0.9240098  0.8908889
  2                  100      0.9775766  0.9339219  0.8895556
  2                  150      0.9782565  0.9376679  0.9006667
  3                   50      0.9754686  0.9330379  0.8948889
  3                  100      0.9786717  0.9418388  0.8997778
  3                  150      0.9788557  0.9431624  0.8933333

Tuning parameter 'shrinkage' was held constant at a value of 0.1
Tuning
 parameter 'n.minobsinnode' was held constant at a value of 10
ROC was used to select the optimal model using the largest value.
The final values used for the model were n.trees = 150, interaction.depth = 3, shrinkage =
 0.1 and n.minobsinnode = 10.
```

Figure 2.35: SMOTE output

In the preceding example, we saw how to use SMOTE to balance the data.

Activity 8: Oversampling and Undersampling using SMOTE

The **mushrooms** dataset contains imbalanced data and has a property named **bruises**, which we will oversample and undersample in this activity.

The dataset can be found at https://github.com/TrainingByPackt/Practical-Machine-Learning-with-R/blob/master/Data/mushrooms.csv.

These are the steps that will help you solve the activity:

1. Read the **mushrooms.csv** file using the **read.csv()** command, and save the value in the **ms** variable.

2. Perform downsampling on **bruises**.

3. Perform oversampling on **bruises**.

The output will be oversampled as shown in the following:

```
   f    t
4748 4748
```

> **Note**
>
> The solution for this activity can be found on page 329.

Activity 9: Sampling and Oversampling using ROSE

We want to use the German Credit dataset to make predictions relating to class in the German Credit dataset. However, the dataset does not have a good balance of *Good* and *Bad* values. We want to use ROSE to perform sampling to balance the class values so that the dataset is balanced.

The dataset can be found at https://github.com/TrainingByPackt/Practical-Machine-Learning-with-R/blob/master/Data/GermanCredit.csv.

These are the steps that will help you solve the activity:

1. Load the dataset.

2. View samples from the data.

3. Check the count of unbalanced classes using the `summary()` method.

4. Use ROSE to balance the numbers.

The balanced data sampled using ROSE will look as follows:

```
Good   Bad
 480   520
```

> **Note**
>
> The solution for this activity can be found on page 330.

Summary

In this chapter, we learned how to perform several operations on a data frame, including scaling, standardizing, and normalizing. Also, we covered the sorting, ranking, and joining operations with their implementations in R. We discussed the need for pre-processing of the data; and identified and handled outliers, missing values, and duplicate values.

Next, we moved on to the sampling of data. It is important for the data to contain a reasonable sample of each class that is to be predicted. If the data is imbalanced, it can affect our predictions in a negative manner. Therefore, we can use either the undersampling, oversampling, ROSE, or SMOTE techniques imbalanced to ensure that the dataset is representative of all the classes that we want to predict. This can be done using the `MICE`, `rpart`, `ROSE`, and `caret` packages.

In the next chapter, we will cover feature engineering in detail, where we will focus on extracting features to create models.

3

Feature Engineering

Learning Objectives

By the end of this chapter, you will be able to:

- Interpret date, time series, domain-specific, and datatype-specific data in R.

- Perform numeric and string operations in R.

- Handle categorical variables.

- Generate automated text features in R.

- Identify and add features to an R data frame.

- Implement selection using the correlation analysis, PCA, and RFE approaches.

In this chapter, we will be handling, selecting, and normalizing features required for building a model.

Introduction

We learned about the process of machine learning in *Chapter 1, An Introduction to Machine Learning*, and looked at the different ways to process data in *Chapter 2, Data Cleaning and Pre-processing*. In this chapter, we will delve deep into the feature engineering process. Feature engineering is a process in which we select the attributes that are related to the target field in our dataset. The selection is made using techniques such as correlation analysis, **Principal Component Analysis** (**PCA**), and other techniques. During this process, new features can also be generated that are meaningful and add information to our dataset. In addition to this, we can generate statistics of existing numeric fields as features, as they contain statistical information about the fields or attributes.

In this chapter, we will learn how to create features for date variables, time series data, strings, and numeric variables, and explore text features. Furthermore, we will look at the implementation of new features to an R data frame. We will identify and handle redundant features appropriately. Correlation analysis and PCA will be used to select the required features. The features will be ranked using several techniques, such as learning vector quantization and PCA.

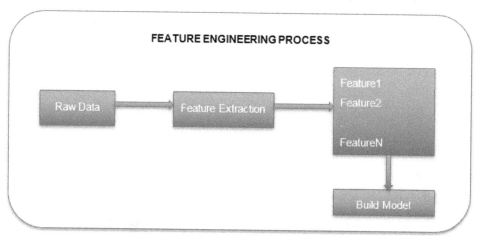

Figure 3.1: The feature engineering process

Figure 3.1 denotes a typical feature engineering process where the extraction of features from raw data is performed before the model building process. In *Figure 3.1*, N number of features are extracted for the model.

The datasets being used are shown in the following table:

Dataset	Description	Output Field
PimaIndiansDiabetes	This data contains diabetes-related information in 9 variables. It has 768 observations.	The diabetes column is the output variable which contains the test result of diabetes (positive or negative).
Sonar	This data contains numerical columns of 61 variables. It has 208 observations.	The class column is the output predictor variable.
GermanCredit	The data has variables that characterizes the credit worthiness in 62 variables Has 1000 observations	Class column is the output predictor variable which takes values "good" and "bad"

Figure 3.2: The description and output variable fields for datasets

In the next section, we will discuss the domain-specific features in detail.

Types of Features

We have two types of features:

- **Generic features, or datatype-specific features**: These are features based on the datatype of the field.

- **Domain-specific features**: These are features that are dependent upon the domain of the data. Here, we derive some features from the data based on our business knowledge or the domain.

Datatype-Based Features

Features can be extracted from the existing features. For instance, when we consider a date variable, we can extract the year from the entire date. From these datatypes, it is essential to extract the feature.

Date and Time Features

Imagine that you have a dataset containing information such as dates, months, and years in a non-numerical format; for example, 31/05/2019. We cannot feed this information to a machine learning algorithm, as such algorithms will not understand date-type values. Thus, converting date and time into machine-readable data format is an important skill for a machine learning engineer.

We can extract the year, month, day of the month, quarter, week, day of the week, the difference between two dates, and the hour, minute, and season. We can also find out whether the given date is a weekend or not, whether the time falls between business hours or not, whether it is a public holiday, and whether the year is a leap year. In the next exercise, we will extract the year, month, day, and weekday of the present time.

Exercise 23: Creating Date Features

In this exercise, we will use the date feature in R and extract the year, month, day, and weekday using the **POSIXlt()** function.

1. Fetch the current date using the following command:

```
#Fetch the current date
current_date <- Sys.time()
current_date
```

The output is as follows:

```
## [1] "2019-03-18 00:28:09 IST"
```

The **Sys.time()** function returns the time at the moment the command is executed.

> **Note**
>
> The output for *Exercises 1* and *2* will depend on the **current_date** variable that is shown in the preceding code. The year, month, date, minutes, and seconds will be different each time.

2. Use the **POSIXlt()** function to extract the local time:

```
# print the date
formatted_date <- as.POSIXlt(current_date)
formatted_date
```

The output is as follows:

```
## [1] "2019-03-18 00:28:09 IST"
```

We will be making use of the **POSIXlt** class, which is a subset of the **POSIXt** class. **POSIXlt** returns the local time, which contains the year, month of the year, day of month, hours, minutes, seconds, day of week, day of year, and a daylight savings indicator.

3. Fetch the year using the following command:

```
#Fetch the year
year <- format(formatted_date, "%Y")
year
```

The output is as follows:

```
## [1] "2019"
```

The **format()** function takes the date and the section of date that is required and returns the specified value.

4. Fetch the month using the following command:

```
#Fetch the month
month <- format(formatted_date, "%m")
month
```

The output is as follows:

```
## [1] "03"
```

5. Fetch the date using the following command:

```
#Fetch the date
day <- format(formatted_date, "%d")
day
```

The output is as follows:

```
## [1] "18"
```

As can be seen from the output, it is the 18th day of the month.

6. Fetch the day of the week using the following command:

```
#Fetch the day of week
weekday <- format(formatted_date, "%w")
weekday
```

The output is as follows:

```
## [1] "1"
```

The output is the first day of the week.

Thus, we have used the built-in functions to find the current time, date, day, and day of the week.

Note

The values of the variables are also displayed in the **Environment** tab of RStudio.

In the next exercise, we will extract the time and date. This is important for when we want to use time information in our features.

Exercise 24: Creating Time Features

In this exercise, we will use the time feature in R and extract the hour and minute using the **lubridate** library.

1. Install and attach the **lubridate** package:

```
install.packages("lubridate")
library(lubridate)
```

The **lubridate** package helps fetch time features. It can be installed using the **install.packages("lubridate")** command. The methods in the **lubridate** package, such as **hour()** and **minute()**, are simple to use.

2. Fetch the hour using the following command:

```
#Hour of Day
#hour<-hour(formatted_date)
```

The output is as follows:

```
## [1] 0
```

3. Fetch the minutes using the following command:

```
#Extract Minute
min <- minute(formatted_date)
```

The output is as follows:

```
## [1] 28
```

Thus, we have used the **lubricate** package to find the hour and minute from a given time.

Time Series Features

Time series data is a special type of data where some quantities are measured over time, and therefore it contains data along with the timestamp. An examples would be stock prices and forecasting of the market, where we would have a stock name, stock value, and time as the time series data.

The following figure presents some time series features:

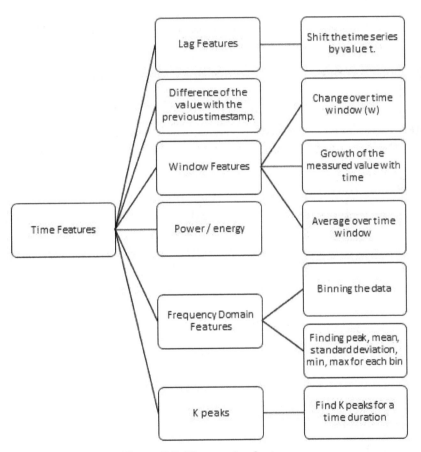

Figure 3.3: Time series features

The time series features are as follows:

1. **Lag features**: Using the lag feature of time series data, we can shift the time series data values by a specific value.

2. **Difference in value of timestamp**: In time series data, it is important to derive the difference between timestamps.

3. **Window Features**: Window features are features that tend to change over a fixed interval of time (window). These could be measured using the change over time window, growth of measured value with time, or average over time window.

4. **Power/Energy**: This features denotes the power consumption over a fixed time.

5. **Frequency Domain Features**: These features summarize the data by creating bins and then finding peak, mean, standard deviation, min, and max for each bin.

6. **K peaks**: For continuous data, it refers to picking the data point that have the highest value.

In this chapter, we will cover frequency domain features. In the next exercise, we will be learning about the binning feature from the frequency domain features.

Exercise 25: Binning

In this exercise, we will look at the binning feature. We will be performing binning on Age data from the **PimaIndianDiabetes** dataset. Binning helps in visualizing the data.

1. Attach the following packages:

```
library(caret)
library(mlbench)
#Install caret if not installed
#install.packages('caret')
```

2. Load the **PimaIndiansDiabetes** dataset:

```
data(PimaIndiansDiabetes)
age <- PimaIndiansDiabetes$age
```

3. Check the data summary as follows:

```
summary(age)
```

The output is as follows:

```
Min. 1st Qu.  Median    Mean 3rd Qu.    Max.
21.00   24.00   29.00   33.24   41.00   81.00
```

4. Create the bins (intervals):

```
#Creating Bins
# set up boundaries for intervals/bins
breaks <- c(0,10,20,30,40,50,60,70,80)
```

5. Create labels:

```
# specify interval/bin labels
labels <- c("<10", "10-20", "20-30", "30-40", "40-50", "50-60", "60-70",
"70-80")
```

6. Bucket the data points into the bins:

```
bins <- cut(age, breaks, include.lowest = T, right=FALSE, labels=labels)
```

7. Find the **summary** of the bins:

```
summary(bins)
```

The output is as follows:

```
<10 10-20 20-30 30-40 40-50 50-60 60-70 70-80  NA's
  0     0   396   165   118    57    29     2    1
```

8. Plot the bins:

```
plot(bins, main="Binning for Age",  ylab="Total Count of
People",col="bisque",xlab="Age",ylim=c(0,450))
```

The output is as follows:

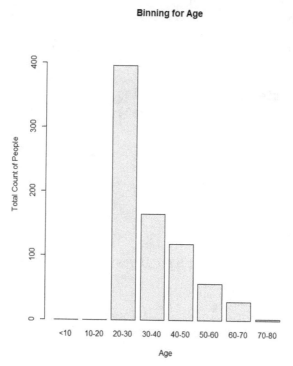

Figure 3.4: Binning the data

We have the maximum values for the age between 20 to 30. Binning has helped to categorize the continuous values and also to derive insights. In the following activity, we will be dealing with a **GermanCredit** dataset and creating bins.

Activity 10: Creating Time Series Features – Binning

In this activity, we will create bins for a continuous numeric field called **Duration** (this is the duration of credit for the customer) in the **GermanCredit** dataset. Often, we have lots of continuous data values; these values are binned to understand the **Data** column better. The dataset can be found at https://github.com/TrainingByPackt/Practical-Machine-Learning-with-R/blob/master/Data/GermanCredit.csv.

These are the steps that will help you solve the activity:

1. Attach the **caret** package.

2. Load the **GermanCredit** data from the **caret** package. (Hint: use **read.csv()**.)

3. Print the summary of the duration columns. (Hint: use **summary()**.)

4. Use **ggplot2** to plot **Duration** (Hint: use of the **gglplot2** package was covered in *Chapter 1, An Introduction to Machine Learning.*)

5. Set up bins using [breaks <- c(0,10,20,30,40,50,60,70,80)].

6. Set up labels, such as labels <- c("<10", "10-20", "20-30", "30-40", "40-50", "50-60", "60-70", "70-80").

7. Create a new set of bins for the preceding labels using bins <- cut(duration, breaks, include.lowest = T, right=FALSE, labels=labels).

8. Print summary of bins.

9. Use plot() to plot the frequency of the new bin's variable.

Once you complete the activity, you should obtain the following output:

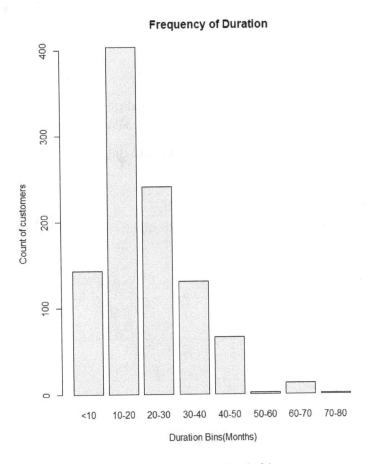

Figure 3.5: Plot of duration in bins

Note

The solution for this activity can be found on page 331.

Summary Statistics

The following are some of the summary statistics that can be derived for numeric features:

1. **Mean**: Calculates the average for the values in the field.

2. **Standard Deviation**: This defines spread of the data points around the mean.

3. **Minimum**: The lowest value in the field is the minimum value.

4. **Maximum**: The highest value in the field is the maximum value.

5. **Skewness**: The distribution is used to identify the asymmetry of the data.

In the following exercises, we will be finding descriptions of features in the GermanCredit dataset.

Exercise 26: Finding Description of Features

In this exercise, we will calculate the mean, standard deviation, minimum, maximum, and skewness of the dataset. These numeric features can be calculated as follows:

1. Attach the **caret** package and the GermanCredit dataset:

```
library(caret)
data(GermanCredit)
```

2. Check the structure of the GermanCredit dataset:

```
#See the structure of the dataset
str(GermanCredit)
```

The output is as follows:

```
'data.frame':   1000 obs. of  62 variables:
 $ Duration                        : int  6 48 12 42 24 36 24 36 12 30 ...
 $ Amount                          : int  1169 5951 2096 7882 4870 9055 2835 6948 3059 5234 ...
 $ InstallmentRatePercentage       : int  4 2 2 2 3 2 3 2 2 4 ...
 $ ResidenceDuration               : int  4 2 3 4 4 4 4 2 4 2 ...
 $ Age                             : int  67 22 49 45 53 35 53 35 61 28 ...
 $ NumberExistingCredits           : int  2 1 1 1 2 1 1 1 1 2 ...
 $ NumberPeopleMaintenance         : int  1 1 2 2 2 2 1 1 1 1 ...
 $ Telephone                       : num  0 1 1 1 1 0 1 0 1 1 ...
 $ ForeignWorker                   : num  1 1 1 1 1 1 1 1 1 1 ...
 $ Class                           : Factor w/ 2 levels "Bad","Good": 2 1 2 2 1 2 2 2 2 1 ...
 $ CheckingAccountStatus.lt.0      : num  1 0 0 1 1 0 0 0 0 0 ...
 $ CheckingAccountStatus.0.to.200  : num  0 1 0 0 0 0 0 1 0 1 ...
 $ CheckingAccountStatus.gt.200    : num  0 0 0 0 0 0 0 0 0 0 ...
 $ CheckingAccountStatus.none      : num  0 0 1 0 0 1 1 0 1 0 ...
 $ CreditHistory.NoCredit.AllPaid  : num  0 0 0 0 0 0 0 0 0 0 ...
 $ CreditHistory.ThisBank.AllPaid  : num  0 0 0 0 0 0 0 0 0 0 ...
 $ CreditHistory.PaidDuly          : num  0 1 0 1 0 1 1 1 1 0 ...
 $ CreditHistory.Delay             : num  0 0 0 0 1 0 0 0 0 0 ...
 $ CreditHistory.Critical          : num  1 0 1 0 0 0 0 0 0 1 ...
 $ Purpose.NewCar                  : num  0 0 0 0 1 0 0 0 0 1 ...
 $ Purpose.UsedCar                 : num  0 0 0 0 0 0 0 1 0 0 ...
 $ Purpose.Furniture.Equipment     : num  0 0 1 0 0 1 0 0 0 ...
 $ Purpose.Radio.Television        : num  1 1 0 0 0 0 0 1 0 ...
```

Figure 3.6: Section of the GermanCredit dataset

From the structure, we can identify the numeric fields.

3. Calculate the mean of the **Amount** values in the **GermanCredit** dataset:

```
#Calculate mean
mean <- mean(GermanCredit$Amount)
mean
```

The output is as follows:

```
[1] 3271.258
```

4. Calculate the standard deviation of the **Amount** values in the **GermanCredit** dataset:

```
#Calculate standard deviation
standard_dev <- sd(GermanCredit$Amount)
standard_dev
```

The output is as follows:

```
[1] 2822.737
```

5. Calculate the median of the **Amount** values in the **GermanCredit** dataset:

```
#Calculate median
median <- median(GermanCredit$Amount)
median
```

The output is as follows:

```
[1] 2319.5
```

6. Calculate the maximum **Amount** in the **GermanCredit** dataset:

```
#Identify maximum
min <- max(GermanCredit$Amount)
max
```

The output is as follows:

```
[1] 18424
```

7. Calculate the minimum **Amount** in the **GermanCredit** dataset:

```
#Identify minimum
min <- min(GermanCredit$Amount)
min
```

The output is as follows:

```
[1] 250
```

8. Calculate the skewness of the **Amount** values in the **GermanCredit** dataset. The **e1071** package contains implementations of many statistical functions (such as skewness) in R:

```
library(e1071)              # load e1071
skewness<-skewness(GermanCredit$Amount)
skewness
```

The output is as follows:

```
[1] 1.943783
```

In this exercise, we have descriptions of the features. In the next section, we will cover the standardizing technique.

Standardizing and Rescaling

Standardization contains two steps:

1. Subtract the mean from the value (if x is the value, then $x-mean$)

2. Then, divide by the standard deviation (($x-mean$)/standard deviation).

At times, features have to be scaled to lie within the same range. For instance, **Age** and **Income** will have different range of values; they could be scaled to [0-1] or any standard range such as [-1,1].

The steps to rescale are as follows:

1. Subtract the value by the minimum value, *x-min*; in our case, -1

   Numerator = x-(-1)

2. Subtract the max range and the min range; that is, 1 – (-1)

   Denominator = 1-(-1)

3. Divide the numerator by the denominator to get the rescaled value.

Handling Categorical Variables

Categorical variables are a list of string values or numeric values for an attribute. For instance, gender can be "Male" or "Female". There are two types of categories: nominal and ordinal. In nominal categorical data, there is no ordering among the values in that attribute. This is the case with gender values. Ordinal categories have some order within the set of values. For instance, for temperature "Low," "Medium," and "High" have an order.

- **Label Encoding:** String literals needs to be converted to numeric values, where "Male" can take value 1 and "Female" can take value 2. This is called integer encoding or label encoding. The integer values have a natural ordering so this may be suitable in cases dealing with categorical data, which is ordinal.

- **One-Hot Encoding:** For nominal categories, label encoding is not suitable as the natural order of the numbers may be learned by the machine learning model. Therefore, the integers are encoded into binary values. For instance, 1 representing "Male" becomes 00 and 2 representing "Female" becomes 01.

- **Hashing: Hashing:** Hashing is an approach where the categories are given hash values. There will be some information loss due to collision, but it works well with nominal and ordinal categories.

- **Count Encoding:** This is a technique where the categories are replaced with their counts. A log transformation is used to reduce the effect of outliers.

- **Binning: Binning:** Binning is an approach in which numeric values are converted to categorical values, such as discrete values. For example, "Age" can take a value from 1-100. 1-25 can be categorized as "young," 25-50 as "middle-aged," and 50-75 as "old age."

- **Variable Transformation: Many**

  Many modeling techniques require data to have a normal distribution, so we transform data to a normal distribution wherever possible. Data is considered highly skewed if the skewness value is less than –1 or greater than 1.

Skewness

Skewness denotes the alignment of the values in the specified column. A negative skewness value means that the data is skewed to the left and a positive skewness value means that the data is skewed to the right. We would not want the data to be skewed for the model. So, we will often try to reduce the skewness in the data.

Exercise 27: Computing Skewness

In this exercise, we will find the skewness of the **V4** column of the **Sonar** dataset. The **Sonar** dataset contains patterns of signals obtained from bouncing rocks and mines. The columns contain the pattern information. The "M" label indicates a mine and the "R" label indicates a rock.

1. Attach the **mlbench** package:

   ```
   library(mlbench)
   library(lattice)
   library(caret)
   library(e1071)
   ```

2. Load the **Sonar** dataset:

   ```
   data(Sonar)
   ```

3. Find the skewness of the **V4** column:

   ```
   skewness(Sonar$V4)
   ```

   The skewness is 0.5646697.

4. Plot the histogram:

   ```
   histogram(Sonar$V4,xlab="V4")
   ```

The histogram is as follows:

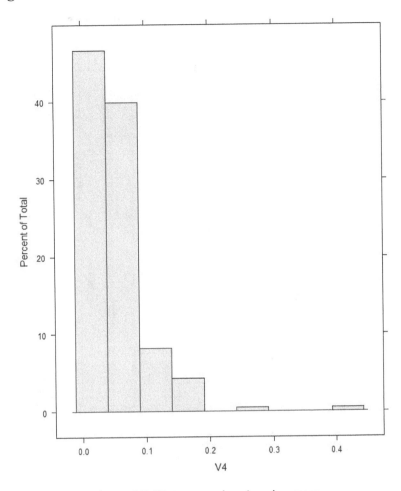

Figure 3.7: Histogram showing skewness

The histogram denotes skewness. The positive skewness value means that the graph is skewed to the right, as you can see in the preceding plot.

Activity 11: Identifying Skewness

In this activity, we will identify the skewness of the **glucose** column in the **PimaIndiansDiabetes** dataset. We will then compare it with the skewness of the **age** column. The dataset can be found at https://github.com/TrainingByPackt/Practical-Machine-Learning-with-R/blob/master/Data/GermanCredit.csv.

These are the steps that will help you solve the activity:

1. Attach the **mlbench** package and load the **PimaIndiansDiabetes** data. (Hint: use `library()` and `read.csv()`.)

2. Print the skewness for the durations of the **glucose** and **age** columns. (Hint: use `skewness(<<column name>>)`.)

3. Use `histogram()` to visualize the two columns.

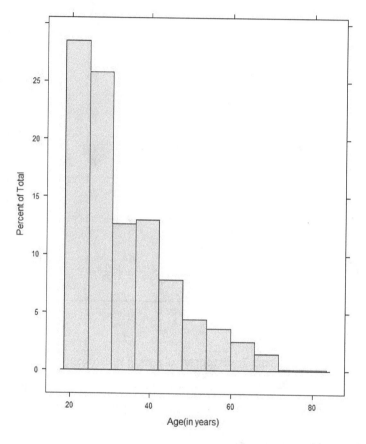

Figure 3.8: Histogram of the age values of the PimaIndiansDiabetes dataset

---

Note

The solution for this activity can be found on page 334.

Reducing Skewness Using Log Transform

When a continuous variable has a skewed distribution, we can log-transform it to reduce skewness. This will make the distribution normal. The **log()** function is used to log-transform the values.

Exercise 28: Using Log Transform

In this exercise, we will reduce the skewness of the data using log transform

1. Calculate the **log()** of the values:

    ```
    #Log Transformation
    transformed_data <- log(PimaIndiansDiabetes$age)
    ```

2. Plot the transformed data using the **histogram()** function:

    ```
    #View histogram
    histogram(transformed_data)
    ```

    The output is as follows:

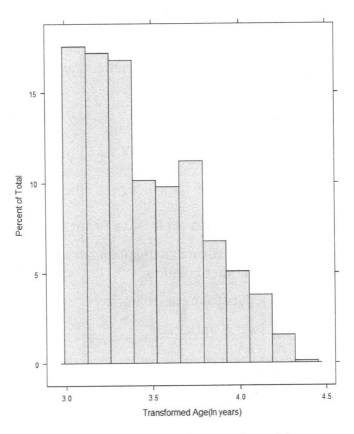

Figure 3.9: Histogram of log-transformed data

As we can see, the data distribution is now looking much better; it now follows a more normal distribution.

This is a transformation that transforms a skewed distribution to a distribution closer to a normal distribution.

Derived Features or Domain-Specific Features

These are features that are derived from data that requires an understanding of the business domain.

Let's imagine a dataset that contains data for the sale prices of houses in different areas of a city and that our goal is to predict the future price of any house. For this dataset, the input fields are area code, size of the house, floor number, type of house (individual/apartment), age of the property, renovated status, and so on, along with the sale price of the house. The derived features in this scenario are as follows:

- Total sales in the area for the past week, month, and so on

- Location of the house (central area or suburb, based on the area code)

- Livability index (based on the **age** and **renovated** columns)

Another example of deriving domain-specific features would be deriving a person's age from their birth date and the current date in a dataset containing information about people.

Adding Features to a Data Frame

We will look at the code to add new columns to an R data frame. A new column may be a new feature or a copy of an existing column. We'll look at an example in the following exercise. Adding new features can help in improving the efficiency of a model.

Exercise 29: Adding a New Column to an R Data Frame

In this exercise, we will add columns to an existing R data frame. These new columns can be dummy values or copies of other columns.

1. Add a new feature to the R data frame, as follows:

```
#Adding new features to a R datadrame
library(caret)
```

2. Load the **GermanCredit** dataset:

```
data(GermanCredit)
```

3. Assign the **GermanCredit** value to a new field:

```
#Assign the value to the new field
GermanCredit$NewField1 <- 1
```

4. Print the **GermanCredit** string:

```
str(GermanCredit)
```

The output is as follows:

```
$ OtherDebtorsGuarantors.None              : num  1 1 1 0 1 1 1 1 1 1 ...
$ OtherDebtorsGuarantors.CoApplicant       : num  0 0 0 0 0 0 0 0 0 0 ...
$ OtherDebtorsGuarantors.Guarantor         : num  0 0 0 1 0 0 0 0 0 0 ...
$ Property.RealEstate                      : num  1 1 1 0 0 0 0 0 1 0 ...
$ Property.Insurance                       : num  0 0 0 1 0 0 1 0 0 0 ...
$ Property.CarOther                        : num  0 0 0 0 0 0 0 1 0 1 ...
$ Property.Unknown                         : num  0 0 0 0 1 1 0 0 0 0 ...
$ OtherInstallmentPlans.Bank               : num  0 0 0 0 0 0 0 0 0 0 ...
$ OtherInstallmentPlans.Stores             : num  0 0 0 0 0 0 0 0 0 0 ...
$ OtherInstallmentPlans.None               : num  1 1 1 1 1 1 1 1 1 1 ...
$ Housing.Rent                             : num  0 0 0 0 0 0 0 1 0 0 ...
$ Housing.Own                              : num  1 1 1 0 0 0 1 0 1 1 ...
$ Housing.ForFree                          : num  0 0 0 1 1 1 0 0 0 0 ...
$ Job.UnemployedUnskilled                  : num  0 0 0 0 0 0 0 0 0 0 ...
$ Job.UnskilledResident                    : num  0 0 1 0 0 1 0 0 1 0 ...
$ Job.SkilledEmployee                      : num  1 1 0 1 1 0 1 0 0 0 ...
$ Job.Management.SelfEmp.HighlyQualified   : num  0 0 0 0 0 0 0 1 0 1 ...
$ NewField                                 : num  1 1 1 1 1 1 1 1 1 1 ...
```

Figure 3.10: Section showing the added NewField

5. Copy an existing column into a new column, as follows:

```
#Copy an existing column into a new column
GermanCredit$NewField2 <- GermanCredit$Purpose.Repairs
```

6. Print the **GermanCredit** string:

```
str(GermanCredit)
```

The output is as follows:

```
$ OtherDebtorsGuarantors.None             : num  1 1 1 0 1 1 1 1 1 1 ...
$ OtherDebtorsGuarantors.CoApplicant      : num  0 0 0 0 0 0 0 0 0 0 ...
$ OtherDebtorsGuarantors.Guarantor        : num  0 0 0 1 0 0 0 0 0 0 ...
$ Property.RealEstate                     : num  1 1 1 0 0 0 0 0 1 0 ...
$ Property.Insurance                      : num  0 0 0 1 0 0 1 0 0 0 ...
$ Property.CarOther                       : num  0 0 0 0 0 0 0 1 0 1 ...
$ Property.Unknown                        : num  0 0 0 0 1 1 0 0 0 0 ...
$ OtherInstallmentPlans.Bank              : num  0 0 0 0 0 0 0 0 0 0 ...
$ OtherInstallmentPlans.Stores            : num  0 0 0 0 0 0 0 0 0 0 ...
$ OtherInstallmentPlans.None              : num  1 1 1 1 1 1 1 1 1 1 ...
$ Housing.Rent                            : num  0 0 0 0 0 0 0 1 0 0 ...
$ Housing.Own                             : num  1 1 1 0 0 0 1 0 1 1 ...
$ Housing.ForFree                         : num  0 0 0 1 1 1 0 0 0 0 ...
$ Job.UnemployedUnskilled                 : num  0 0 0 0 0 0 0 0 0 0 ...
$ Job.UnskilledResident                   : num  0 0 1 0 0 1 0 0 1 0 ...
$ Job.SkilledEmployee                     : num  1 1 0 1 1 0 1 0 0 0 ...
$ Job.Management.SelfEmp.HighlyQualified  : num  0 0 0 0 0 0 0 1 0 1 ...
$ NewField                                : num  1 1 1 1 1 1 1 1 1 1 ...
$ NewField2                               : num  0 0 0 0 0 0 0 0 0 0 ...
```

Figure 3.11: Section showing the added NewField2

We have added two new features to the dataset.

Handling Redundant Features

Redundant features are those that are highly correlated with each other. They will contain similar information with respect to their output variables. We can remove such features by finding correlation coefficients between features.

Exercise 30: Identifying Redundant Features

In this exercise, we will find redundant features, select any one among them, and remove them.

1. Attach the **caret** package:

    ```
    #Loading the library
    library(caret)
    ```

2. Load the **GermanCredit** dataset:

    ```
    # load the German Credit Data
    data(GermanCredit)
    ```

3. Create a correlation matrix:

    ```
    # calculating the correlation matrix
    correlationMatrix <- cor(GermanCredit[,1:9])
    ```

4. Print the correlation matrix:

```
# printing the correlation matrix
print(correlationMatrix)
```

The output is as follows:

```
                             Duration       Amount
Duration                   1.00000000   0.62498420
Amount                     0.62498420   1.00000000
InstallmentRatePercentage  0.07474882  -0.27131570
ResidenceDuration          0.03406720   0.02892632
Age                       -0.03613637   0.03271642
NumberExistingCredits     -0.01128360   0.02079455
NumberPeopleMaintenance   -0.02383448   0.01714215
Telephone                 -0.16471821  -0.27699511
ForeignWorker              0.13819629   0.05005001
                           InstallmentRatePercentage
Duration                                  0.07474882
Amount                                   -0.27131570
InstallmentRatePercentage                 1.00000000
ResidenceDuration                         0.04930237
Age                                       0.05826568
NumberExistingCredits                     0.02166874
NumberPeopleMaintenance                  -0.07120694
Telephone                                -0.01441288
ForeignWorker                             0.09002443
                           ResidenceDuration           Age
Duration                          0.03406720  -0.036136374
Amount                            0.02892632   0.032716417
InstallmentRatePercentage         0.04930237   0.058265684
ResidenceDuration                 1.00000000   0.266419184
Age                               0.26641918   1.000000000
NumberExistingCredits             0.08962523   0.149253582
NumberPeopleMaintenance           0.04264343   0.118200833
Telephone                        -0.09535937  -0.145258701
ForeignWorker                     0.05409740   0.006151396
                           NumberExistingCredits
Duration                            -0.011283597
Amount                               0.020794552
InstallmentRatePercentage            0.021668743
ResidenceDuration                    0.089625233
Age                                  0.149253582
NumberExistingCredits                1.000000000
NumberPeopleMaintenance              0.109666700
Telephone                           -0.065553213
ForeignWorker                        0.009716975
                           NumberPeopleMaintenance
Duration                             -0.02383448
Amount                                0.01714215
InstallmentRatePercentage            -0.07120694
ResidenceDuration                     0.04264343
Age                                   0.11820083
NumberExistingCredits                 0.10966670
NumberPeopleMaintenance               1.00000000
Telephone                             0.01475344
ForeignWorker                        -0.07707085
                             Telephone ForeignWorker
Duration                   -0.16471821   0.138196285
Amount                     -0.27699511   0.050050007
InstallmentRatePercentage  -0.01441288   0.090024429
ResidenceDuration          -0.09535937   0.054097396
Age                        -0.14525870   0.006151396
NumberExistingCredits      -0.06555321   0.009716975
NumberPeopleMaintenance     0.01475344  -0.077070853
Telephone                   1.00000000  -0.107400909
ForeignWorker              -0.10740091   1.000000000
```

Figure 3.12: The correlation matrix

5. To find attributes that have high correlation, set the cutoff as **0.5**.

```
# finding the attributes that are highly corrected
filterCorrelation <- findCorrelation(correlationMatrix, cutoff=0.5)
```

6. Print the indexes that have a high level of correlation.

```
# print indexes of highly correlated fields
print(filterCorrelation)
```

The output is as follows:

```
[1] 2
```

7. Print the correlation matrix:

```
print(correlationMatrix)
```

The correlation matrix is as follows:

```
> print(correlationMatrix)
                           Duration       Amount  InstallmentRatePercentage  ResidenceDuration
Duration                 1.00000000   0.62498420                 0.07474882         0.03406720
Amount                   0.62498420   1.00000000                -0.27131570         0.02892632
InstallmentRatePercentage 0.07474882 -0.27131570                 1.00000000         0.04930237
ResidenceDuration        0.03406720   0.02892632                 0.04930237         1.00000000
>
```

Figure 3.13: The correlation matrix with a cutoff of 0.5

The output is the index of the highly correlated field; here it is **Amount**. If the fields are highly correlated, we can remove one of them. Now that we have covered redundant features, we will move on to text features.

Text Features

Text features are generated for purely textual content, such as a data containing user blogs or user feedback regarding a product on a web page. The following are some text features:

- **N-grams**: N-grams form features. Using unigrams means splitting text into separate, individual words. For instance, "The product is extremely functional" will create the unigrams "The," "product," "is," "extremely," and "functional." The bigram of this textual data is "The product," "product is," "is extremely," "extremely functional." N-grams is splitting the text into n grams.

- **TF-IDF**: This means **Term Frequency-Inverse Document Frequency**. Term frequency is the number of times a term is repeated in text data. Inverse document frequency is the importance of a term in a text.

- **Levenshtein Distance**: This is a distance metric that is calculated at the character-level. It is the minimum edits needed to convert a string to another.

- **Cosine Similarity**: This is a distance metric where two words are compared and the similarity is measured. Cosine similarity measures the angle of similarity between the words by projecting the words on vectors in a multi-dimensional space.

- **Number of words**: The words will be separated using a space.

- **Number of characters**: Each character will be counted in this case.

- **Number of stop words**: The stop words will be counted. A stop word is a word that is used very often, such as "a", "the", and "as."

- **Number of special characters**: Special characters such as !, @, and $.

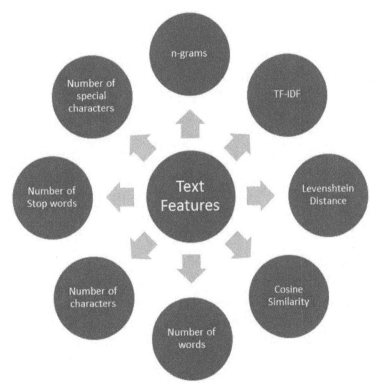

Figure 3.14: Text features

Automated feature engineering is a process where generic features are calculated for a field by a pre-defined package. For text features, the package used is **textfeatures**. This R package generates the common text features used to train a machine learning model with textual data. This process is important because it saves us the time it takes to implement numerous text features.

> **Note**
>
> Using the **textfeatures** package requires R version 3.1 or above.

Exercise 31: Automatically Generating Text Features

In this exercise, we will use the **textfeatures** package to find text features.

1. Install the **itunesr**, **textfeatures**, and **tidyverse** packages:

   ```
   install.packages("itunesr")
   install.packages("textfeatures")
   install.packages("tidyverse")
   ```

2. Attach the **itunersr**, **textfeatures**, and **tidyverse** pacakge:

   ```
   library(itunesr)
   library(textfeatures)
   library(tidyverse)
   ```

3. Create a **text_data** character vector with a few lines of text:

   ```
   ## the text is a review of a product
   text_data <- c(
     "This product was delivered very fast",
     "IT'S A GREAT DAY TODAY!",
     paste("The product works very efficiently"),
     paste("The product saves us a lot of time"),
     paste("The seller arranged a timely delivery")
   )
   ```

4. Use the **`textfeatures()`** function on **`text_data`**:

```
## get the text features of a sample character vector
textfeatures(text_data)
```

The output is as follows:

```
  |==========================================================================================| 100%
  |==========================================================================================| 100%Warni
ng in get_dtm(corp) : dtm has 0 rows. Empty iterator?
  |========================================                                                  |  45%
INFO [2019-03-14 15:51:27] iter 10 loglikelihood = 0.000
  |==========================================================================================| 100%INFO
[2019-03-14 15:51:27] early stopping at 10 iteration

# A tibble: 5 x 31
  id    n_urls n_hashtags n_mentions n_chars n_commas n_digits n_exclaims n_extraspaces n_lowers n_lowersp n_periods n_words n_caps n_nonasciis
  <chr>  <dbl>      <dbl>      <dbl>   <dbl>    <dbl>    <dbl>      <dbl>         <dbl>    <dbl>     <dbl>     <dbl>   <dbl>  <dbl>       <dbl>
1 1          0          0          0   0.611        0        0     -0.447             0    0.470     0.449         0    0     -0.447           0
2 2          0          0          0  -0.111        0        0      1.79              0   -1.79     -1.79          0    0      1.79            0
3 3          0          0          0   0.296        0        0     -0.447             0    0.448     0.447         0   -1.41  -0.447           0
4 4          0          0          0  -1.66         0        0     -0.447             0    0.379     0.441         0    1.41  -0.447           0
5 5          0          0          0   0.869        0        0     -0.447             0    0.491     0.451         0    0     -0.447           0
# ... with 16 more variables: n_puncts <dbl>, n_capsp <dbl>, n_charsperword <dbl>, sent_afinn <dbl>, sent_bing <dbl>, n_polite <dbl>,
#   n_first_person <dbl>, n_first_personp <dbl>, n_second_person <dbl>, n_second_personp <dbl>, n_third_person <dbl>, n_tobe <dbl>,
#   n_prepositions <dbl>, V3 <dbl>, w1 <dbl>, w2 <dbl>
```

Figure 3.15: Text features of text_data

5. Create a data frame with the **`text`** character vector:

```
## data frame with a character vector named "text"
df <- data.frame(
  id = c(1, 2, 3),
  text = c("this is A!\t sEntence https://github.com about #rstats @
github",
           "and another sentence here",
           "The following list:\n- one\n- two\n- three\nOkay!?!"),
  stringsAsFactors = FALSE
)
```

6. Generate the text features using the **`textfeatures()`** function:

```
## Generate the text features
Features <- textfeatures(df)
```

7. Print the text features using the **`glimpse()`** function:

```
#print the text features
glimpse(features)
```

The output is as follows:

```
Observations: 3
Variables: 30
$ id                     <dbl> 1, 2, 3
$ n_urls                 <dbl> 1.1547005, -0.5773503, -0.5773503
$ n_hashtags             <dbl> 1.1547005, -0.5773503, -0.5773503
$ n_mentions             <dbl> 1.1547005, -0.5773503, -0.5773503
$ n_chars                <dbl> -0.7915877, -0.3322458, 1.1238335
$ n_commas               <dbl> 0, 0, 0
$ n_digits               <dbl> 0, 0, 0
$ n_exclaims             <dbl> 0.1726115, -1.0750696, 0.9024581
$ n_extraspaces          <dbl> 0.4446494, -1.1452089, 0.7005594
$ n_lowers               <dbl> -1.0828248, 0.1941117, 0.8887132
$ n_lowersp              <dbl> -0.08713506, 1.04071627, -0.95358121
$ n_periods              <dbl> 0, 0, 0
$ n_words                <dbl> -0.1891344, -0.8919272, 1.0810616
$ n_caps                 <dbl> 0.5773503, -1.1547005, 0.5773503
$ n_nonasciis            <dbl> 0, 0, 0
$ n_puncts               <dbl> -0.5773503, -0.5773503, 1.1547005
$ n_capsp                <dbl> 1.0744449, -0.9035230, -0.1709219
$ n_charsperword         <dbl> -0.4231694, 1.1420124, -0.7188430
$ sent_afinn             <dbl> -0.5773503, -0.5773503, 1.1547005
$ sent_bing              <dbl> 0, 0, 0
$ n_polite               <dbl> 0.5773503, 0.5773503, -1.1547005
$ n_first_person         <dbl> 1.1547005, -0.5773503, -0.5773503
$ n_first_personp        <dbl> 0, 0, 0
$ n_second_person        <dbl> 0, 0, 0
$ n_second_personp       <dbl> 0, 0, 0
$ n_third_person         <dbl> 0, 0, 0
$ n_tobe                 <dbl> 1.1547005, -0.5773503, -0.5773503
$ n_prepositions         <dbl> 1.1547005, -0.5773503, -0.5773503
$ v2                     <dbl> 0, 0, 0
$ w1                     <dbl> 0, 0, 0
```

Figure 3.16: Glimpse of the text features

The output shows the features generated for the text data that we provided. Three of the feature has been explained below:

- **n_hashtags**: This feature value is based on the number of hashtags in the text.

- **n_commas**: This feature value is based on the number of commas in the text.

- **n_digits**: This feature value is based on the number of numerical digits in the text.

In the next section, we will discuss in detail the various feature selection approaches.

Feature Selection

There are two types of feature selection techniques: forward selection and backward selection.

- **Forward Selection**: This is an approach that can be used for a labeled dataset. Basically, we start with one feature and build the model. We add more features in an incremental fashion and make a note of the accuracy as we go. We then select the combination of features that gave the highest level of accuracy while training the model. One con of this technique is that for a dataset with a large set of features, this is an extremely time-consuming process. Also, if an already-added feature is causing degradation of the performance of the model, we will not know it.

- **Backward Selection**: In this approach, we will need a labeled dataset. All the features will be used to build the model. We will iteratively remove features to observe the performance of the model. We can then select the best combination (the combination that produced the highest performance). The con of this approach is that for a dataset with a large set of features, this is an extremely time-consuming process.

In the selection of features, it is useful to find the correlation between the values. In the next section, we will look at correlation analysis, which helps us determine the correlation between two values.

Correlation Analysis

The correlation between two variables plays an important part in feature selection. If two features are correlated with each other and they are linearly dependent on each other, then one of the features can be dropped as it has the same relationship with the output variable as the other. The linear dependency can be in the form of positive correlation or negative correlation. A positive correlation between fields x and y means that as x increases, y also increases. A negative correlation between x and y means that as x increases, y decreases.

Exercise 32: Plotting Correlation between Two Variables

In this exercise, we will plot the correlation between two variables.

1. Load the **PimaIndiansDiabetes** dataset from the **mlbench** packages:

    ```
    library(mlbench)
    data(PimaIndiansDiabetes)
    ```

2. Use **plot()** with an additional parameter, **main = "Pearson Correlation"**, to plot the correlation between the **glucose** and **pressure** fields:

    ```
    #Correlation Analysis between glucose and pressure
    plot(PimaIndiansDiabetes$glucose, PimaIndiansDiabetes$pressure, col="red",
    xlab = "Glucose", ylab = "Pressure", pch=16, main = "Pearson Correlation")
    ```

3. Load the **Sonar** dataset from the **mlbench** library:

    ```
    data(Sonar)
    ```

4. Use **plot()** with an additional parameter, **main = "Pearson Correlation"**, to plot the correlation between the **V3** and **V4** fields:

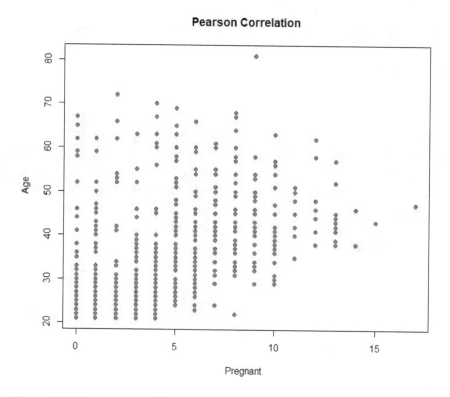

Figure 3.17: Pearson correlation in the PimaIndiansDiabetes dataset between
the Pregnant and Age variables

The correlation between **glucose** and **pressure** is 0.544, which means there is a moderate positive correlation:

5. Use **plot()** with an additional parameter, **main = "Pearson Correlation"**, to plot the correlation between the **glucose** and **pressure** fields:

```
plot(Sonar$V4, Sonar$V3, col="red", xlab = "V4",
     ylab = "V3", pch=16, main = "Pearson Correlation")
```

The output is as follows:

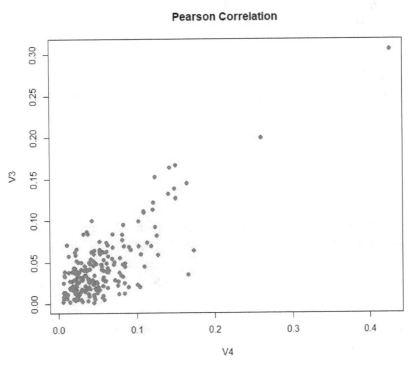

Figure 3.18: Pearson correlation between Sonar v3 and v4

The correlation value between **v3** and **v4** is 0.78, which means there is a strong positive correlation, which means that as **v3** increases, **v4** also increases. Since they are strongly correlated and since these are two input fields, we can drop one and retain another.

P-Value

When we want to know whether a feature is correlated with the output variable in the *real world*, it is not enough to calculate the *correlation coefficient* for the two variables in the dataset, as these might not be representative of the real world. We also need to account for things such as the size of our dataset and the probability of the variables being correlated in our dataset by chance.

The p-value is the probability (0–1) that, given that the **null hypothesis** is true (that there is **no** correlation), we would see a correlation coefficient with the same magnitude as the one in our dataset, or higher, simply due to the random selection of observations from the target population (the real world). If the p-value is below a threshold, such as 0.05, we say that the correlation is significant. Note that *significant* does **not** mean *important* in this context. It instead means that we have strong evidence against the null hypothesis, meaning we can reasonably reject the null hypothesis. The p-value does not address the probability of the alternative hypothesis (that there **is** a correlation) directly, but by rejecting the null hypothesis, the alternative hypothesis becomes more viable. Importantly, a p-value greater than 0.05 does **not** mean that the two variables are not correlated in the real world, as we might just have too few datapoints to say so.

P-values are highly debated in many scientific fields. They are commonly misunderstood and misused, and it is recommended that you read up on them if you will be relying on them in your work.

It is possible for a feature to be useful in a model without being significantly correlated to the output variable. We therefore decide whether or not we should include it in the model based on whether it makes the model better at predicting the output variable in a test set. We will do this in the *Recursive Feature Elimination* section.

The `cor.test()` function in R is used to calculate the Pearson's product moment correlation coefficient between two variables. It outputs a correlation estimate and a p-value.

Exercise 33: Calculating the P-Value

In this exercise, we are finding the p-value for a correlation coefficient between two variables.

1. Attach the **caret** package:

```
library(caret)
```

2. Calculate the p-value for the **V3** and **V4** fields:

```
#Calculating P-Value
component=cor.test(Sonar$V4, Sonar$V3)
print(component)
```

The output is as follows:

```
        Pearson's product-moment correlation

data:  Sonar$V4 and Sonar$V3
t = 17.995, df = 206, p-value < 2.2e-16
alternative hypothesis: true correlation is not equal to 0
95 percent confidence interval:
 0.7225966 0.8295954
sample estimates:
     cor
0.781786
```

Figure 3.19: P-value

`cor.test()` in R is used to calculate the Pearson's product moment correlation coefficient between two fields. The two fields can be any two fields for which we need to find the correlation. It can be two input fields or one input and one output field. It will output a correlation estimate and a p-value.

3. Print the p-value:

```
#Print the P value
component$p.value
```

The output is as follows:

```
[1] 3.918396e-44
```

4. Print the correlation:

```
#Print the Correlation
component$estimate
```

The output is as follows:

```
     cor
0.781786
```

The p-value of 3.918396e-44 suggests that we have strong evidence against the null hypothesis and have no reason not to trust the correlation coefficient of 0.781786. With such a high correlation, it is likely a good feature to include in our model.

Recursive Feature Elimination

Recursive Feature Elimination (**RFE**) is a recursive method used for feature selection in R's **caret** package. This method uses all possible combinations of the subset of the features to train models and accordingly drop features. The algorithms used here are linear regression, random forest, naïve Bayes, and bagged trees. This method will build models with the subset of columns and the best subset size will be printed as output.

In the following example, nine features from the **GermanCredit** dataset have been provided as input to the function. RFE selects the top five features that are important.

Exercise 34: Implementing Recursive Feature Elimination

In this exercise, we will be eliminating features using the recursive feature elimination technique. The top features will be selected for training the model.

1. Install the **e1071** and **randomforest** packages:

```
set.seed(7)
install.packages("e1071")
install.packages("randomForest")
```

2. Attach the **e1071** and **randomForest** packages:

```
library(e1071)
library(randomForest)
```

3. Attach the **mlbench** and **caret** packages:

```
# Attach the packages
library(mlbench)
library(caret)
```

4. Load the German credit data:

```
# load the German Credit Data
data("GermanCredit")
```

5. Use the **rfeControl()** function with the parameter as **rfFuncs**, the **method** parameter as **cv**, and the **number** parameter as 9.

```
# Use random forest as the method
method_fn <- rfeControl(functions=rfFuncs, method="cv", number=9)
```

The **rfeControl()** function in R creates a control object through which we can specify a function for prediction/model fitting, a method that is a sampling method, and the number of folds or iterations.

6. Run the recursive elimination function using the random forest function with the `GermanCredit[,1:9]` data frame for model training, and `GermanCredit[,10]` as the outcomes of the features mentioned in sizes.

```
# run the Recursive Feature Elimination algorithm
output <- rfe(GermanCredit[,1:9], GermanCredit[,10], sizes=c(1:9),
rfeControl=method_fn)
```

The `rfe()` function in R performs recursive feature elimination.

7. Print the output:

```
# print the output
print(output)
```

The output is as follows:

```
Recursive feature selection

Outer resampling method: Cross-Validated (9 fold)

Resampling performance over subset size:
```

Variables	Accuracy	Kappa	AccuracySD	KappaSD	Selected
1	0.7000	0.07993	0.01450	0.05992	
2	0.6841	0.11776	0.03479	0.09647	
3	0.6900	0.08827	0.03138	0.08838	
4	0.6781	0.13250	0.03428	0.10378	
5	0.7130	0.20887	0.03098	0.09935	
6	0.7271	0.23200	0.03680	0.11610	
7	0.7280	0.21180	0.02549	0.09123	
8	0.7230	0.20408	0.02081	0.08139	
9	0.7281	0.23882	0.03347	0.10788	*

```
The top 5 variables (out of 9):
    Duration, Amount, Age, NumberPeopleMaintenance, Telephone
```

8. Print the selected features:

```
predictors(output)
```

The output is as follows:

```
[1] "Duration"                  "Amount"                        "Age"
"NumberPeopleMaintenance"
[5] "Telephone"                 "InstallmentRatePercentage"
"ResidenceDuration"            "NumberExistingCredits"
[9] "ForeignWorker"
```

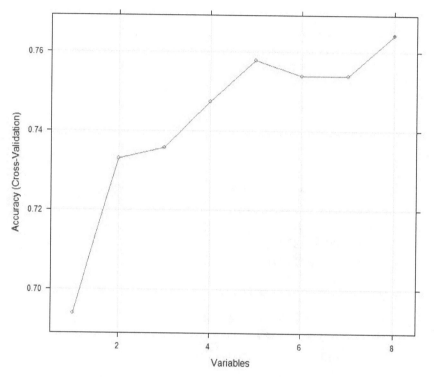

Figure 3.20: Plot of accuracy versus variables

The preceding plot shows the accuracy values for each of the different variables chosen for the model. For instance, with these two variables, the accuracy is 0.73.

PCA

We visited PCA in *Chapter 2, Data Cleaning and Pre-Processing*, where we used PCA for pre-processing. In this chapter, we will delve into the details of this technique. PCA basically reduces the dimensionality of our data. For instance, if our data contains 20 columns, we can reduce it to 5 key fields generated from the 20 columns. These 5 key fields will now represent the data. Basically, PCA forms a linear combination of the data where the generated components will not be correlated with each other. These five values will also have maximum variance.

If our data has many dimensions, such as a large number of fields, then this technique can help to reduce the dimensions by generating the principal components. These components will represent most of the information from our high dimensional dataset. To perform PCA, there is first a check for correlation between all the fields, and then the important fields are chosen, and a linear combination of those fields is created to represent all the information from the fields. In this way, PCA helps to perform feature selection and is also known as a dimensionality reduction technique. PCA can even be applied to unlabeled data.

Exercise 35: Implementing PCA

In this exercise, we will be using PCA to find the principal components in the **PimaIndiansDiabetes** dataset.

1. Load the **PimaIndiansDiabetes** data:

   ```
   #PCA Analysis
   data(PimaIndiansDiabetes)
   ```

2. Create a subset of the first nine columns into another variable named **PimaIndiansDiabetes_subset**:

   ```
   #Use the
   PimaIndiansDiabetes_subset <- PimaIndiansDiabetes[,1:8]
   ```

3. Find the principal components:

   ```
   #Find out the Principal components
   principal_components <- prcomp(x = PimaIndiansDiabetes_subset, scale. = T)
   ```

   The **prcomp()** function performs PCA for the data in R.

4. Print the principal components:

```
#Print the principal components
print(principal_components)
```

The output is as follows:

```
Standard deviations (1, .., p=8):
[1] 1.4471973 1.3157546 1.0147068 0.9356971 0.8731234 0.8262133 0.6479322 0.6359733

Rotation (n x k) = (8 x 8):
               PC1        PC2        PC3        PC4        PC5        PC6        PC7        PC8
pregnant -0.1284321  0.5937858 -0.01308692  0.08069115 -0.4756057  0.193598168  0.58879003  0.117840984
glucose  -0.3930826  0.1740291  0.46792282 -0.40432871  0.4663280  0.094161756  0.06015291  0.450355256
pressure -0.3600026  0.1838921 -0.53549442  0.05598649  0.3279531 -0.634115895  0.19211793 -0.011295538
triceps  -0.4398243 -0.3319653 -0.23767380  0.03797608 -0.4878621  0.009589438 -0.28221253  0.566283799
insulin  -0.4350262 -0.2507811  0.33670893 -0.34994376 -0.3469348 -0.270650609  0.13200992 -0.548621381
mass     -0.4519413 -0.1009598 -0.36186463  0.05364595  0.2532038  0.685372179  0.03536644 -0.341517637
pedigree -0.2706114 -0.1220690  0.43318905  0.83368010  0.1198105 -0.085784088  0.08609107 -0.008258731
age      -0.1980271  0.6205885  0.07524755  0.07120060 -0.1092900 -0.033357170 -0.71208542 -0.211661979
```

Figure 3.21: Principal components of the PrimaIndiansDiabetes dataset

The principal components are PC1, PC2,.. PC8, in their order of importance. These components are calculated from multiple fields and can be used as features on their own.

Activity 12: Generating PCA

In this activity, we will use the **GermanCredit** dataset and find the principal components. These values can be used instead of the features. The dataset can be found at https://github.com/TrainingByPackt/Practical-Machine-Learning-with-R/blob/master/Data/GermanCredit.csv.

These are the steps that will help you solve the activity:

1. Load the **GermanCredit** data.

2. Create a subset of the first nine columns into another variable named **GermanCredit_subset**.

3. Use **prcomp(x = GermanCredit_subset, scale. = T)** to generate the principal components.

4. Print the generated **principal_components**.

5. Interpret the results.

The PCA values will look as follows:

```
Standard deviations (1, .., p=9):
[1] 1.3505916 1.2008442 1.1084157 0.9721503 0.9459586 0.9317018 0.9106746 0.8345178 0.5211137

Rotation (n x k) = (9 x 9):
                             PC1         PC2         PC3         PC4         PC5         PC6         PC7         PC8         PC9
Duration               0.58346016 -0.20189333  0.12607255 -0.21394820 -0.36935166  0.007214856 -0.18401918 -0.07228018 -0.61772568
Amount                 0.63752012 -0.19597234 -0.20145979  0.01877283 -0.06099068  0.031119661 -0.10715380 -0.09832788  0.69884609
InstallmentRatePercentage -0.11091325  0.21017115  0.63060195 -0.35109100 -0.49102817  0.231088890  0.14106768  0.04384568  0.32598981
ResidenceDuration      0.15008720  0.50427875  0.08265692  0.43069132 -0.18654202 -0.221281544 -0.42182623  0.51846212  0.01859594
Age                    0.12965396  0.59827665 -0.05602464  0.24438107 -0.08053172  0.038094595  0.11150502 -0.73307644 -0.06799295
NumberExistingCredits  0.08144692  0.40299991 -0.14933373 -0.59017205  0.42288252  0.339609189 -0.40121515  0.06984228 -0.01839272
NumberPeopleMaintenance 0.01856789  0.26671893 -0.48949217 -0.42738113 -0.29772936 -0.473379812  0.39954279  0.18380489  0.01044675
Telephone             -0.39964528 -0.17281706 -0.11414936 -0.16231291 -0.30734854 -0.337741629 -0.65030093 -0.35155164  0.12660953
ForeignWorker          0.18657318  0.03188044  0.51083921 -0.16759647  0.46425426 -0.664581419  0.02974633 -0.12136714  0.04809892
```

Figure 3.22: Principal components of the GermanCredit dataset

> **Note**
>
> The solution for this activity can be found on page 337.

Ranking Features

While building certain models such as decision trees and random forests, the features that are important to the model (for instance, the features that have good correlation with the output variable) are known. These features are then ranked by the model. We will look at a few examples of ranking features automatically using machine learning models.

Variable Importance Approach with Learning Vector Quantization

In **Learning Vector Quantization** (**LVQ**) , we rank features based on their importance. LVQ and the variable importance function, `varImp()`, will be used to fetch the important variables. The `GermanCredit` dataset is used to demonstrate LVQ. For simplicity's sake, we are choosing the first ten columns in the `GermanCredit` dataset. The 10th column contains the class values for prediction.

Exercise 36: Implementing LVQ

In this exercise, we will implement LVQ for the `GermanCredit` dataset and use the variable importance function to list the importance of the fields in this dataset.

1. Attach the **mlbench** and **caret** packages.

```
set.seed(9)
# loading the libraries
library(mlbench)
library(caret)
```

2. Load the **GermanCredit** dataset.

```
# load the German Credit dataset
data("GermanCredit")
```

3. Set the parameters for training using the **trainControl()** function.

```
#Setting parameters for training
control <- trainControl(method="repeatedcv", number=10, repeats=3)
```

4. Train the model.

```
# training the model
model <- train(Class~., data=GermanCredit[,1:10], method="lvq",
preProcess="scale", trControl=control)
```

5. Find the importance of the variables:

```
# Getting the variable importance

importance <- varImp(model, scale=FALSE)
```

6. Print the importance of the variables:

```
# print the variable importance
print(importance)
```

7. Plot the importance:

```
# plot the result
plot(importance)
```

The output is as follows:

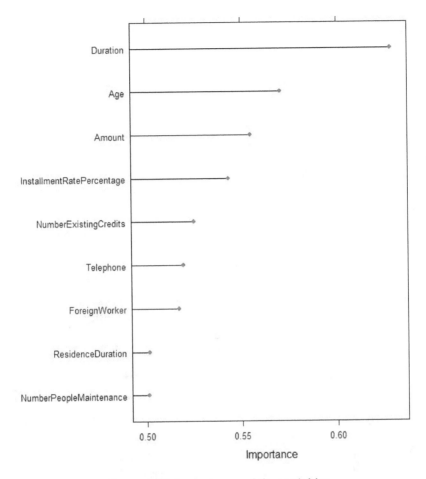

Figure 3.23: Importance of the variables

8. Print the importance.

```
print(importance)
```

The output is as follows:

```
ROC curve variable importance
```

	Importance
Duration	0.6286
Age	0.5706
Amount	0.5549
InstallmentRatePercentage	0.5434
NumberExistingCredits	0.5251
Telephone	0.5195
ForeignWorker	0.5169
ResidenceDuration	0.5015
NumberPeopleMaintenance	0.5012

An importance score has been assigned to each variable. The **Duration**, **Age**, and **Amount** variables are the most important variables. The least important variables are **ResidenceDuration** and **NumberPeopleMaintenance**.

Variable Importance Approach Using Random Forests

When using random forests to determine variable importance, multiple trees are trained. After creating the forest, it will also show the importance of variables used in the data. A tree-based model takes into consideration non-linear relationships. The features used in the split are highly relevant to the output variable. We should also make sure that we avoid overfitting, and therefore the depth of the tree should be small.

Exercise 37: Finding Variable Importance in the PimaIndiansDiabetes Dataset

In this exercise, we will find variable importance in the **PimaIndiansDiabetes** dataset using random forests.

1. Attach the necessary packages.

```
library(mlbench)
library(caret)
library(randomForest)
```

2. Load the **PimaIndiansDiabetes** data.

```
data(PimaIndiansDiabetes)
```

3. Train a random forest model using **randomForest(Class~., data= PimaIndiansDiabetes)**.

```
random_forest <- randomForest(Class~., data= PimaIndiansDiabetes)
```

4. Invoke **importance()** for the trained **random_forest**.

```
# Create an importance based on mean decreasing gini
importance(random_forest)
```

The output is as follows:

```
          MeanDecreaseGini
pregnant       28.60846
glucose        88.03126
pressure       29.83910
triceps        23.92739
insulin        25.89228
mass           59.12225
pedigree       42.86284
age            48.09455
```

5. Use the **varImp()** function to view the list of important variables.

```
varImp(random_forest)
```

The importance of the variables is as follows:

```
          Overall
pregnant 28.60846
glucose  88.03126
pressure 29.83910
triceps  23.92739
insulin  25.89228
mass     59.12225
pedigree 42.86284
age      48.09455
```

The features that are important have higher scores and those features can be selected for the model.

Activity 13: Implementing the Random Forest Approach

In this activity, we will use the **GermanCredit** dataset and perform a random forest approach on the dataset to find the features with the highest and lowest importance. The dataset can be found at https://github.com/TrainingByPackt/Practical-Machine-Learning-with-R/blob/master/Data/GermanCredit.csv.

These are the steps that will help you solve the activity:

1. Load the **GermanCredit** data.

2. Create a subset to load the first ten columns into **GermanCredit_subset**.

3. Attach the **randomForest** package.

4. Train a random forest model using **random_forest<-randomForest(Class~., data=GermanCredit_subset)**.

5. Invoke **importance()** for the trained **random_forest**.

6. Invoke the **varImp()** function, as in **varImp(random_forest)**.

7. Intepret the results.

The expected output of variable importance will be as follows:

	Overall
Duration	70.380265
Amount	121.458790
InstallmentRatePercentage	27.048517
ResidenceDuration	30.409254
Age	86.476017
NumberExistingCredits	18.746057
NumberPeopleMaintenance	12.026969
Telephone	15.581802
ForeignWorker	2.888387

> **Note**
>
> The solution for this activity can be found on page 338.

Variable Importance Approach Using a Logistic Regression Model

We have seen the importance score provided by random forests; in this exercise, a logistic regression model is trained for the data to identify variable importance. We will use **varImp()** to show the relative importance of the columns. This model will help to provide us with the importance of the fields in a dataset.

Exercise 38: Implementing the Logistic Regression Model

In this exercise, we will implement a logistic regression model.

1. Create a subset of the **GermanCredit** data excluding the first element.

    ```
    GermanCredit_subset <- GermanCredit[,1:10]
    ```

2. Attach the **mlbench** package.

    ```
    library(mlbench)
    ```

3. Load **GermanCredit_subset**.

    ```
    data(GermanCredit_subset)
    ```

4. Create a dataframe using the **as.data.frame()** function.

    ```
    data_lm = as.data.frame(GermanCredit_subset)
    ```

5. Fit a logistic regression model.

    ```
    # Fit a logistic regression model
    log_reg = glm(Class~.,GermanCredit_subset,family = "binomial")
    ```

6. Attach the **caret** package.

    ```
    library(caret)
    ```

7. Use the **varImp()** function to list out the importance of the variables.

    ```
    # Using varImp() function
    varImp(log_reg)
    ```

The output is as follows:

```
                                Overall
Duration                        3.0412079
Amount                          2.7164175
InstallmentRatePercentage       2.9227186
ResidenceDuration               0.6339908
Age                             2.7370544
NumberExistingCredits           1.1394251
NumberPeopleMaintenance         0.6952838
Telephone                       2.5708235
ForeignWorker                   1.9652732
```

After building a logistic regression model, the importance of each variable is given a score. The higher the score is, the more important the variable is. The variables that are most important can be used for the model.

Determining Variable Importance Using rpart

Using **varImp()**, we can list the features with their importance. *rpart* stands for Recursive Partitioning and Regression Trees. This package contains an implementation of a tree algorithm in R, specifically known as **Classification and Regression Trees (CART)**. In the following exercise, we will be using the **rpart** package in R.

Exercise 39: Variable Importance Using rpart for the PimaIndiansDiabetes Data

In this exercise, we will be finding the variable importance using **rpart**. Finding the importance of variables helps to select the correct variables.

1. Install the following packages:

```
install.packages("rpart")
install.packages("randomForest")
set.seed(10)

library(caret)
library(mlbench)
```

2. Load the dataset and create a subset:

```
data(PimaIndiansDiabetes)
PimaIndiansDiabetes_subset <- PimaIndiansDiabetes[,1:9]
PimaIndiansDiabetes_subset
```

3. Train the **rpart** model:

```
#Train a rpart model
rPartMod <- train(diabetes ~ ., data=PimaIndiansDiabetes_subset,
method="rpart")
```

4. Find the variable importance:

```
#Find variable importance
rpartImp <- varImp(rPartMod)
```

5. Print the variable importance:

```
#Print variable importance
print(rpartImp)
```

The output is as follows:

```
rpart variable importance

          Overall
glucose   100.000
mass       65.542
age        52.685
pregnant   30.245
insulin    16.973
pedigree    7.522
triceps     0.000
pressure    0.000
```

6. Plot the top five variables' importance:

```
#Plot top 5 variable importance
plot(rpartImp, top = 5, main='Variable Importance')
```

The plot is as follows:

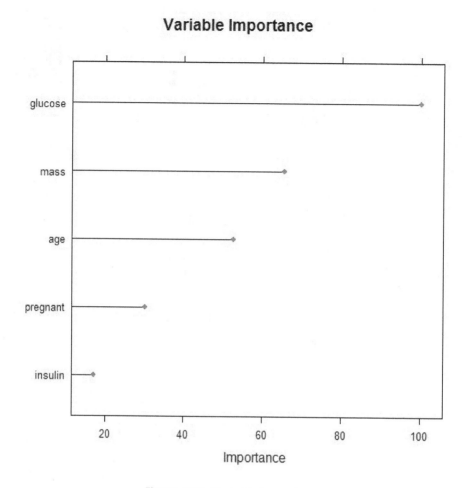

Figure 3.24: Variable importance

From the preceding plot, it can be noted that glucose, mass, and age are most important for the output, and should therefore be included for the modeling. In the next activity, we will be selecting features using variable importance.

Activity 14: Selecting Features Using Variable Importance

In this activity, we will use the **GermanCredit** dataset and find the variable importance using **rpart**. The dataset can be found at https://github.com/TrainingByPackt/Practical-Machine-Learning-with-R/blob/master/Data/GermanCredit.csv.

These are the steps that will help you solve the activity:

1. Attach the **rpart** and **caret** packages.

2. Load the **GermanCredit** data.

3. Create a subset to load the first 10 columns into `GermanCredit_subset`.

4. Train an **rpart** model using `rPartMod <- train(Class ~ ., data=GermanCredit_subset, method="rpart")`.

5. Invoke the `varImp()` function, as in `rpartImp <- varImp(rPartMod)`.

6. Print `rpartImp`.

7. Plot `rpartImp` using `plot()`.

8. Interpret the results.

The expected output of variable importance will be as follows:

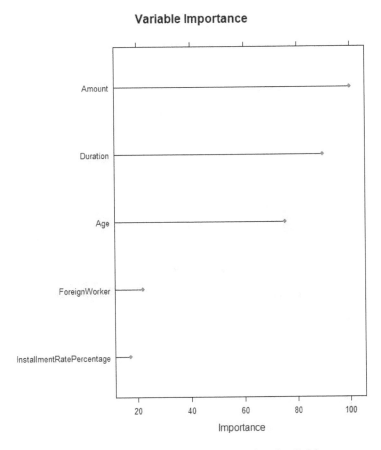

Figure 3.25: Variable importance for the fields

Note

The solution for this activity can be found on page 339.

Here is a table that summarizes the techniques we have looked at and the features we can select using these techniques:

Sr no	Technique	Feature selected (GermanCredit Dataset)				
1	RFE	Duration	Amount	Age	Number People Maintenance	Telephone
2	PCA	PCA1	PCA2	PCA3	PCA4	PCA5
3	LVQ	Duration	Age	Amount	Installment Rate Percentage	Number Existing Credits
4	Random Forest	Duration	Amount	Installment Rate Percentage	Residence Reduction	Age
5	Variable Importance using logic Regression	Duration	Amount	Installment Rate Percentage	Residence Reduction	Age
6	Variable Importance using rpart	Amount	Duration	Age	ForeignWorker	Installment Rate Percentage

Figure 3.26: Summary of the models

Thus, we can see that most methods suggest the Duration, Amount, and Age as the features.

Summary

In this chapter, we have learned about the different types of features that are generated to train a model. We have derived domain-specific features and datatype-specific features. Also, we explored an automated technique for generating text features. The feature engineering process is essential for obtaining the best model performance. We delved into two variable transformation techniques and learned about techniques to identify redundant features and handle them in a dataset.

We have learned about forward and backward feature selection approaches and have performed correlation analysis through detailed examples. We implemented the calculation of p-values in R and looked at its significance to the process of the selection of features. Recursive feature elimination is another way that we saw to find the best combination of features for a model. We delved into a dimensionality reduction approach, known as PCA, that drastically reduces the number of features needed, as it calculates the principal components in a dataset.

We explored several techniques for ranking the features in R. LVQ and random forests were implemented in R to observe the ranking for the features in the `GermanCredit` dataset. We also learned how to use the variable importance function in R to list the importance of all the variables in a dataset.

In the next chapter, we will use neural networks to solve classification problems. Along with this, we will also evaluate the models using cross-validation.

4

Introduction to neuralnet and Evaluation Methods

Learning Objectives

By the end of this chapter, you will be able to:

- Use a neural network to solve a classification problem by using the neuralnet package.
- Create balanced partitions from a dataset, while decreasing leakage, with the groupdata2 package.
- Evaluate and select between models using cross-validation.
- Explain the concept of multiclass classification.

In this chapter, we aim to equip you with a practical understanding of neural networks.

Introduction

While neural networks have been around in some form since the mid-twentieth century, they have recently surged in popularity. Be it self-driving cars or healthcare technologies, neural networks are fundamental to some of the most innovative products being developed.

In this chapter, we will train a neural network to predict whether a loan applicant in the GermanCredit dataset has a good or bad credit rating. To do this, we will partition the dataset into a training set, a development set, and a validation set. The neural network will be trained on the training set, and we will evaluate whether it makes good predictions on the development and validation sets. We will use cross-validation, along with four different evaluation metrics, to select between different neural network architectures.

Classification

The goal of **classification** is to create a model that can *predict* classes in never-before-seen data. This means that the model should *generalize* beyond the training data. As the data we work with is supervised, meaning that we already know the answer to our question (does the applicant have a good or bad credit rating?), it is rarely interesting to have a model that can merely repeat that. Instead, we need the model to classify the unlabeled data we gather in the future. We will discuss this further when covering under- and overfitting.

The datasets being used are the following:

Dataset	Description	Output Variable
PimaIndiansDiabetes2 [mlbench]	This dataset contains 9 variables related to diabetes. It has 768 observations. The dataset contains missing data.	The "diabetes" column is the output variable. It contains the results of a diabetes test.
GermanCredit [caret]	This dataset has 62 variables that characterize the creditworthiness of loan applicants. It has 1000 observations.	The "Class" column is the output variable with the values "Good" and "Bad".

Figure 4.1: Datasets

Binary Classification

In **binary classification**, our question is of the *either or* type. There are only two options, either *yes* or *no*; not *maybe* and not both *yes* and *no*. In **multiclass classification**, we can have more than two options, though we can only choose one of them. In **multilabel classification**, it is possible to predict both *yes* and *no* at the same time, hence an observation can have multiple labels. We will discuss multiclass classification later, but multilabel classification is outside the scope of this chapter.

Exercise 40: Preparing the Dataset

In this exercise, we will load and assess the GermanCredit dataset. If the data has inappropriately biasing features, we will remove them:

1. Attach the required packages:

    ```
    # Attaching the packages
    library(caret)
    library(groupdata2)
    ```

2. Load the **GermanCredit** dataset:

    ```
    # Load the GermanCredit dataset
    data(GermanCredit)
    ```

3. We can inspect the structure of the dataset. We will only check a subset, as the rest of the columns are all **numerics (num)**, valued either 0 or 1. Feel free to check them yourself:

    ```
    str(GermanCredit[,1:10])
    ```

    The output is as follows:

    ```
    ## 'data.frame':     1000 obs. of  10 variables:
    ##  $ Duration                : int  6 48 12 42 24 36 24 36 12 30 ...
    ##  $ Amount                  : int  1169 5951 2096 7882 4870 9055 2835
    6948 3059 5234 ...
    ##  $ InstallmentRatePercentage: int  4 2 2 3 2 3 2 2 4 ...
    ##  $ ResidenceDuration       : int  4 2 3 4 4 4 4 2 4 2 ...
    ##  $ Age                     : int  67 22 49 45 53 35 53 35 61 28 ...
    ##  $ NumberExistingCredits   : int  2 1 1 1 2 1 1 1 1 2 ...
    ##  $ NumberPeopleMaintenance : int  1 1 2 2 2 2 1 1 1 1 ...
    ```

```
##  $ Telephone      : num  0 1 1 1 1 0 1 0 1 1 ...
##  $ ForeignWorker  : num  1 1 1 1 1 1 1 1 1 1 ...
##  $ Class          : Factor w/ 2 levels "Bad","Good": 2 1 2 2
     1 2 2 2 2 1 ...
```

4. To avoid unfair discrimination, we will not use the **Age** feature. It is not always straightforward to explain *why* a neural network makes a certain prediction; hence it can be useful to discuss the inclusion/exclusion of features. In many contexts, we would like to avoid biasing the model against certain groups of people (for instance, young people):

```
# Remove the Age column
GermanCredit$Age <- NULL
```

We have assessed the **GermanCredit** dataset and removed the **Age** feature to avoid biasing our models against a specific age group.

> **Note**
>
> To get a sense of a feature's importance, we can train models with and without it, and see whether their predictions differ. Be aware that interpretation can be difficult, as the different features can interact in nontransparent ways. If we include a feature, we can alter the value of that feature for an applicant and see how it changes the prediction. If we have a gender variable, for instance, we can change it from male to female to see whether the applicant would have gotten the loan if they were of a different gender.

Balanced Partitioning Using the groupdata2 Package

We wish to partition the data into a training set (60%), a development set (20%), and a validation set (20%). We will train our models on the training set and select the model that performs best on the development set. Once we have selected the best model, we will evaluate it on the validation set. We will treat the development and validation sets as if they were collected after we trained our model on the training set. This means that any preprocessing parameters (such as for scaling and centering) will be found for the training set and applied to all three partitions.

For the partitioning, we will use the **groupdata2** package, which contains multiple functions for *balanced* grouping and splitting of data. A dataset can be balanced or imbalanced in multiple ways. In our case, we will balance our partitions by having the same ratio of *Good* and *Bad* loan applicants in the three partitions. This makes it easier to compare the evaluations of the different partitions and ensures that each partition contains both *Good* and *Bad* loan applicants. Alternatively, we could ensure that the development and validation sets have the same number of observations per class. We will also discuss how to avoid leakage in *repeated measures* datasets, although this does not apply to our dataset.

> **Note**
>
> The groupdata2 package was created by one of the authors of this book, Ludvig Renbo Olsen.

Exercise 41: Partitioning the Dataset

In this exercise, we will partition the dataset into a training set with 60% of the observations, a development set with 20% of the observations, and a validation set with the remaining 20% of the observations. In this exercise, we will partition the dataset without balancing it on the target variable. In the following exercise, we will then make balanced partitions and compare the results of the two approaches.

1. Attach the **groupdata2** package:

    ```
    # Attach groupdata2
    library(groupdata2)
    ```

2. Set the seed value:

    ```
    # Set seed for reproducibility and easier comparison
    set.seed(1)
    ```

3. Partition the data:

    ```
    # Simple partitioning
    # Note that we only need to specify the 2 first partition sizes
    # as the remaining observations are put into a third partition.
    partitions <- partition(GermanCredit, p = c(0.6, 0.2))
    ```

The **partition()** function splits the data into groups. We specify the data we wish to partition and the list of partition sizes (as percentages between 0 and 1 in this case). Note that we only specify the first two partitions, as the remaining 20% will automatically be placed in a third partition.

4. Assign each partition to a variable name:

```
# This returns a list with three data frames.
train_set <- partitions[[1]]
dev_set <- partitions[[2]]
valid_set <- partitions[[3]]
```

5. Count the number of observations from each class in the training and test sets:

```
# Count the number of observations from each class
# in the training and test sets.
train_counts <- table(train_set$Class)
dev_counts <- table(dev_set$Class)
valid_counts <- table(valid_set$Class)
```

6. For each partition, print the counts of the two classes:

Inspect the class counts from the training set:

```
train_counts
```

The output is as follows:

```
##   Bad Good
##   188  412
```

7. Inspect the class counts from the development set:

```
dev_counts
```

The output is as follows:

```
##   Bad Good
##    60  140
```

8. Inspect the class counts from the validation set:

```
valid_counts
```

The output is as follows:

```
##   Bad Good
##    52  148
```

9. For each partition, print the ratios of the two classes:

Inspect the ratio of the two classes in the training set:

```
train_counts/max(train_counts)
```

The output is as follows:

```
##         Bad       Good
## 0.4563107 1.0000000
```

10. Inspect the ratio of the two classes in the development set:

```
dev_counts/max(dev_counts)
```

The output is as follows:

```
##         Bad       Good
## 0.4285714 1.0000000
```

11. Inspect the ratio of the two classes in the validation set:

```
valid_counts/max(valid_counts)
```

The output is as follows:

```
##         Bad       Good
## 0.3513514 1.0000000
```

In this exercise, we used the **partition()** function to split the dataset into three subsets (partitions). The outputs from steps 9, 10, and 11 show that we have different ratios of *Good* and *Bad* loan applicants in our partitions.

In the next exercise, we will include the **cat_col** argument, which takes the name of a categorical column and tries to balance it so that there is the same ratio of the classes in all partitions.

> **Note**
>
> What happens when we specify the **cat_col** argument in **partition()**?
> First, the dataset is subset by each class level. In our case, we will have one subset with all the applicants with *Good* credit ratings and another subset with the applicants with *Bad* credit ratings. Then, both subsets are partitioned and merged, so that partition one from the *Good* subset is merged with partition one from the *Bad* subset, and so on.

Exercise 42: Creating Balanced Partitions

In this exercise, we will load the **GermanCredit** dataset and use **partition()** to create balanced training (60%), development (20%), and validation (20%) sets. In this case, *balanced* means that the ratios of the two classes should be similar in all three partitions. Also, remember to remove the **Age** column:

1. Attach the packages:

   ```
   # Attaching the packages
   library(caret) # GermanCredit
   library(groupdata2) # partition()
   ```

2. Load the **GermanCredit** dataset:

   ```
   # Load the German Credit dataset
   data("GermanCredit")
   ```

3. Remove the **Age** column:

   ```
   # Remove the Age column
   GermanCredit$Age <- NULL
   ```

4. Partition the data:

   ```
   # Partition into train, dev and valid sets.
   partitions <- partition(GermanCredit, p = c(0.6, 0.2),
                           cat_col = "Class")
   ```

   The **partition()** function splits the data into groups. We specify the data we wish to partition, the list of partition sizes, and the categorical column to balance the partitions by.

5. Assign each partition to a variable name:

   ```
   # Assign each partition to a variable name
   train_set <- partitions[[1]]
   dev_set <- partitions[[2]]
   valid_set <- partitions[[3]]
   ```

6. Count the number of observations from each class in the three partitions:

```
# Count the number of observations from each class
# in the training and test sets.
train_counts <- table(train_set$Class)
dev_counts <- table(dev_set$Class)
valid_counts <- table(valid_set$Class)
```

7. Inspect the class counts from the training set:

```
train_counts
```

The output is as follows:

```
Bad Good
180  420
```

8. Inspect the class counts from the development set:

```
dev_counts
```

The output is as follows:

```
## Bad Good
##  60  140
```

9. Inspect the class counts from the validation set:

```
valid_counts
```

The output is as follows:

```
## Bad Good
##  60  140
```

10. For each partition, print the ratios of the two classes. Inspect the ratio of the two classes in the training set:

```
train_counts/max(train_counts)
```

The output is as follows:

```
##        Bad      Good
## 0.4285714 1.0000000
```

11. Inspect the ratio of the two classes in the development set:

```
dev_counts/max(dev_counts)
```

The output is as follows:

```
##        Bad      Good
## 0.4285714 1.0000000
```

12. Inspect the ratio of the two classes in the validation set:

```
valid_counts/max(valid_counts)
```

The output is as follows:

```
##        Bad      Good
## 0.4285714 1.0000000
```

Notice how the ratios of the two classes are now the same for all partitions.

In this exercise, you created balanced partitions using the **partition()** function from **groupdata2**. You will likely do this very often in your future machine learning practices.

Leakage

As noted previously, we should treat the development and validation sets as if they were independent of the training set. In practice, they might not be so, but when creating the partitions, it is worth discussing whether there is any *leakage* between the partitions. One such example could be that we had recorded multiple loans per loan applicant. In that case, we would have an **ID** column with multiple rows per applicant ID. We refer to this as *repeated measures* data. In this case, the same applicant should not be in both the training set and one of the test sets, as we wish to test how well our model performs on new applicants, not the applicants it encountered during training. The **id_col** argument in the **partition()** function ensures that all rows with the same applicant ID are placed in only one of the partitions.

The following code shows how we would specify the **id_col** argument in **partition()**, if we had an **ApplicantID** column in our dataset.

```
# Avoiding ID leakage
# NOTE: Can't be run as we don't actually have an ApplicantID column
partition(GermanCredit, p = c(0.6, 0.2),
          cat_col = "Class",
```

```
        id_col = "ApplicantID")
# With this, each applicant would have all their observations/rows
# in the same partition!
```

> **Note**
>
> What happens when we specify the **id_col** argument in **partition()**? First, we extract a list of the unique IDs. Then, that list is partitioned and the rows are put in the partition of their ID.
> What happens when we specify both the **cat_col** and **id_col** arguments in **partition()**?
> First, the dataset is subset by each class level. For each subset, we extract and partition the list of unique IDs. Finally, the rows are put in the partition of their ID. This will ensure that all rows with the same ID are put in the same partition, while also balancing the ratios of each class between the folds. Note that this approach requires all rows with the same ID to have the same value in the **cat_col** column.

Exercise 43: Ensuring an Equal Number of Observations Per Class

In this exercise, we will partition the dataset such that the development and validation sets have an equal number of observations per class. This makes our evaluation metrics easier to interpret. We can do this by first specifying the number of observations per class for the two test partitions and then use the rest of the observations as the training set. Note that if you specify the **id_col** argument, this will put that number of individuals (per class) into the partitions. Also note that the training set is now the third element in the list of partitions.

1. Attach the necessary packages:

   ```
   # Attach groupdata2
   library(groupdata2)
   ```

2. Set the seed value for reproducibility and easier comparison:

   ```
   # Set seed for reproducibility and easier comparison
   set.seed(1)
   ```

3. Partition the data to have the same number (**50**) of observations per class in the test partitions:

```
# Partition with an equal number of observations (50) per class in
# the development and validation sets
# The remaining observations will end up in a third partition,
# which will be our training set
partitions_equal <- partition(GermanCredit, p = c(50, 50),
                              cat_col = "Class")
```

4. Assign each partition to a variable name:

```
dev_set_equal <- partitions_equal[[1]]
valid_set_equal <- partitions_equal[[2]]
train_set_equal <- partitions_equal[[3]]
```

5. Count the number of observations from each class in the three partitions:

```
# Count the number of observations from each class
# in the training and test sets.
train_counts_equal <- table(train_set_equal$Class)
dev_counts_equal <- table(dev_set_equal$Class)
valid_counts_equal <- table(valid_set_equal$Class)
```

6. Inspect the number of observations per class in each of the partitions:

7. Inspect the class counts from the training set:

```
train_counts_equal
```

The output is as follows:

```
##    Bad Good
##    200  600
```

8. Inspect the class counts from the development set:

```
dev_counts_equal
```

The output is as follows:

```
##    Bad Good
##     50   50
```

9. Inspect the class counts from the validation set:

   ```
   valid_counts_equal
   ```

   The output is as follows:

   ```
   ##   Bad Good
   ##    50   50
   ```

Notice how the development and validation sets both have 50 *Good* and 50 *Bad* loan applicants.

In this exercise, we have partitioned the dataset such that the development and validation sets have an equal number of observations per class, and everything else is the training set.

Standardizing

We will work with the partitions from *Exercise 42, Creating Balanced Partitions*. A few of the features could benefit from being standardized, and the rest are already one-hot encoded. We only run the **preProcess()** function on the training set to find the scaling and centering parameters, which are then applied to all three partitions:

```
# Find scaling and centering parameters for the first 6 columns

params <- preProcess(train_set[, 1:6], method=c("center", "scale"))
```

The **predict()** function uses the parameters in the **params** object to apply the preprocessing transformations to the specified dataset:

```
# Transform the training set

train_set[, 1:6] <- predict(params, train_set[, 1:6])
```

```
# Transform the development set

dev_set[, 1:6] <- predict(params, dev_set[, 1:6])
```

```
# Transform the validation set

valid_set[, 1:6] <- predict(params, valid_set[, 1:6])
```

Neural Networks with neuralnet

We are now ready to train a classifier to predict whether an applicant is creditworthy or not. The **neuralnet** package makes it easy to specify and train an artificial neural network. The first argument in the **neuralnet()** function is the model formula. Here, we tell our model to predict whether **Class** is *Good* or *Bad*. The tilde ~ means *predicted by*, and the variables to the right of it are the predictors. If we wish to use all the variables (excluding the target variable) as predictors, we can use a dot (y~.).

To begin with, we specify a simple formula with only **Duration** and **Amount** as predictors:

```
# Attaching neuralnet
library(neuralnet)


# Set seed for reproducibility and easier comparison
set.seed(1)
# Classifying if class is "Good"
nn1 <- neuralnet(Class == "Good" ~ Duration + Amount,
                 train_set, linear.output = FALSE)


plot(nn1, rep="best", fontsize = 10)
```

The output is as follows:

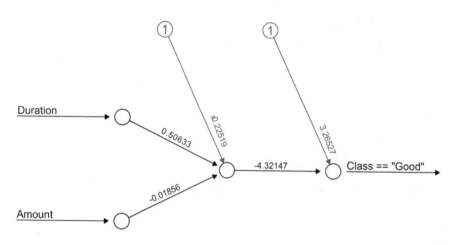

Error: 59.630264   Steps: 2350

Figure 4.2: Neural network architecture with trained weights, error, and number of training steps.

The plot shows the neural network with three layers (input, hidden, output), from left to right. We have two nodes (also called neurons) in the input layer. The values in these nodes are multiplied by the weights (the numbers on the lines) going into the hidden layer with one node. The output layer has one node as well, which is our probability of **Class** being *Good*. The last two layers also have bias parameters (the "1" nodes). At the bottom of the plot, we see the training error, along with the number of training steps.

We can also get the error from the result matrix in the model object:

```
train_error <- nn1$result.matrix[1]

train_error

## [1] 59.630264
```

Now we will use columns 11 to 20 as predictors (remember to include column 9, as that's the target variable – **Class**). With the regular **plot()** function, the plot gets very messy with larger networks, so we will use the **plotnet()** function from the **NeuralNetTools** package. Let's see whether our error is reduced:

```
# Attach packages
library(neuralnet)
library(NeuralNetTools)


# Set seed for reproducibility and easier comparison
set.seed(1)


# Classifying if class is "Good"
# Using columns 11 to 20
# Notice that we choose the predictors by subsetting the data frame
# and use every column as predictor with the dot "~."
nn2 <- neuralnet(Class == "Good" ~ ., train_set[, c(9, 11:20)],
                 linear.output = FALSE)


plotnet(nn2, var_labs = FALSE)
```

The output is as follows:

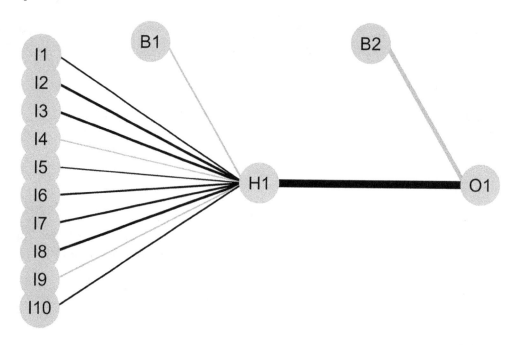

Figure 4.3: Neural network architecture using columns 11- 20 as predictors

The plot produced by **plotnet()** does not show the weights by numbers but by line thickness and nuance (gray is negative and black is positive). Let's check the error:

```
train_error <- nn2$result.matrix[1]

train_error
```

The output is as follows:

```
## [1] 52.13454
```

Choosing these predictors lowered our error. In the next activity, we will train a neural network and calculate the training error.

Activity 15: Training a Neural Network

In this activity, we will train the neural network using the German Credit dataset found at https://github.com/TrainingByPackt/Practical-Machine-Learning-with-R/blob/master/Data/GermanCredit.csv.

We will preprocess the **GermanCredit** dataset and train a neural network to predict creditworthiness. Feel free to reuse the code from *Exercise 42, Creating Balanced Partitions*, so that you get to train multiple neural networks.

Expected output: we expect the training error to be close to 62.15447. Note that, depending on the version of R and the packages installed, the results might vary.

Here are the steps that will help you complete the activity:

1. Attach the **caret**, **groupdata2**, **neuralnet**, and **NeuralNetTools** packages.

2. Set the random seed to 1.

3. Load the **GermanCredit** dataset with **read.csv()**.

4. Remove the **Age** column.

5. Partition the dataset into a training set (60%), a development set (20%), and a validation set (20%). Use the **cat_col** argument to balance the ratio of the two classes.

6. Find the preprocessing parameters for scaling and centering from the training set.

7. Apply standardization to the first six predictors in all three partitions using the **preProcess** parameters from the previous step.

8. Train a neural network using the **InstallmentRatePercentage**, **ResidenceDuration**, and **NumberExistingCredits** variables as predictors. The goal is to classify whether or not **Class** is *Good*. Feel free to experiment with the other predictors as well and see whether you can obtain a lower error.

9. Plot the neural network and print the error.

The random initialization of the neural network weights can lead to slightly different results from one training to another. To avoid this, we use the **set.seed()** function at the beginning of the script, which helps when comparing models. We could also train the same model architecture with five different seeds to get a better sense of its performance.

> **Note**
>
> The solution for this activity can be found on page 342.

Model Selection

Now that we know how to train a classifier, we will revise how to evaluate and choose between models. First, we will cover four common metrics: Accuracy, Precision, Recall, and F_1, and then we will discuss cross-validation as a good tool for model comparison.

Evaluation Metrics

We use a confusion matrix to split the predictions into True Positives, False Positives, True Negatives, and False Negatives. In our case, True Positives are the applicants that were *correctly* identified as being "Good," False Positives are the applicants that were *incorrectly* identified as being "Good," True Negatives are the applicants that were *correctly* identified as "Bad," while False Negatives are the applicants that were *incorrectly* identified as "Bad."

True / Predicted	Positive	Negative
Positive	True Positive	False Negative
Negative	False Positive	True Negative

Figure 4.4: Confusion matrix

In *Figure* 4.4, the rows are the true classes, while the columns are the predicted classes. If the true class is *Positive* and the model predicts *Positive*, that prediction is a True Positive.

Accuracy

Accuracy: what percentage of the predictions were correct?

$$\text{Accuracy} = \frac{\text{True Positives} + \text{True Negatives}}{\text{True Positives} + \text{True Negatives} + \text{False Positives} + \text{False Negatives}}$$

Figure 4.5: Accuracy formula

Precision

Precision: of all the *Good* predictions, how many were actually *Good*?

Note that we can choose to use the other class, *Bad*, as the *Positive* class. In that case, we would be asking how many of the *Bad* predictions actually *were Bad*.

$$\text{Precision} = \frac{\texttt{True Positives}}{\texttt{True Positives} + \texttt{False Positives}}$$

Figure 4.6: Precision formula

Recall

Recall: how many of the applicants with a *Good* credit rating were correctly identified?

$$\text{Recall} = \frac{\texttt{True Positives}}{\texttt{True Positives} + \texttt{False Negatives}}$$

Figure 4.7: Recall formula

Header F_1: the harmonic mean of precision and recall, which is a common way to merge the two scores into one, making it easier to compare models.

$$F_1 = 2 \cdot \frac{\texttt{Precision} \cdot \texttt{Recall}}{\texttt{Precision} + \texttt{Recall}}$$

Figure 4.8: F$_1$ formula

It is easier to visualize the difference between the F_1 score and a simple average of the two metrics than to explain it in words:

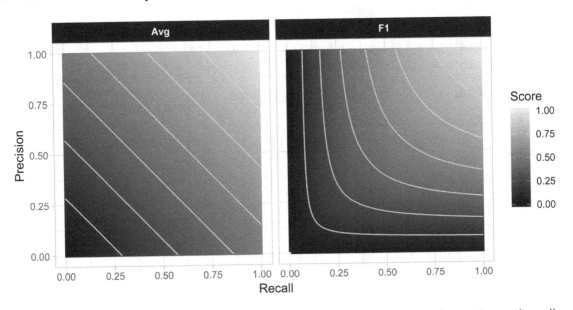

Figure 4.9: Contour plots comparing the F$_1$ score to the simple averaging of precision and recall

Figure 4.9 shows that the F_1 score rewards models where both the precision and recall scores are decent, whereas the simple average does not take an imbalance between the metrics into account.

Exercise 44: Creating a Confusion Matrix

In this exercise, we will find the confusion matrix for a trained neural network. We will use the trained neural network from *Activity 15, Training a neural network*, to predict the development set. From these predictions, we will create a confusion matrix. The **confusionMatrix()** function from the **caret** package also calculates our evaluation metrics:

1. Attach the **caret** package:

    ```
    # Attach caret
    library(caret)
    ```

2. Create a one-hot encoding of the **Class** variable:

    ```
    # Create a one-hot encoding of the Class variable
    # ifelse() takes the arguments: "If x, then a, else b"
    true_labels <- ifelse(dev_set$Class == "Good", 1, 0)
    ```

3. Predict the class in the development set, using the trained neural network from *Activity 15, Training a neural network*:

    ```
    # Predict the class in the dev set
    # It returns probabilities that the observations are "Good"
    predicted_probabilities <- predict(nn, dev_set)
    predictions <- ifelse(predicted_probabilities > 0.5, 1, 0)
    ```

4. Create a confusion matrix with the predictions:

    ```
    # Create confusion matrix
    confusion_matrix <- confusionMatrix(as.factor(predictions),
                                as.factor(true_labels),
                                mode="prec_recall", positive = "1")
    ```

5. Print the confusion matrix and try to interpret it:

    ```
    confusion_matrix
    ```

The output is as follows:

```
## Confusion Matrix and Statistics
##
##              Reference
## Prediction   0    1
##           0  0    0
##           1  60  140
##
##                    Accuracy : 0.7
##                      95% CI : (0.6314, 0.7626)
##         No Information Rate : 0.7
##         P-Value [Acc > NIR] : 0.5348
##
##                       Kappa : 0
##    Mcnemar's Test P-Value : 2.599e-14
##
##                   Precision : 0.7000
##                      Recall : 1.0000
##                          F1 : 0.8235
##                  Prevalence : 0.7000
##              Detection Rate : 0.7000
##        Detection Prevalence : 1.0000
##           Balanced Accuracy : 0.5000
##
##            'Positive' Class : 1
##
```

If we look at the metrics, our model has an accuracy of 70%, precision of 70%, recall of 100%, and an F_1 score of 82.35%. This seems pretty good, but when we look at the predictions in the confusion matrix, we see that the model simply predicts *Good* for all observations. With the imbalance in the training set, where we have 420 *Good* and 180 *Bad* observations, the model will get a decent error by simply predicting *Good*. This especially happens if our features do not provide enough information about the classes to get a smaller error. Another possible reason is that the model is simply not big enough (the number of nodes and layers) to extract useful information from the features. In that case, we would say that the model is *underfitting* the data.

An important point to take away from this example is that we can get seemingly high accuracies, precision scores, and so on, when our dataset is imbalanced, even though our model is useless. It is always a good idea to look at the confusion matrix to check that this isn't the case. In the upcoming exercise, we will create baseline evaluations so that we have something to compare our models against.

Exercise 45: Creating Baseline Evaluations

In this exercise, we will create and evaluate three sets of predictions in order to know what accuracy we should beat to be better than chance, or the discussed "one-class-predictor." The three sets of predictions are 1) all "Good" predictions, 2) all "Bad" predictions, and 3) random predictions, preferably repeated 100 times or more:

1. Attach caret:

   ```
   # Attach caret
   library(caret)
   ```

2. Create a one-hot encoding of the target variable:

   ```
   # Create one-hot encoding of Class variable
   true_labels <- ifelse(dev_set$Class == "Good", 1, 0)
   ```

3. Specify the number of predictions to make. This is the same as the number of true labels:

   ```
   # The number of predictions to make
   num_total_predictions <- 200  # Alternatively: length(true_labels)
   ```

4. Create the set of "**All Good**" predictions by simply repeating "1" 200 times:

   ```
   # All "Good"
   good_predictions <- rep(1, num_total_predictions)
   ```

5. Create a confusion matrix and inspect the results:

   ```
   # Create confusion Matrix
   confusion_matrix_good <- confusionMatrix(as.factor(good_predictions),as.
   factor(true_labels),mode="prec_recall",positive = "1")
   confusion_matrix_good
   ## Confusion Matrix and Statistics
   ##
   ##           Reference
   ## Prediction   0   1
   ##          0   0   0
   ##          1  60 140
   ##
   ```

```
##                   Accuracy : 0.7
##                     95% CI : (0.6314, 0.7626)
##        No Information Rate : 0.7
##        P-Value [Acc > NIR] : 0.5348
##
##                      Kappa : 0
##    Mcnemar's Test P-Value : 2.599e-14
##
##                  Precision : 0.7000
##                     Recall : 1.0000
##                         F1 : 0.8235
##                 Prevalence : 0.7000
##             Detection Rate : 0.7000
##       Detection Prevalence : 1.0000
##          Balanced Accuracy : 0.5000
##
##           'Positive' Class : 1
##
```

6. Create the set of **"All Bad"** predictions by simply repeating "0" 200 times:

```
# All "Bad"
bad_predictions <- rep(0, num_total_predictions)
Create a confusion matrix and inspect the results:
# Create confusion Matrix
confusion_matrix_bad <- confusionMatrix(
    as.factor(bad_predictions), as.factor(true_labels),
    mode="prec_recall", positive = "1")
confusion_matrix_bad
```

The output is as follows:

```
## Confusion Matrix and Statistics
##
##             Reference
## Prediction    0    1
##           0  60 140
##           1   0    0
##
##                   Accuracy : 0.3
##                     95% CI : (0.2374, 0.3686)
##        No Information Rate : 0.7
##        P-Value [Acc > NIR] : 1
##
```

```
##                       Kappa :  0
##    Mcnemar's Test P-Value :  <2e-16
##
##                   Precision :  NA
##                      Recall :  0.0
##                          F1 :  NA
##                  Prevalence :  0.7
##              Detection Rate :  0.0
##        Detection Prevalence :  0.0
##           Balanced Accuracy :  0.5
##
##               'Positive' Class :  1
```

Note that the precision and F_1 scores could not be calculated, as the precision calculation becomes $\frac{0}{0}$ and the F_1 metric uses precision in its calculation. By default, the **confusionMatrix()** function would set **Bad** as the **positive** class, but we are using **positive = "1"**. If you wanted to know how precise the model is at finding **Bad** applicants, you could set **positive = "0"**.

For the random predictions, we could either sample and evaluate within a loop and find the average evaluation, or, as we will do in this example, we could sample the number of predictions 100 times and repeat the **true_labels** vector 100 times. The method to use depends on the chosen set of evaluation metrics.

7. Set the random seed for reproducibility:

```
# Set seed for reproducibility
set.seed(1)
```

8. Set the number of evaluations to perform. We will perform 100 evaluations with random predictions:

```
# The number of evaluations to do
num_evaluations <- 100
```

9. Repeat the true labels vector 100 times:

```
# Repeat the true labels vector 100 times
true_labels_100 <- rep(true_labels, num_evaluations)
```

10. Draw 100*200 random predictions and ensure that they are either 0 or 1:

```
# Random predictions
# Draw random predictions (either 1 or 2, hence the "-1")
random_predictions <- sample.int(
    2, size = num_total_predictions * num_evaluations,
    replace = TRUE) - 1
head(random_predictions)
```

The output is as follows:

```
## [1] 0 0 1 1 0 1
```

11. Find the average number of times the prediction is *Good*. It should be about half of the 200 predictions:

```
# Average number of times predicting "Good"
sum(random_predictions) / num_evaluations
```

The output is as follows:

```
## [1] 99.59
```

12. Create a confusion matrix and inspect the results:

```
# Create confusion matrix
confusion_matrix_random <- confusionMatrix(
    as.factor(random_predictions),
    as.factor(true_labels_100),
    mode = "prec_recall",
    positive = "1")
confusion_matrix_random
```

The random confusion matrix is as follows:

```
## Confusion Matrix and Statistics
##
##              Reference
## Prediction     0     1
##            0 3020 7021
##            1 2980 6979
##
##                 Accuracy : 0.5
##                   95% CI : (0.493, 0.5069)
##      No Information Rate : 0.7
##      P-Value [Acc > NIR] : 1
##
```

```
##                          Kappa : 0.0015
##      Mcnemar's Test P-Value : <2e-16
##
##                      Precision : 0.7008
##                         Recall : 0.4985
##                             F1 : 0.5826
##                     Prevalence : 0.7000
##                 Detection Rate : 0.3489
##           Detection Prevalence : 0.4980
##              Balanced Accuracy : 0.5009
##
##                 'Positive' Class : 1
##
```

When randomly predicting the class of the applicants, we get around 50% accuracy, 50% recall, 70% precision, and an F_1 score of 58%. Hence, our model should perform better than this, before its predictions are more useful than if we simply *guessed*.

Over and Underfitting

Underfitting happens when a model is too simple to use the information in the training data. Conversely, overfitting happens when a model is too complex and learns too much from the dataset, which does not generalize to new data.

Finding the right number of nodes and layers in a neural network can be a long, tedious process with a lot of trial and error. If we increase the size of the network, we can handle more advanced tasks but risk overfitting, whereas if we make it smaller, we risk making the model too simple to solve our task (underfitting). We need to find the middle ground, usually by **increasing the network size until overfitting and then dialing it back some**. We must also consider that larger networks can take longer to train and take up more disk space. If, for instance, we intend to run a model on a smartphone, we might sacrifice a bit of accuracy in order to have the model run faster and save some megabytes:

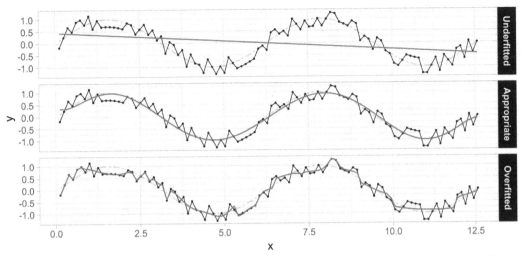

Black line with points: sin(x) + noise ; Solid magenta line: predict(x) ; Dashed grey line: sin(x)

Figure 4.10: Three examples of curve fitting

Figure 4.10 shows three examples of curve fitting. The black line with points shows the training data, which is a sine wave with random noise. The dashed grey line shows the pure sine wave, which is the formula the model should learn. The solid magenta line shows the predicted values for each x. We wish to avoid underfitting and overfitting as their predictions do not generalize to new data.

Adding Layers and Nodes in neuralnet

So far, we have only one node in one layer (excluding the input and output layers) in our neural networks. Adding nodes and layers is very simple and can decrease the error a lot. We simply pass a vector with the number of nodes per layer in the **hidden** argument. Let's create a model with two layers with two nodes each. We can have thousands of nodes in tens or even hundreds of layers, but that would take too long to train for this example (and would most likely overfit):

```
# Attach neuralnet

library(neuralnet)


# Set seed for reproducibility and easy comparison

set.seed(1)
```

Train the neural network:

```
# Classifying if class is "Good"
nn3 <- neuralnet(Class == "Good" ~ ., train_set[, c(9, 11:20)],
                 linear.output = FALSE, hidden = c(2,2))
```

Plot the trained model:

```
plotnet(nn3, var_labs = FALSE)
```

The output is as follows:

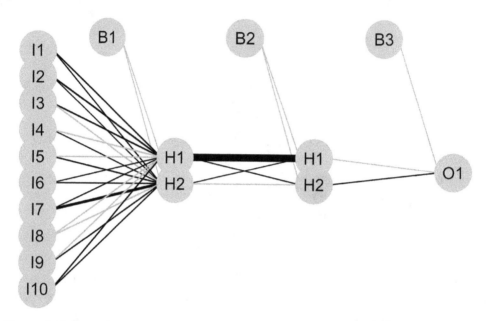

Figure 4.11: Neural network architecture with two hidden layers with two nodes each.

Calculate the training error:

```
# Print the training error
train_error <- nn3$result.matrix[1]
train_error
```

The output is as follows:

```
## [1] 48.42343
```

We get a lower error, but we have no real indication of whether it is underfitting or overfitting.

Cross-Validation

Cross-validation (CV) is a common technique used when deciding between model architectures. We split the training set into a number (k) of groups called folds. We train a model k times, using a different fold as the test set each time, while the other folds constitute the CV training set.

> **Note**
>
> The CV training set is not to be confused with the overall training set that we used to create the folds.

Say we use 4 folds ($k = 4$). We train the first instance of the model on folds 2, 3, and 4 and evaluate on fold 1. Then, we train a model instance on folds 1, 3, and 4 and evaluate on fold 2. Once all the folds have been used as test folds, we average the results and compare them to the cross-validation results of the other model architectures. Finally, we train an instance of the best-performing model architecture on the entire training set and test it on the validation set.

An alternative approach to averaging the results from each iteration is to collect the predictions from all iterations and evaluate once.

When working with a small development set, we risk it not being representative of our data distribution. In cross-validation, we evaluate our model architecture on **all observations** in the training set. We learn how well the model architecture can be fitted to multiple subsets of the training set instead of just a single subset. We can also detect inconsistencies in our data if, for instance, we get a very low accuracy when evaluating one of the folds compared to the others.

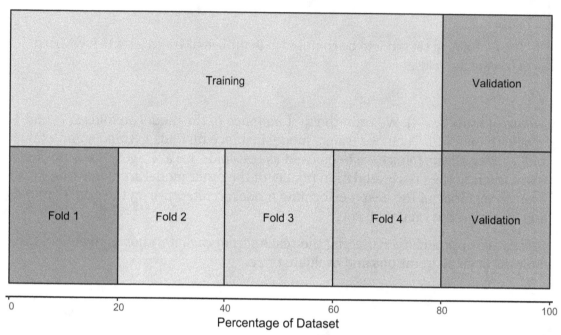

Top row: Training set (80%) and Validation set (20%).
Bottom row: Four folds (20% each) and Validation set (20%).

Figure 4.12: The percentages of the dataset assigned to the partitions and folds

Figure 4.12 shows the percentage split of the dataset into, first, the training and validation sets, and second, the 4 folds. *Figure* 4.13 shows how these folds are used in the cross-validation training loop:

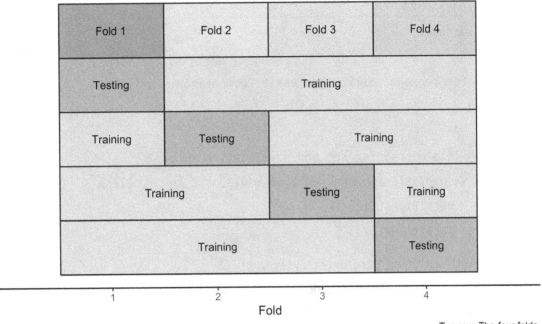

Top row: The four folds.
Four bottom rows: Use of the folds for either training or testing per iteration.

Figure 4.13: The usage of each fold per cross-validation iteration

Similar to when we created the partitions, we would like to have balanced ratios of the classes and avoid leakage between the folds. For this purpose, **groupdata2** has a **fold()** function, working similarly to **partition()**. Instead of returning a list of folds though, it simply creates a column with the fold identifiers in our data frame, called .**folds**.

There are multiple variations of cross-validation. We are using **stratified cross-validation**, as we are balancing the ratio of the classes between the folds. Another method is called **leave-one-out cross-validation**, where we would treat each observation as a fold. In situations where that would lead to leakage between the folds, we can use **leave-one-group-out cross-validation**, where, for instance, each applicant is treated as a fold (containing all their loan applications). A fourth method is **repeated cross-validation**, where we repeat the fold creation step multiple times, compared to just once. We create the folds, run cross-validation, create new folds, run cross-validation, and so on. This allows us to evaluate a lot more combinations of our observations.

Creating Folds

We will create and preprocess a training and validation set and create four folds from the training set. It is common to use 10 folds, but there are no hard rules:

```
# Attach groupdata2
library(groupdata2)


# Set seed for reproducibility and easier comparison
set.seed(1)


# Partition into a training set and a validation set
partitions <- partition(GermanCredit, p = 0.8, cat_col = "Class")
train_set <- partitions[[1]]
valid_set <- partitions[[2]]
```

Find scaling and centering parameters:

```
# Note: We could also decide to do this inside the training loop!
params <- preProcess(train_set[, 1:6], method=c("center", "scale"))
```

Transform the training set:

```
train_set[, 1:6] <- predict(params, train_set[, 1:6])


# Transform the validation set
valid_set[, 1:6] <- predict(params, valid_set[, 1:6])
```

To create four folds, we will use k = 4:

```
# Create folds for cross-validation
# Again balanced on the Class variable
train_set <- fold(train_set, k=4, cat_col = "Class")
```

> **Note**
>
> This creates a factor in the dataset called ".folds". Take care not to use this as a predictor.

Exercise 46: Writing a Cross-Validation Training Loop

In this exercise, we will perform cross-validation with a simple **for** loop. For each iteration, we subset the cross-validation training and test sets, train our model on the training set, and evaluate the model on the test set. We then find the average accuracy and error:

1. Initialize two vectors for collecting errors and accuracies:

   ```
   # Initialize vectors for collecting errors and accuracies
   errors <- c()
   accuracies <- c()
   ```

2. Start the training for loop. We have four folds, so we need four iterations:

   ```
   # Training loop
   for (part in 1:4){
   ```

3. Assign the chosen fold as the **test_set** and the rest of the folds as the **train_set**; Write this term in the same line be aware of the indentation:

   ```
   # Assign the chosen fold as test set
   # and the rest of the folds as train set
   cv_test_set <- train_set[train_set$.folds == part,]
   cv_train_set <- train_set[train_set$.folds != part,]
   ```

4. Train the neural network on predictors 11 – 20:

   ```
   # Train neural network classifier
   # Make sure not to include the ".folds" column as a predictor!
   nn <- neuralnet(Class == "Good" ~ .,
                   cv_train_set[, c(9, 11:20)],
                   linear.output = FALSE)
   ```

5. Append the error to the **errors** vector:

   ```
   # Append error to the errors vector
   errors <- append(errors, nn$result.matrix[1])
   ```

6. Create one-hot encoding of the target variable in the CV test set:

   ```
   # Create one-hot encoding of Class variable
   true_labels <- ifelse(cv_test_set$Class == "Good", 1, 0)
   ```

7. Use the trained neural network to predict the target variable in the CV test set:

```
# Predict the class in the test set
# It returns probabilities that the observations are "Good"
predicted_probabilities <- predict(nn, cv_test_set)
predictions <- ifelse(predicted_probabilities > 0.5, 1, 0)
```

8. Calculate the accuracy. We could also use **confusionMatrix()** here if we wanted other metrics:

```
# Calculate accuracy manually
# Note: TRUE == 1, FALSE == 0
cv_accuracy <- sum(true_labels == predictions) / length(true_labels)
```

9. Append the calculated accuracy to the accuracies vector:

```
# Append the accuracy to the accuracies vector
accuracies <- append(accuracies, cv_accuracy)
```

10. Close the for loop:

```
}
```

11. Calculate the average error and accuracy and print them. Note that we could also have gathered the predictions from all the folds and calculated the accuracy only once:

```
# Calculate average error and accuracy
# Note that we could also have gathered the predictions from all the
folds and calculated the accuracy only once. This could lead to slightly
different results, if, for instance, the folds were not exactly the same
size.

average_error <- mean(errors)
average_error
## [1] 51.47703

average_accuracy <- mean(accuracies)
average_accuracy
## [1] 0.74375
```

Once we have found the model architecture that gives the best average accuracy (or some other chosen metric), we can train this model on the entire training set and evaluate it on the validation set.

As we will be rerunning the cross-validation training loop again and again when comparing multiple model architectures, it would make sense to convert this code into a function, taking the arguments for **neuralnet()** and returning the average accuracy and error. A function in R is defined like this:

```
# Basic function in R

function_name <- function(arg1, arg2){


  # Do something with the arguments

  result <- arg1 + arg2


  # Return the result

  return(result)

}
```

In the upcoming activity, we will be training neural networks.

Activity 16: Training and Comparing Neural Network Architectures

In this activity, we will predict whether a diabetes test is positive or negative based on eight predictors. We will be using the **PimaIndiansDiabetes2** dataset from https://github.com/TrainingByPackt/Practical-Machine-Learning-with-R/blob/master/Data/PimaIndiansDiabetes2.csv.

The dataset has missing data, which you will need to handle. A quick solution would be to remove the columns with many missing values and the rows with missing data in the other columns. Let's summarize the dataset and discuss this before diving into the activity:

```
# Attach packages

library(groupdata2)

library(caret)

library(mlbench)

library(neuralnet)


# Load the data
```

```
PimaIndiansDiabetes2 <- read.csv("PimaIndiansDiabetes2.csv")
```

```
# Summarize the dataset
summary(PimaIndiansDiabetes2)
```

```
##       pregnant          glucose          pressure         triceps
## Min.    : 0.000   Min.    : 44.0   Min.    : 24.00   Min.    : 7.00
## 1st Qu.: 1.000   1st Qu.: 99.0   1st Qu.: 64.00   1st Qu.:22.00
## Median : 3.000   Median :117.0   Median : 72.00   Median :29.00
## Mean    : 3.845   Mean    :121.7   Mean    : 72.41   Mean    :29.15
## 3rd Qu.: 6.000   3rd Qu.:141.0   3rd Qu.: 80.00   3rd Qu.:36.00
## Max.    :17.000   Max.    :199.0   Max.    :122.00   Max.    :99.00
##                   NA's    :5      NA's    :35      NA's    :227
##
##       insulin          mass          pedigree           age
## Min.    : 14.00   Min.    :18.20   Min.    :0.0780   Min.    :21.00
## 1st Qu.: 76.25   1st Qu.:27.50   1st Qu.:0.2437   1st Qu.:24.00
## Median :125.00   Median :32.30   Median :0.3725   Median :29.00
## Mean    :155.55   Mean    :32.46   Mean    :0.4719   Mean    :33.24
## 3rd Qu.:190.00   3rd Qu.:36.60   3rd Qu.:0.6262   3rd Qu.:41.00
## Max.    :846.00   Max.    :67.10   Max.    :2.4200   Max.    :81.00
## NA's    :374     NA's    :11
##
## diabetes
## neg:500
## pos:268
```

Two of the predictors (**triceps** and **insulin**) contain a lot of NAs ("Not Available"). If we remove these, we can either try to infer the other missing values or simply remove the rows containing NAs. This is up to you.

The **diabetes** column is the target variable that we wish to predict.

The main purpose of this activity is to train and compare multiple neural network architectures. Try changing the number of layers and nodes and compare them on accuracy, precision, recall, and F_1.

Here are the steps that will help you complete the activity. Note that these do not include cross-validation, which will be performed in the next activity:

1. Attach the packages.

2. Set the random seed to 1.

3. Load the **PimaIndiansDiabetes2** dataset.

4. Summarize the dataset.

5. Handle the missing data (possible solution: remove the **triceps** and **insulin** columns and use **na.omit()** on the dataset).

6. Partition the dataset into a training set (60%), development set (20%), and validation set (20%). Use **cat_col="diabetes"** to balance the ratios of each class between the partitions.

7. Assign the partitions to variable names.

8. Find the **preProcess** parameters for scaling and centering on the training set and apply them to all partitions.

9. Train multiple neural network architectures. Adjust them by changing the number of nodes and/or layers. In the model formula, use **diabetes == "pos"**.

10. Evaluate each model on the development set using the **confusionMatrix()** function.

11. Evaluate the best model on the validation set.

12. Plot the best model.

13. Consider/discuss whether the model is underfitting or overfitting the training set based on the validation set results.

The output will be similar to the following:

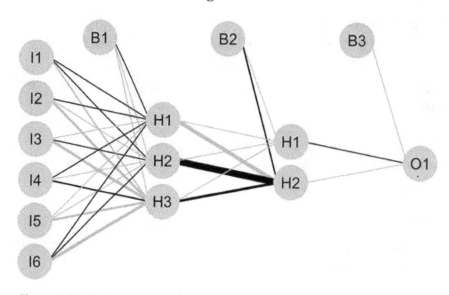

Figure 4.14: The best neural network architecture without cross-validation

In this activity, we have trained multiple neural network architectures and evaluated the best model on the validation set.

Note

The solution for this activity can be found on page 344.

Activity 17: Training and Comparing Neural Network Architectures with Cross-Validation

In this activity, we will perform the same operations as in the previous activity, Activity 16, *Training and Comparing Neural Network Architectures*, but instead of using a development set, we will use cross-validation to select the best model. We will be using the cross-validation code from Exercise 6, *Writing a Cross-validation Training Loop*.

We will be using the PimaIndiansDiabetes2 dataset from https://github.com/TrainingByPackt/Practical-Machine-Learning-with-R/blob/master/Data/PimaIndiansDiabetes2.csv.

Here the steps to complete the activity:

1. Attach the **groupdata2**, **caret**, **neuralnet**, and **mlbench** packages.

2. Set the random seed to 1.

3. Load the **PimaIndiansDiabetes2** dataset.

4. Handle the missing data (quick solution: remove the **triceps** and **insulin** columns and use **na.omit()** on the dataset).

5. Partition the dataset into a training set (80%) and a validation set (20%). Use **cat_col="diabetes"** to balance the ratios of each class between the partitions.

6. Assign the partitions to variable names.

7. Find the preProcess parameters for scaling and centering on the training set and apply them to both partitions.

8. Create four folds in the training set, using the **fold()** function. Use **cat_col="diabetes"** to balance the ratios of each class between the folds.

9. Use the cross-validation training loop code to cross-validate your models. In the model formula, use **diabetes == "pos"**. Also, remember to not use the **.folds** column as a predictor.

10. Select the best performing model and train it on the entire training set.

11. Evaluate the best model on the validation set.

12. Plot the best model.

13. Consider/discuss whether the model is underfitting or overfitting the training set based on the validation set results.

The output will be similar to the following:

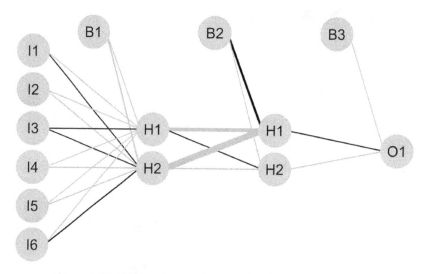

Figure 4.15: The best neural network with cross-validation

In this activity, we used cross-validation to evaluate the performance of neural networks, and then we evaluated the best model on the validation set. In the provided solution, we only showed one model architecture, so you might have found another model architecture that performs better.

> **Note**
>
> The solution for this activity can be found on page 351.

Multiclass Classification Overview

When we have more than two classes, we have to modify our approach slightly. In the output layer of the neural network, we now have the same number of nodes as the number of classes. The values in these nodes are normalized using the *softmax* function, such that they all add up to 1. We can interpret these normalized values as probabilities, and the node with the highest probability is our predicted class. The *softmax* function is given by $\sigma(\mathbf{z})_i = \frac{e^{z_i}}{\sum_{j=1}^{k} e^{z_j}}$, where $\mathbf{Z}$ is the vector of output nodes.

When evaluating the model, we have to increase the size of our confusion matrix. *Figure 4.16* shows a confusion matrix with three classes. The "Yay!" boxes contain the counts of correct predictions, while the "Nope!" boxes contain the counts of incorrect predictions:

True / Predicted	Class 1	Class 2	Class 3
Class 1	Yay!	Nope!	Nope!
Class 2	Nope!	Yay!	Nope!
Class 3	Nope!	Nope!	Yay!

Figure 4.16: The confusion matrix with three classes

With this, we can calculate both overall metrics and one-vs-all metrics. In one-vs-all evaluations, we have one class (such as class 2) against all the other classes combined as one negative class (class 1 + class 3). We can then use the metrics we know.

For "class 2-vs-all", we would use the confusion matrix in *Figure 4.17*:

True / Predicted	Class 1	Class 2	Class 3
Class 1	True Negative	False Negative	True Negative
Class 2	False Positive	True Positive	False Positive
Class 3	True Negative	False Negative	True Negative

Figure 4.17: The confusion matrix for the one-vs-all evaluation for Class 2

We can average the metrics from the one-vs-all evaluations. We can also calculate an overall accuracy, which is simply all the predictions in the diagonal "Yay!" boxes divided by the total number of predictions. Both the average and overall accuracy metrics can inform us of the model performance. How we interpret them depends on how balanced the validation set is. If one class has 90% of the observations, the overall accuracy could be 90% by simply predicting that class all the time, while the average accuracy would be much lower.

By looking at the confusion matrix and the one-vs-all metrics, we can gain an understanding of which classes might be difficult to differentiate. This might suggest that we need to collect more data from these classes, or that the classes are very similar on the chosen features.

Summary

In this chapter, you trained, evaluated, and compared multiple neural network architectures on the **GermanCredit** and **PimaIndiansDiabetes2** classification tasks. To achieve this, you created balanced partitions and folds with the **groupdata2** package. You used the **neuralnet** package to specify and train neural networks and used those trained models to predict the classes in the development and validation sets. Both in theory and by using caret's **confusionMatrix** function, you learned how to calculate accuracy, precision, recall, and F_1 metrics. You implemented a cross-validation training loop and used it to compare multiple model architectures. Finally, we introduced multiclass classification and the **softmax** function.

If you wish to build more advanced neural networks while keeping the code simple, the **keras** package would be a good place to start.

In the next chapter, you will learn how to fit and interpret linear and logistic regression models. We will use the **cvms** package to easily cross-validate multiple model formulas at once, without having to write a training loop ourselves.

5

Linear and Logistic Regression Models

Learning Objectives

By the end of this chapter, you will be able to:

- Implement and interpret linear and logistic regression models
- Compare linear and logistic regression models with cvms
- Implement a random forest model
- Create baseline evaluations with cvms
- Select nondominated models, when metrics rank models differently

In *Chapter 1, An Introduction to Machine Learning*, we were introduced to linear and logistic regression models. In this chapter, we will expand our knowledge of these tools and use cross-validation to compare and choose between a set of models.

Introduction

While neural networks are often better than linear and logistic regression models at solving regression and classification tasks, respectively, they can be very difficult to interpret. If we wish to test the hypothesis that people drink more water when the temperature rises, it's important that we can extract this information from our model. A neural network with many layers might be very good at predicting the water consumption of a person, based on features such as age, gender, weight, height, humidity, and temperature, but it would be difficult to say how temperature alone affects the prediction. Linear regression would tell us specifically how temperature contributed to the prediction. So, while we might get a worse prediction, we gain an insight into the data and, potentially, the real world. Logistic regression, which we use for binary classification, is similarly easier to interpret.

In this chapter, we will implement and interpret linear and logistic regression models. Linear regression is used to predict continuous variables, while logistic regression is used for binary classification. We will use two methods of model building, one where features (which we will also refer to as "predictors") are incrementally added based on theoretical relevance, and one where all possible models are compared with cross-validation, using the `cvms` package. We will learn how to compare our models to baseline models, similar to what we did in *Chapter 4, Introduction to neuralnet and Evaluation Methods*, but this time using the **baseline()** function from **cvms**. We will also compare the models against random forest models. Finally, we will learn how to identify the nondominated models, when our evaluation metrics do not agree on what model is best.

Regression

Regression models are used to predict the value of a dependent variable from a set of independent variables, and to inform us about the strengths and forms of the potential relationships between each independent variable and the dependent variable in our dataset. While we will only cover linear and logistic regression in this chapter, it is worth noting that there are more types of regression, such as **Poisson regression**, for predicting *count* variables, such as the number of tattoos a person has, and **ordinal regression**, for predicting *ranked* variables, such as questionnaire answers ("Really Bad", "Bad", "Decent", "Good", "Really Good"), where the difference between "Decent" and "Good" is not necessarily the same as between "Really bad" and "Bad".

Each of these regression models relies on a set of assumptions about the data. For instance, in order to meaningfully use and interpret a *linear* regression model, we should make sure the phenomenon we are modeling is actually somewhat *linear* in nature. If these assumptions do not hold true for our data, we cannot reliably interpret our models.

> **Note**
>
> We will not cover these assumptions *extensively* in this chapter, so we highly recommend learning more about them elsewhere, for instance, in Discovering Statistics using R, by Andy Field (2012), or the in-depth YouTube video "Regression V: All regression assumptions explained!" by the channel **zedstatistics**. Here is the link to the video: https://www.youtube.com/watch?v=0MFpOQRY0rw

In *Chapter 3, Feature Engineering*, we learned about feature selection. In this chapter, we will use two different approaches to choose the predictors for our model. One is to use whatever domain-specific theory we have about our task to incrementally add the most meaningful predictors. We then compare this model to the previous models on a set of metrics, to test whether the model is better with or without the added predictor. This approach is meaningful when we have a specific hypothesis we wish to test, and when the models take a long time to train. One of the disadvantages of this approach is that the process might take a long time when we have many potential predictors. Also, it can be hard to know whether we have missed any meaningful combinations of the predictors.

A second approach is to try as many models as possible and choose the model that performs best on a test set (for instance by using cross-validation). Suppose we have five potential predictors available. This leaves us with **31** different models to test and compare. If we allow for two- and three-way interactions between predictors (we will discuss these later in the *Interactions* section), this increases the number of models to **5,160**. If we have even more predictors available, this number can quickly explode. Hence, it makes sense to combine the two approaches by using domain-specific knowledge to limit the number of models to test, for instance, *by only including theoretically meaningful predictors*.

While the second approach tells us, which model is best at predicting the dependent variable in our test set, we do risk ending up with a model that is less theoretically meaningful. A variable can be a good predictor of another variable without there being a causal relationship between the two. For instance, we could probably (to some degree) predict how much sun we had during the summer months from the color of the grass. However, since changing the color of the grass would not affect the amount of sunshine, this is not a causal relationship. Conversely, if we were to predict the color of the grass, the amount of sun in the previous months could potentially be a causal effect.

We should also be aware that while cross-validation reduces the risk of overfitting, it does not eliminate it. When trying a high number of models, there is a risk that some of them are better due to overfitting.

In this chapter, we will start out with the incremental model-building approach, interpreting each model along the way, and then use cross-validation to test all possible models and interpret the one that performs best. We do this for pedagogical reasons but be aware that we would usually find the best model first, before starting the interpretation process.

The following datasets will be used in this chapter:

Dataset	Description	Output Variable
Sacramento	This dataset contains 932 rows with 9 columns related to housing prices in Sacramento CA area.	The "price" column is the main output variable included. It contains house prices in US dollars.
cars	This dataset contains 18 variables describing 804 cars from GM.	The "price" column is the output variable.
amsterdam.listings	This dataset contains 17,318 AirBnB listings in Amsterdam, with 8 variables describing the listings.	We use the "room_type" column as output variable.

Figure 5.1: Datasets

Linear Regression

When performing linear regression, we are trying to find linear relationships between variables. Suppose we have a cat shelter and want to know how many extra cans of cat food we need to buy after receiving new cats. A simple approach would be to find the average number of cans a cat eats per day (**z**) and multiply it by the number of new cats (**x**). This is a linear relationship: if the number of cats increases by **x**, make sure to buy **x** times **z** cans of cat food. Of course, other variables might affect how much a new cat eats, such as age, breed, and weight at birth. We could possibly make a better linear model by adding these as predictors.

Imagine we had measured the amount of food eaten by **85** cats, along with their weight at birth (in grams). For budgeting reasons, we wish to predict the amount of food (number of cans) a newborn cat will eat per day when it grows up. We can plot these variables against each other, as shown in *Figure 5.2*:

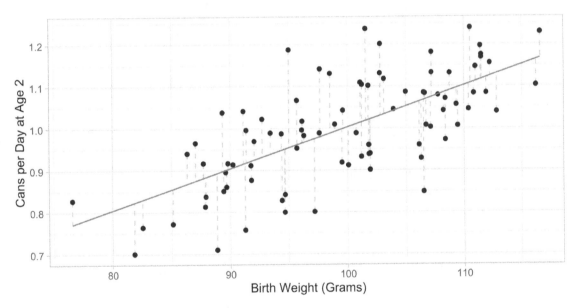

Figure 5.2: Cans of cat food eaten per day at age 2 by birth weight

On the *x-axis*, we have the weight at birth in grams. On the *y-axis*, we have the number of cans eaten per day when the cat is two years old. The black points are the measurements, while the solid line represents the linear predictions. The dashed lines show the distance between each measurement and the predicted value at that birth weight. These distances are called the **residuals**.

Our (simulated) data seems to indicate that a heavier newborn cat will eat more at two years old than a lighter one. The residuals (the vertical, dashed lines) are used to calculate the error metrics, such as **Mean Absolute Error** (**MAE**) and **Root Mean Square Error** (**RMSE**). The smaller the residuals (on a test set), the better the model is. We can plot these residuals as shown in the following figure:

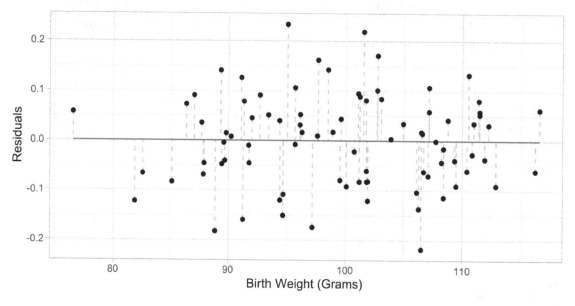

Figure 5.3: Residuals

The solid line lies at **0**, as the residuals (the dashed lines) are the distances to that line. In this plot, the residuals seem to be distributed fairly similarly on both sides of the solid line. The model simply uses the average amount of cat food eaten per cat to create this line, so the sum of distances is the same on each side. Sometimes, though, we can have large outliers (greatly diverging data points) on one side, pushing the line away from the more regular data points. Imagine we had a cat that ate six cans per day. That would increase the average, causing the model to make poorer predictions about the more typical one-can-per-day cats. The fewer cats we had measured, the bigger impact such an outlier would have. When our sample size is small, it is therefore important to check that the residuals are somewhat *normally distributed* (like a bell curve) around **0**. This means that most of the residuals should be close to the prediction line, with fewer and fewer residuals the further away we get from the line.

We can visualize the distribution of the residuals with a density plot. This visualizes the concentrations of continuous values in a vector. Imagine pushing the points in *Figure 5.3* all the way to the left and rotating the plot by **-90** degrees. We then add the density plot to show the distribution of the points at the bottom:

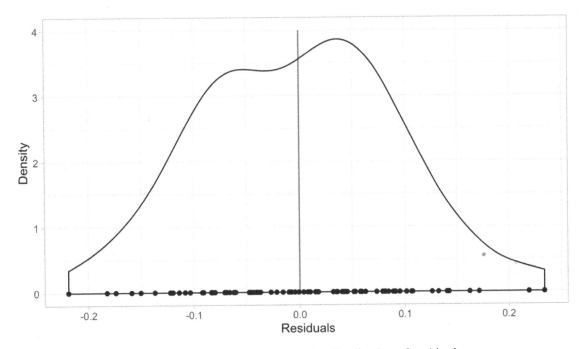

Figure 5.4: Density plot showing the distribution of residuals

The black curvy line (the density plot) shows the shape of the distribution. We want this distribution to resemble a normal distribution (bell curve) with a median of around 0 (the vertical line). There are other types of plots commonly used to inspect *normality* (that the distribution is normal), as well as a set of statistical tests, such as the **Shapiro-Wilk Normality Test**. As we will be working with a dataset with more than a few hundred observations, we will not perform these tests or further discuss the assumption of normality in this chapter.

When interpreting our regression model, we are often interested in the relation between each predictor and the dependent variable. We ask how the dependent variable changes when a predictor increases by one unit. This interpretation relies on the assumption that the predictors are independent of each other. If a predictor can itself be predicted by a linear combination of the other predictors (**multicollinearity**), the predictor's information is redundant and non-independent. In that case, we cannot properly interpret the effects of the single predictors. Importantly, multicollinearity does not necessarily make the model worse at predicting the dependent variable.

The assumption of **homoscedasticity** is that the variance of the residuals should be similar for different values of our predictors. We shouldn't, for instance, be very good at predicting the amount of cat food when the cat weighed 90 grams at birth but be really bad when the cat weighed 110 grams at birth.

The assumption of no **auto-correlation** is that the **residuals** must be independent of each other. This means that we should not be able to predict the value of a residual from the other residuals.

Having briefly explained some of the assumptions of regression, we again recommend reading up on the assumptions of the regression models you intend to use. We will now move ahead and train a linear regression model.

Exercise 47: Training Linear Regression Models

In this exercise, we will load, inspect, and prepare the Sacramento dataset from the **caret** package. It contains prices for 932 houses in the Sacramento CA area, across a 5-day period. Then, we will train and interpret a simple linear regression model:

1. Attach the **caret**, **groupdata2**, and **cvms** packages:

   ```
   # Attach Packages
   library(caret)
   library(groupdata2)
   library(cvms)
   ```

2. Set the random seed to **1**:

   ```
   set.seed(1)
   ```

3. Load the Sacramento dataset:

   ```
   # Load Sacramento dataset
   data(Sacramento)
   ```

4. Assign/copy the dataset to another variable name:

```
# Assign data to variable name
full_data <- Sacramento
```

5. Summarize the dataset:

```
# Summarize the dataset
summary(full_data)
```

The summary is as follows:

```
##             city           zip           beds          baths
##   SACRAMENTO    :438   z95823 :  61   Min.   :1.000   Min.   :1.000
##   ELK_GROVE     :114   z95828 :  45   1st Qu.:3.000   1st Qu.:2.000
##   ROSEVILLE     : 48   z95758 :  44   Median :3.000   Median :2.000
##   CITRUS_HEIGHTS: 35   z95835 :  37   Mean   :3.276   Mean   :2.053
##   ANTELOPE      : 33   z95838 :  37   3rd Qu.:4.000   3rd Qu.:2.000
##   RANCHO_CORDOVA: 28   z95757 :  36   Max.   :8.000   Max.   :5.000
##   (Other)       :236   (Other):672
##       sqft                type           price         latitude
##   Min.   : 484   Condo        : 53   Min.   : 30000   Min.   :38.24
##   1st Qu.:1167   Multi_Family : 13   1st Qu.:156000   1st Qu.:38.48
##   Median :1470   Residential :866   Median :220000   Median :38.62
##   Mean   :1680                       Mean   :246662   Mean   :38.59
##   3rd Qu.:1954                       3rd Qu.:305000   3rd Qu.:38.69
##   Max.   :4878                       Max.   :884790   Max.   :39.02
##
##     longitude
##   Min.   :-121.6
##   1st Qu.:-121.4
##   Median :-121.4
##   Mean   :-121.4
##   3rd Qu.:-121.3
##   Max.   :-120.6
```

The **city** column contains multiple cities, some of which only appear a few times.

6. Count the appearances of each city with **table()**. Use **sort()** to order the counts:

```
# Count observations per city
sort( table(full_data$city) )
```

The output is as follows:

```
##
##            COOL DIAMOND_SPRINGS        FORESTHILL   GARDEN_VALLEY
##               1               1                1               1
##       GREENWOOD          MATHER    MEADOW_VISTA          PENRYN
##               1               1                1               1
##    WALNUT_GROVE       EL_DORADO           LOOMIS     GRANITE_BAY
##               1               2                2               3
##   POLLOCK_PINES RANCHO_MURIETA WEST_SACRAMENTO         ELVERTA
##               3               3                3               4
##      GOLD_RIVER          AUBURN           WILTON   CAMERON_PARK
##               4               5                5               9
##       FAIR_OAKS     PLACERVILLE       ORANGEVALE       RIO_LINDA
##               9              10               11              13
##          FOLSOM         ROCKLIN       CARMICHAEL            GALT
##              17              17               20              21
## NORTH_HIGHLANDS         LINCOLN EL_DORADO_HILLS RANCHO_CORDOVA
##              21              22               23              28
##        ANTELOPE CITRUS_HEIGHTS        ROSEVILLE       ELK_GROVE
##              33              35               48             114
##      SACRAMENTO
##             438
```

Some cities have only one observation, which is not nearly enough to train a model on. As these cities might be very diverse, it can seem a bit artificial to group them together as one condition. On the other hand, doing so might show us some general tendencies of home prices in and outside Sacramento.

7. Create a one-hot encoded column called **in_sacramento**, describing whether a home is located in Sacramento:

```
# Create one-hot encoded factor column describing
# if the city is Sacramento or not
full_data$in_sacramento <- factor(
  ifelse(full_data$city == "SACRAMENTO", 1, 0)
)
```

8. Count the homes in and outside Sacramento:

```
# Count observations per city condition
table(full_data$in_sacramento)
##
##   0   1
## 494 438
```

9. Partition the dataset into a training set (**80%**) and a validation set (**20%**). Balance the ratios of the two **in_sacramento** conditions between the partitions and assign each partition to a variable name:

```
partitions <- partition(full_data, p = 0.8,
                        cat_col = "in_sacramento")
train_set <- partitions[[1]]
valid_set <- partitions[[2]]
```

Now, we can train a linear regression model with the **in_sacramento** column as a predictor of **price**. We use the **lm()** function for this. Similar to the **neuralnet()** function in *Chapter 4, Introduction to neuralnet and Evaluation Methods*, we first have a model formula: **price ~ in_sacramento** (read as "**price** *predicted by* **in_sacramento**"). We use the **summary()** function to view the fitted model parameters.

10. Fit a linear model where **price** is predicted by the **in_sacramento** variable:

```
# Fit model where price is predicted by in_sacramento
lin_model <- lm(price ~ in_sacramento, data = train_set)
```

11. Inspect the model summary:

```
# Inspect the model summary
summary(lin_model)
```

The summary is as follows:

```
##
## Call:
## lm(formula = price ~ in_sacramento, data = train_set)
##
## Residuals:
##      Min      1Q  Median      3Q     Max
## -261719  -82372  -25719   54491  593071
##
## Coefficients:
##                 Estimate Std. Error t value Pr(>|t|)
## (Intercept)       291719       6214   46.94   <2e-16 ***
## in_sacramento1    -91427       9067  -10.08   <2e-16 ***
## ---
## Signif. codes:  0 '***' 0.001 '**' 0.01 '*' 0.05 '.' 0.1 ' ' 1
##
## Residual standard error: 123500 on 743 degrees of freedom
## Multiple R-squared:  0.1204, Adjusted R-squared:  0.1192
## F-statistic: 101.7 on 1 and 743 DF,  p-value: < 2.2e-16
```

Now, let's learn how to interpret the output. In the top of the output, we have the `Call` section. This simply repeats how we called the `lm()` function.

Next, we have summary statistics of the residuals. The median residual (**-25719**) is negative, meaning that most data points lie below the prediction line. Interestingly, the most positive residual (**593071**) has more than double the magnitude of the most negative residual (**-261719**).

In the *Coefficients* section, we see the coefficient estimations, along with their standard errors and significance tests. The coefficient estimates can be thought of as the neural network weights we saw in the previous chapter. For this model, the *Intercept* tells us the average home price (**$291,719**) in the smaller cities. The estimate for homes in Sacramento tells us that the average price in Sacramento is **$91,427** less! So, on average, it is cheaper to buy a house in Sacramento than in one of the other cities.

The coefficient **standard error** (**std. error**) is an estimate of how uncertain the model is about the coefficient estimate. As we are working with a random sample of houses from the Sacramento area, we do not know the **true** coefficient, and were we to collect a different sample of houses, the coefficient estimate would almost certainly be different from our current estimate. To get closer to the true coefficient, we could collect a lot of these samples and find the average coefficient estimate. As this could be expensive and time-consuming, we would like to have an estimate of how close to the true coefficient we think the model is. The standard error helps us by estimating the standard deviation of the coefficient estimates if we were to gather a lot of samples from the real world. In our summary, the standard error for `in_sacramento` (**$9,067**) is a lot smaller than the coefficient estimate (**$-91,427**). This tells us that we should expect the true coefficient to be within **$9,067** of the current coefficient estimate 68% of the time, and within twice that amount ~95% of the time.

The p-value (**Pr(>|t|)**) tells us that the difference between living in and outside Sacramento is *statistically significant* (<2e-16). This means that we have strong evidence against the null hypothesis (that there is no difference between prices in and outside Sacramento) and can reasonably reject it. If the houses in our training set are representative of the real world, and the many assumptions of the model are met, this means that accepting the alternative hypothesis (that the difference between prices in and outside Sacramento exists) will only make us look stupid 5% of the time (that is, if our significance threshold is $p=0.05$, we would get a significant effect 5% of the time by chance). Note that the size of the coefficient estimate is just as important as the p-value when deciding whether to believe the alternative hypothesis. If we have enough data points, even very small coefficients can be significant. Whether it is meaningful or not depends on the context.

In the *Signif. codes* section below the coefficients, we see different significance thresholds, each symbolized by a number of asterisks. We should generally decide on a threshold before running the analysis. We will use the 0.05 threshold (one asterisk), but which threshold is appropriate will depend on the context.

Finally, we get a few metrics about the model, such as **adjusted R-squared**. This tells us that the model can explain ~11.92% of the variance in the dependent variable in the training set.

R^2

The coefficient of determination, R^2, or R-squared, tells us how much of the variance in the dependent variable can be explained by the predictors in our model, as a percentage between 0 and 1. Although we want this to be as large as possible, even a seemingly small R^2 can be good if the phenomenon we're modeling is very complex. A model with a high R^2 is generally better suited for making predictions, whereas a model with a small R^2 can still be useful for describing the effect of the various predictors. When we add predictors to a model, R^2 increases as well, even if the model is overfitted. To account for this, the adjusted R^2 only increases if the added predictor actually makes the model better (that is, it increases R^2 more than adding a random variable as a predictor would), and can even decrease, if it doesn't.

In the previous chapter, we talked about the importance of comparing our models on their performances on a test set (either in cross-validation or a development set). The R^2 metric is usually calculated on the training set, although a Predicted R^2 metric does exist. We will therefore **not** use R^2 for model selection.

In the following exercise, we will visualize the predictions our model makes on the training set.

Exercise 48: Plotting Model Predictions

In this exercise, we will plot our model's predictions of home prices on top of our training data using **ggplot2**. While we have used **ggplot2** in the previous chapters, let's quickly refresh the basics.

We first create a **ggplot** object. We then use the **+** operator to add layers to the object. These layers can be boxes, lines, points, or many other *geoms* (from *geometry*). We specify the variables for the *x* and *y* axes via the **aes()** function ("aes" is from "*aesthetic mapping*"). We can also change the colors and sizes of the added geoms:

1. Attach the **ggplot2** package:

   ```
   # Attach ggplot2
   library(ggplot2)
   ```

2. Assign/copy the training set to a new name:

```
# Assign/copy the training set to a new name
plotting_data <- train_set
```

3. Use the model to predict prices in the training set:

```
# Use the model to predict prices in the training set
plotting_data$predicted_price <- predict(lin_model, train_set)
```

4. Create a **ggplot** object. Specify the mapping between the variables and the axes. Remember the **+**:

```
# Create ggplot object and specify the data and x,y axes
ggplot(data = plotting_data,
        mapping = aes(x = in_sacramento, y = price)) +
```

5. Add each observation in the training set as a point with **geom_point()**. Change the color and size as well. It is also possible to use the name of a common color, such as "green". Remember the **+**:

```
# Add the training set observations as points
geom_point(color = '#00004f', size = 0.4) +
```

6. Add a prediction line with **geom_line()**. Because the *x-axis* is the **in_sacramento** factor, the line will start at the predicted value when **in_sacramento** is 0 and end at the predicted value when **in_sacramento** is 1. Remember the **+**:

```
# Add the predictions as a line
# Notice that we convert in_sacramento to the
# type "numeric", as this allows us to draw the
# line in-between the two binary values
geom_line(color = '#d8007a',
          aes(x = as.numeric(in_sacramento),
              y = predicted_price)) +
```

7. Add the **light** theme. There is a set of themes for **ggplot2** plots to choose from. Do not add a **+**, as this is the last layer of our plot:

```
# Add a theme to make our plot prettier
theme_light()
```

The output is as follows:

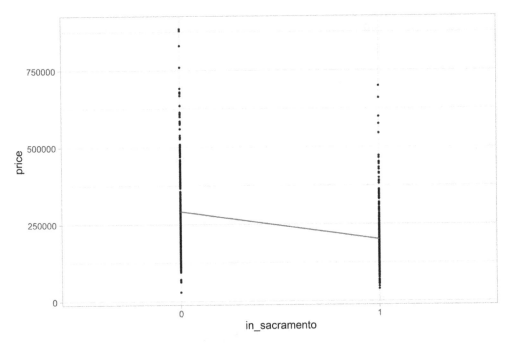

Figure 5.5: Plot of price predicted by in_sacramento

The points are the actual prices in the training set, while the solid line is what our model would predict in the two conditions. The "line" of black points in the right column seems to be shifted slightly downward from the left column, although a lot of the points are in the same range across the two conditions. The points in the left column cover a larger range of prices, which makes sense because we artificially grouped the cities together. Given that the points with similar values are all stacked on top of each other, it can be hard to tell their actual distribution. For that, we will add a *violin plot* behind the points.

1. We wish to add a **geom_violin()** layer to the beginning of our plot. Instead of rewriting every step, just add the new layer to our code.

2. You should have this code *before* the new layer:

```
# Create ggplot object and specify the data and x,y axes
ggplot(data = plotting_data,
       mapping = aes(x = in_sacramento, y = price)) +
```

3. Add this code to create the new layer:

```
# Add violin plot of the training data
geom_violin(color = '#00004f', size = 0.4) +
```

4. You should have the following code *after* the new layer:

```
# Add the training data as points
geom_point(color = '#00004f', size = 0.4) +
# Add the predictions as a line
# Notice that we convert in_sacramento to the
# type "numeric", as this allows us to draw the
# line in-between the two binary values
geom_line(color = '#d8007a',
            aes(x = as.numeric(in_sacramento),
                y = predicted_price)) +
# Add a theme to make our plot prettier
theme_light()
```

The output will appear as follows:

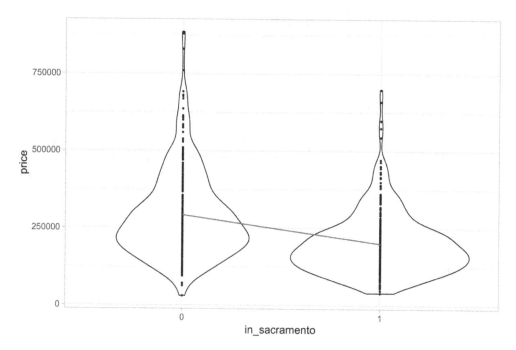

Figure 5.6: Improved plot of price predicted by in_sacramento

Similar to the density plot we saw previously, the broader the "violins" are, the greater number of data points have approximately that value. As the right violin (when in_sacramento is 1) is broadest at a lower point than the left violin (when in_sacramento is 0), we can tell that the bulk of Sacramento prices lie below those outside Sacramento. We can also tell though that using only this predictor in our model would not make it very successful at estimating the price of a specific home.

In this exercise, we learned how to plot the predictions against the actual observations. In the next exercise, we will learn how to incrementally add predictors.

Exercise 49: Incrementally Adding Predictors

In this exercise, we will add predictors to our linear regression model one at a time and see how the model summary changes. We have three additional predictors that are likely to impact the home price. First, the size (in sqft), then, the number of bedrooms (beds), and finally, the number of bathrooms (baths). We also have the type of house, but because it is so imbalanced, we will leave it out. As larger houses tend to have more beds and baths than smaller houses, we might hypothesize that our predictors are correlated. As you may recall, one of the assumptions of linear regression is that there is not a high degree of multicollinearity. If this assumption is not met, we need to be careful when interpreting the summaries. There are multiple approaches to checking for multicollinearity.

A simple first check is whether the predictors correlate with one another. If two predictors are highly correlated, we should consider removing one of them. Correlation is not enough though, as multicollinearity can also stem from a linear combination of multiple predictors. To check for this, it is common to calculate the **Variance Inflation Factor (VIF)**. Let's first check the correlation between predictors, and then the VIF:

1. Attach the **car** package:

   ```
   # Attach car
   library(car)
   ```

2. Find the correlation coefficients between **sqft**, **beds**, and **baths**:

   ```
   cor(train_set[, c(3:5)])
   ```

   The correlation coefficients are as follows:

   ```
   ##                 beds       baths       sqft
   ## beds    1.0000000 0.6452788 0.7179578
   ## baths  0.6452788 1.0000000 0.7619998
   ## sqft    0.7179578 0.7619998 1.0000000
   ```

The pairwise correlations are **sqft** and **baths** (0.762), **sqft** and **beds** (0.718), and **beds** and **baths** (0.645). These correlation coefficients are fairly high, but not necessarily too high. They are worth bearing in mind, however, when interpreting the model summaries. To assess whether they are too high, or whether we have overly high multicollinearity in other ways, let's use VIF.

3. Train a model with all four predictors and apply the **vif()** function from the **car** package:

```
# Train a linear regression model
# with all four predictors
lin_model_all_predictors <- lm(
    price~in_sacramento + sqft + beds + baths,
    data = train_set)
# Apply the vif() function to the model object
vif(lin_model_all_predictors)
## in_sacramento        sqft        beds       baths
##      1.108431    3.133212    2.196416    2.515782
```

We want the **VIF** values to be as close to 1 as possible. A common rule of thumb is that a **VIF > 5** should be interpreted as there being high multicollinearity. In that case, we could consider removing one of the correlated predictors. In our case, the largest VIF is 3.133, which is acceptable for our analysis. Now, we will start training and interpreting some linear regression models.

4. Train a linear model with **in_sacramento** and **sqft** as predictors of **price**:

```
lin_model_2 <- lm(price ~ in_sacramento + sqft,
                  data = train_set)
summary(lin_model_2)
```

The summary of the model is as follows:

```
##
## Call:
## lm(formula = price ~ in_sacramento + sqft, data = train_set)
##
## Residuals:
##       Min      1Q  Median      3Q      Max
## -198778   -51380  -11981   35566   403189
##
## Coefficients:
##                   Estimate Std. Error t value Pr(>|t|)
## (Intercept)       43421.47    9118.38   4.762 2.31e-06 ***
## in_sacramento1   -35732.88    6306.19  -5.666 2.09e-08 ***
```

```
## sqft               131.09      4.29  30.558  < 2e-16 ***
## ---
## Signif. codes:  0 '***' 0.001 '**' 0.01 '*' 0.05 '.' 0.1 ' ' 1
##
## Residual standard error: 82240 on 742 degrees of freedom
## Multiple R-squared:  0.6105, Adjusted R-squared:  0.6095
## F-statistic: 581.6 on 2 and 742 DF,  p-value: < 2.2e-16
```

Adding the size in square feet changed the summary quite a lot. Our intercept is now the price when living outside Sacramento with a home size of 0 square feet. For every extra square foot, we have to add **$131.09** to the price. The estimated effect of living in Sacramento has now become smaller as well, though it's still statistically significant. Finally, we see that the adjusted R-squared has grown to 60.95%. Now, let's add the number of bedrooms.

5. Train a linear model with **in_sacramento**, **sqft**, and **beds** as predictors of **price**:

```
lin_model_3 <- lm(price ~ in_sacramento + sqft + beds,
                 data = train_set)
summary(lin_model_3)
```

The summary of the model is as follows:

```
##
## Call:
## lm(formula = price ~ in_sacramento + sqft + beds, data = train_set)
##
## Residuals:
##     Min      1Q  Median      3Q     Max
## -197285  -51124  -10338   32609  390503
##
## Coefficients:
##                   Estimate Std. Error t value Pr(>|t|)
## (Intercept)      88084.399  12230.228   7.202 1.46e-12 ***
## in_sacramento1  -32276.138   6225.042  -5.185 2.79e-07 ***
## sqft               154.180      6.025  25.591  < 2e-16 ***
## beds            -26058.703   4861.568  -5.360 1.11e-07 ***
## ---
## Signif. codes:  0 '***' 0.001 '**' 0.01 '*' 0.05 '.' 0.1 ' ' 1
##
## Residual standard error: 80740 on 741 degrees of freedom
## Multiple R-squared:  0.6251, Adjusted R-squared:  0.6235
## F-statistic: 411.8 on 3 and 741 DF,  p-value: < 2.2e-16
```

We get an interesting estimate for the number of bedrooms. It seems that for every bedroom we add to the house, the price drops by **$26,058**. The coefficient tells us that *when we already know the number of square feet*, and whether the house is located in Sacramento, and we know how these variables affect the price, an increase in the number of bedrooms decreases our price expectation. Where a larger number of bedrooms usually implies a larger house and therefore a greater price, we now ask for the effect on price *when more bedrooms do not imply a larger home as well.*

All these effects are significant, and the adjusted R-squared has increased to 62.35%. What happens if we add the number of bathrooms to the model?

6. Train a linear model with **in_sacramento**, **sqft**, **beds**, and **baths** as predictors of **price**:

```
lin_model_4 <- lm(
    price ~ in_sacramento + sqft + beds + baths,
    data = train_set)
summary(lin_model_4)
```

The summary of the model is as follows:

```
##
## Call:
## lm(formula = price ~ in_sacramento + sqft + beds + baths, data = train_
set)
##
## Residuals:
##      Min      1Q  Median      3Q     Max
## -197062  -50856  -10504   32786  389848
##
## Coefficients:
##                     Estimate Std. Error t value Pr(>|t|)
## (Intercept)        88552.649  12780.774   6.929 9.25e-12 ***
## in_sacramento1    -32331.816   6244.561  -5.178 2.90e-07 ***
## sqft                 154.666      7.142  21.656  < 2e-16 ***
## beds              -25916.586   4991.630  -5.192 2.69e-07 ***
## baths               -838.448   6596.329  -0.127    0.899
## ---
## Signif. codes:  0 '***' 0.001 '**' 0.01 '*' 0.05 '.' 0.1 ' ' 1
##
```

```
## Residual standard error: 80800 on 740 degrees of freedom
## Multiple R-squared:  0.6251, Adjusted R-squared:  0.623
## F-statistic: 308.4 on 4 and 740 DF,  p-value: < 2.2e-16
```

When we already know the values of **sqft**, **in_sacramento**, and **beds**, the coefficient estimate for **baths** is not significant (**p=0.899**). The adjusted R-squared is approximately the same.

What would happen if we left out the **sqft** predictor?

7. Train a linear model with **in_sacramento**, **beds**, and **baths** as predictors of **price**:

```
lin_model_5 <- lm(price ~ in_sacramento + beds + baths,
                 data = train_set)
summary(lin_model_5)
```

The summary of the model is as follows:

```
##
## Call:
## lm(formula = price ~ in_sacramento + beds + baths, data = train_set)
##
## Residuals:
##      Min      1Q  Median      3Q     Max
## -271495  -65516  -18642   41358  519964
##
## Coefficients:
##                  Estimate Std. Error t value Pr(>|t|)
## (Intercept)         38812      16060   2.417   0.0159 *
## in_sacramento1     -58566       7825  -7.485 2.04e-13 ***
## beds                24695       5634   4.383 1.34e-05 ***
## baths               75745       7113  10.649  < 2e-16 ***
## ---
## Signif. codes:  0 '***' 0.001 '**' 0.01 '*' 0.05 '.' 0.1 ' ' 1
##
## Residual standard error: 103200 on 741 degrees of freedom
## Multiple R-squared:  0.3875, Adjusted R-squared:  0.385
## F-statistic: 156.2 on 3 and 741 DF,  p-value: < 2.2e-16
```

Removing **sqft** made the coefficient estimate for **baths** significant ($p<2e-16$), and turned both **beds** ($24,695) and **baths** ($75,745) into positive effects. The adjusted R-squared decreased markedly (0.385).

But how do we know which model to trust?

Comparing Linear Regression Models

In *Chapter 4, Introduction to neuralnet and Evaluation Methods*, we used cross-validation to compare our classification models based on their predictions. This technique is also useful for linear regression, although we use a different set of evaluation metrics. Instead of using the long cross-validation training loop code from that chapter, though, we will use the **cvms** package, which is specifically designed for cross-validating linear and logistic regression models. We simply pass it a list of our model formulas as strings, and it gives us the results of the cross-validations.

> **Note**
>
> The **cvms** package was created by the one of the authors of this book, Ludvig Renbo Olsen.

Evaluation Metrics

When evaluating how well our model predicts the dependent variable in the test set, we use the residuals to calculate a set of error metrics. As mentioned previously, the residuals are the differences between the observations and the predicted values. The residuals can be both negative and positive, so we cannot simply add them together, as they might cancel out (if, for instance, one residual is 3 and another is -3, the result of adding them together would be 0). We are instead interested in the magnitudes of the residuals (the absolute values of the residuals). These are what we use in the **Mean Absolute Error** (**MAE**) metric. An alternative approach to making all the errors non-negative is to *square* them. We do this for the **Root Mean Square Error** (**RMSE**) metric. These two metrics are commonly used, and we wish to minimize both as far as possible. As the values of the two metrics depend on the scale of the dependent variable, they can be hard to compare between projects. We therefore mainly use them to compare our model formulas when selecting the best performing model. As we will see in the *Differences between MAE and RMSE* section, a key difference between the two metrics is how they respond to outliers.

MAE

The MAE (Mean Absolute Error) is the average absolute difference between the observed values and the predicted values.

The formula for MAE is as follows:

$$MAE = \frac{\sum_{i=1}^{n} |(y_i - \hat{y}_i)|}{n}$$

Figure 5.7: MAE formula

Here, y is the vector of observations, and $\hat{y}$ is the vector of predictions.

RMSE

The RMSE (Root Mean Square Error) is the square root of the average squared difference between the observed values and the predicted values. If this sounds complicated, here are the four steps involved:

1. Find the residuals by subtracting the observed values from the predicted values.

2. Square the residuals.

3. Find the average squared residual.

4. Take the square root of this average squared residual.

The formula for RMSE is as follows:

$$RMSE = \sqrt{\frac{\sum_{i=1}^{n} (\hat{y}_i - y_i)^2}{n})}$$

Figure 5.8: RMSE formula

Differences between MAE and RMSE

One of the main differences between MAE and RMSE is how they react to outliers. RMSE penalizes large outliers more because it squares the residuals. To get a sense of how they differ, we can add two outliers (one negative and one positive) to the residuals in our cat food data and scale them, such that their magnitudes become increasingly larger than the magnitudes of the other residuals. Let's first visualize our residuals with these additional outliers:

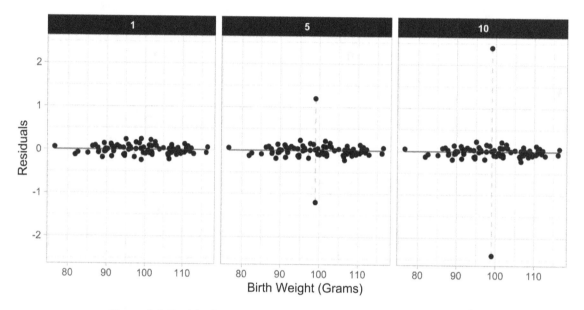

Figure 5.9: Residuals with added outliers at three different scales

Figure 5.9 shows three different scalings of our added outliers. The outliers are simply multiplied by the scaling factors (1, 5, and 10). Now, let's see the effect of these scalings on the RMSE and MAE metrics. We will compare the effect of the outlier scalings to the effect of scaling all the residuals at once:

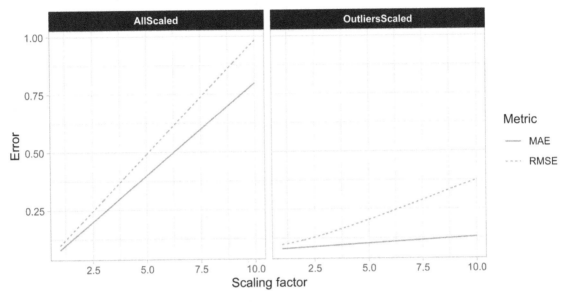

Figure 5.10: Comparison of MAE and RMSE at different outlier scalings

On the left in *Figure* 5.10, we see the effect (*y-axis*) of multiplying all the residuals by different scaling factors (*x-axis*). This shows that RMSE becomes increasingly larger than MAE when the residuals increase in magnitude. On the right, only the two outliers have been scaled. While MAE increases linearly with the total error (in the left-hand plot, it is simply multiplied by the scaling factor), the two outliers affect the increase in RMSE more the larger the scaling factor is.

For the remainder of this chapter, we will use RMSE. This will favor models with fewer large residual outliers (errors). MAE could also be useful if we believe a prediction being $10,000 off is about twice as bad as being $5,000 off. This depends on the context in which we wish to use our model.

Exercise 50: Comparing Models with the cvms Package

In this exercise, we will use the **cvms** package to cross-validate a list of model formulas:

1. Attach the **cvms** and **groupdata2** packages:

   ```
   # Attach packages
   library(cvms)
   library(groupdata2)
   ```

2. Set the random seed to **2**:

   ```
   # Set seed for reproducibility
   set.seed(2)
   ```

3. Create a vector with model formulas:

   ```
   # Create vector with model formulas
   model_formulas <- c(
        "price ~ in_sacramento",
        "price ~ in_sacramento + sqft",
        "price ~ in_sacramento + sqft + beds",
        "price ~ in_sacramento + sqft + beds + baths",
        "price ~ in_sacramento + beds + baths")
   ```

4. Create five folds in the training set. Balance the folds by **in_sacramento**:

   ```
   # Create folds
   train_set <- fold(train_set, k = 5,
                     cat_col = "in_sacramento")
   ```

5. Cross-validate the model formulas with **cross_validate()**. In addition to the dataset and model formulas, we specify the name of the fold column, **.folds**, and the model family, **gaussian**:

   ```
   # Cross-validate our models
   # Note that we specify the model family as "gaussian",
   # which refers to linear regression
   cv_results <- cross_validate(data = train_set,
                                models = model_formulas,
                                fold_cols = ".folds",
                                family = "gaussian")
   ```

6. Print the results:

   ```
   cv_results
   ```

The output is as follows:

```
## # A tibble: 5 x 18
##      RMSE     MAE   r2m   r2c    AIC   AICc    BIC Predictions Results
##     <dbl>   <dbl> <dbl> <dbl>  <dbl>  <dbl>  <dbl> <list>      <list>
## 1 1.23e5 92787. 0.121 0.121 15670. 15670. 15683. <tibble [7… <tibbl…
## 2 8.21e4 59878. 0.610 0.610 15187. 15187. 15204. <tibble [7… <tibbl…
## 3 8.06e4 58516. 0.624 0.624 15166. 15166. 15188. <tibble [7… <tibbl…
## 4 8.08e4 58662. 0.624 0.624 15167. 15167. 15194. <tibble [7… <tibbl…
## 5 1.03e5 75560. 0.387 0.387 15458. 15458. 15480. <tibble [7… <tibbl…
## # … with 9 more variables: Coefficients <list>, Folds <int>, 'Fold
## #   Columns' <int>, 'Convergence Warnings' <dbl>, 'Singular Fit
## #   Messages' <int>, Family <chr>, Link <chr>, Dependent <chr>,
## #   Fixed <chr>
```

The output contains a lot of information. It is worth understanding the content of all the columns, but for now, we will select the metrics and model formulas with **select_metrics()** and discuss them. The other columns are described in the help page, accessed with **?cross_validate**. We will use the **kable()** function from the **knitr** package to spice up the layout of the data frame.

7. Attach the **knitr** package:

```
# Attach knitr
library(knitr)
```

8. Select the metrics and model definitions with **select_metrics()**. Print the output with **kable()**, with numbers rounded to two digits:

```
# Select the metrics and model formulas
# with select_metrics()
# Print with knitr::kable for fanciness,
# and round to 2 decimals.
kable(select_metrics(cv_results), digits = 2)
```

The output is as follows:

RMSE	MAE	r2m	r2c	AIC	AICc	BIC	Dependent	Fixed
123384.99	92787.25	0.12	0.12	15670.11	15670.15	15683.28	price	in_sacramento
82068.24	59877.65	0.61	0.61	15186.51	15186.58	15204.07	price	in_sacramento+sqft
80629.41	58515.89	0.62	0.62	15165.70	15165.80	15187.65	price	in_sacramento+sqft+beds
80849.02	58661.62	0.62	0.62	15167.32	15167.46	15193.66	price	in_sacramento+sqft+beds+baths
102977.53	75559.51	0.39	0.39	15458.23	15458.33	15480.18	price	in_sacramento+beds+baths

Figure 5.11: The metrics in the cross-validation output

As mentioned previously, we will focus on the RMSE metric, but *Figure 5.12* contains the goals for each metric in the output:

Metric	Goal
RMSE	Minimize
MAE	Minimize
r2m	Maximize
r2c	Maximize
AIC	Minimize
AICc	Minimize
BIC	Minimize

Figure 5.12: Goals for each metric

Looking at the cross-validation results in *Figure 5.11*, we see that the third model (the one without the number of bathrooms) has the lowest RMSE. As this is our *selection criterion*, this model is the best of the five. When the models are this close, we can use *repeated cross-validation* to get an even better estimate of the model performances. We will apply this technique later, as well as cover an approach for choosing models by multiple, disagreeing metrics.

Interactions

So far, we have asked whether the price of a home goes up or down when we increase the size or add a bedroom. But what if more bedrooms **increases** the price of a **small** home, and **decreases** it for a **bigger** home? Or vice versa? We couldn't tell! We can ask our model that question, though, through **interaction terms**. An interaction is written as **effect1 : effect2**, and is simply added to the formula as follows:

```
lin_model_6 <- lm(price ~ in_sacramento + sqft + beds + sqft : beds,
                  data = train_set)

summary(lin_model_6)
```

The summary will appear as follows:

```
##
## Call:
## lm(formula = price ~ in_sacramento + sqft + beds + sqft : beds, data =
train_set)
##
##      Min      1Q  Median      3Q      Max
## -202169  -48471  -11623   33049   396985
##
## Coefficients:
##                   Estimate Std. Error t value Pr(>|t|)
## (Intercept)       1237.724  26124.893   0.047 0.962225
## in_sacramento1  -30556.412   6187.792  -4.938 9.75e-07 ***
## sqft               211.963     16.515  12.835  < 2e-16 ***
## beds             -3190.095   7768.994  -0.411 0.681471
## sqft:beds          -14.431      3.845  -3.753 0.000189 ***
## ---
## Signif. codes:  0 '***' 0.001 '**' 0.01 '*' 0.05 '.' 0.1 ' ' 1
##
## Residual standard error: 80040 on 740 degrees of freedom
## Multiple R-squared:  0.6321, Adjusted R-squared:  0.6301
## F-statistic: 317.8 on 4 and 740 DF,  p-value: < 2.2e-16
```

An alternative to the colon (:) operator is the asterisk (*) operator. This operator *unpacks* the interaction such that the predictors are also included in the formula on their own. If we have more than two predictors in our interaction, for instance, **price ~ sqft * beds * baths** (which we refer to as a *three-way interaction*), it will also include all the smaller interactions (the *two-way interactions* in this case). We will use the asterisk operator as it is an easier and cleaner way to write our formulas. We simply replace + with a * between two or more predictors, like so:

```
lin_model_6_2 <- lm(price ~ in_sacramento + sqft * beds,
                    data = train_set)
```

The summary of this model would only differ from the previous summary in the *Call* section.

When our model formula contains interaction terms, we get separate coefficient estimates for the interactions, represented as **effect1:effect2**, and the individual effects. When interpreting the summary, we start with the interaction estimates. If an interaction term is significant, we can reasonably reject the null hypothesis that the effects are not interacting. This changes the interpretation of the two predictors' coefficient estimates because, at least in our dataset, these appear to be dependent on one another and not just linearly correlated with the dependent variable. In our model, the interaction between **sqft** and **beds** is significant. To interpret this, we plot the two variables against each other with the **interplot** package. First, we will plot the effect of **sqft** on the **price** *when the number of bedrooms changes*. Notice that **interplot** creates a **ggplot2** object, to which we can add layers and themes:

```
# Attach interplot
library(interplot)
# Plot the effect of size
# depending on the number of bedrooms
interplot(lin_model_6, "sqft", "beds", hist = TRUE) +

  # Add labels to the axes
  labs(x = "Number of bedrooms", y = "Price") +

  # Add a theme to make our plot prettier
  theme_light()
```

The output will be as follows:

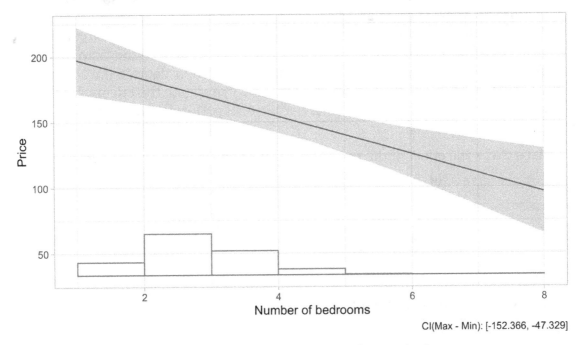

CI(Max - Min): [-152.366, -47.329]

Figure 5.13: Interaction plot for `price` per `sqft` when `beds` changes

The plot contains a black line with a gray boundary (95% confidence interval) and a histogram (the bars at the bottom). Note that the scale of the y-axis (**Price**) is for the line, not the histogram bars.

The histogram tells us the distribution of homes per bedroom count. The black line tells us the estimated price per square foot at the different bedroom counts. When there are few bedrooms, each square foot is worth almost **$200**. The more bedrooms we have, the less each square foot is worth. For a home with eight bedrooms, each square foot is worth less than **$100**.

Does our analysis indicate that we should knock down some walls if we were selling a house? Or does it tell us that the price of homes with eight bedrooms is less affected by the size?

While a house with 8 bedrooms is unlikely to be small and cheap, a home with only one bedroom could be both *small and cheap*, or *large and expensive*. It is also possible that the relationship between price and size is not actually linear. For instance, the gained benefit from adding one square foot to a 200 square-foot home is likely larger than adding it to a 3,000 square-foot home. It is also worth noting from the histogram that we have very few homes with more than five bedrooms in our dataset. If we were a real estate agent working with smaller houses, we could investigate the effect of removing these from the dataset, as they might decrease model performance on the types of houses we care about.

Now, let's check the effect of the bedroom count on the **price** when **size** changes:

```
# Plot the effect of number of bedrooms
# depending on size
interplot(lin_model_6, "beds", "sqft", hist = TRUE) +


  # Add labels to the axes
  labs(x = "Size in square feet", y = "Price") +


  # Add a theme to make our plot prettier
  theme_light()
```

The plot is as follows:

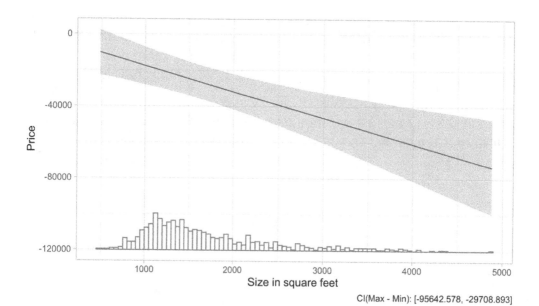

CI(Max - Min): [-95642.578, -29708.893]

Figure 5.14: Interaction plot for **price** per bedroom when **size** changes

In *Figure* 5.14, the black line shows the effect of **beds** on **price** at different house sizes. The histogram is the distribution of homes at different sizes. Again, the scale of the *y-axis* (**Price**) is for the line and not the histogram bars.

The larger our home is, the more each bedroom subtracts from the price! So, if we have a small home, adding a bedroom affects the price less negatively than if the home is big. Again, we could consider whether the effect of **beds** on the **price** is actually linear? Does adding the first bedroom to a home affect the price the same as adding the fifth bedroom?

As most of our homes have a size of between 700 and 3,000 square feet, the few very large homes could bias the model inappropriately. If our real estate agency mostly sells homes in the lower size range, we could try to remove the biggest houses from the model and see whether this changes the model performance on our types of houses.

Exercise 51: Adding Interaction Terms to Our Model

Now that we have a grasp of what interactions are, we return to our proposed models. Are there any other potential interactions we should model? Perhaps even three-way interactions? (These are even harder to interpret!) Instead of adding one interaction at a time, let's create a list of model formulas with all the combinations of the predictors (also called *fixed effects*), including the potential two and three-way interactions. For this task, **cvms** has a function called **combine_predictors()**. It has a few limitations, which you can read about in the help page at **?combine_predictors**. Once created, we will cross-validate all the models and select the best one. As mentioned previously, this approach does not *guarantee* a theoretically meaningful model, which is why we should always think critically about its meaningfulness:

1. Attach the **cvms** and **groupdata2** packages:

    ```
    # Attach packages
    library(cvms)
    library(groupdata2)
    ```

2. Set the random seed to **1**:

    ```
    set.seed(1)
    ```

3. Generate all possible model formulas (with and without two- and three-way interaction terms) from the four predictors (fixed effects) using **combine_predictors()**. This will create **165** formulas:

```
# Create all combinations of the predictors
model_formulas <- combine_predictors(
    dependent = "price",
    fixed_effects = c("in_sacramento",
                      "sqft",
                      "baths",
                      "beds"))
```

4. Print the first 15 model formulas:

```
# Print the generated model formulas
head(model_formulas, 15)
```

The output is as follows:

```
##  [1] "price ~ baths"
##  [2] "price ~ beds"
##  [3] "price ~ in_sacramento"
##  [4] "price ~ sqft"
##  [5] "price ~ baths * beds"
##  [6] "price ~ baths * in_sacramento"
##  [7] "price ~ baths * sqft"
##  [8] "price ~ baths + beds"
##  [9] "price ~ baths + in_sacramento"
## [10] "price ~ baths + sqft"
## [11] "price ~ beds * in_sacramento"
## [12] "price ~ beds * sqft"
## [13] "price ~ beds + in_sacramento"
## [14] "price ~ beds + sqft"
## [15] "price ~ in_sacramento * sqft
```

5. Create five folds in the training set. Balance the folds by **in_sacramento**. As we already have a fold column in the training set, we ask **fold()** to remove it and create a new one:

```
# Create folds
train_set <- fold(
    train_set, k = 5,
    cat_col = "in_sacramento",
    handle_existing_fold_cols = "remove")
```

6. Cross-validate the model formulas:

```
# Cross-validate our models
# Note that we specify the model family as "gaussian",
# which refers to linear regression
cv_results <- cross_validate(data = train_set,
                             models = model_formulas,
                             fold_cols = ".folds",
                             family = "gaussian")
```

7. Order the results by **RMSE**:

```
# Order by RMSE
cv_results <- cv_results[order(cv_results$RMSE),]
```

8. Select the 10 best models:

```
# Select the 10 best models
# (feel free to view them all instead)
cv_results_top10 <- head(cv_results, 10)
```

9. Select the metrics and model definition columns with **select_metrics()** and print them with **kable()**:

```
# Select the metrics and
# model formulas with select_metrics()
# Print the top 10 models with
# knitr::kable for fanciness
kable(select_metrics(cv_results_top10), digits = 2)
```

The output is as follows:

RMSE	MAE	r2m	r2c	AIC	AICc	BIC	Dependent	Fixed
79720.68	57641.84	0.63	0.63	15152.63	15152.88	15187.76	price	baths*in_sacramento+beds*sqft
79773.60	57614.84	0.63	0.63	15152.72	15152.91	15183.45	price	beds*in_sacramento+beds*sqft
79923.41	57757.34	0.63	0.63	15155.55	15155.80	15190.68	price	baths*beds+baths*in_sacramento+sqft
79926.49	57682.50	0.63	0.63	15154.15	15154.45	15193.66	price	baths*beds+bath*sin_sacramento+beds*sqft
79930.89	57731.75	0.63	0.63	15153.66	15153.85	15184.40	price	beds*sqft+in_sacramento*sqft
79962.57	57836.87	0.63	0.63	15154.26	15154.57	15193.78	price	baths*in_sacramento+beds*sqft+in_sacramento*sqft
79972.92	57626.48	0.63	0.63	15154.38	15154.62	15189.50	price	baths+beds*in_sacramento+beds*sqft
79975.30	57824.09	0.63	0.63	15153.52	15153.83	15193.03	price	baths*in_sacramento+beds*in_sacramento+beds*sqft
80043.08	57747.51	0.63	0.63	15154.16	15154.47	15193.67	price	baths*in_sacramento+baths*sqft+beds*sqft
80046.19	57889.13	0.63	0.63	15153.97	15154.21	15189.09	price	beds*in_sacramento+beds*sqft+in_sacramento*sqft

Figure 5.15: Output using kable

The best model has an interaction between **baths** and **in_sacramento** and an interaction between **beds** and **sqft**.

10. Train the best model on the training set and inspect its summary. Try to interpret it:

```
lin_model_7 <- lm(
    "price ~ baths * in_sacramento + beds * sqft",
    data = train_set)
summary(lin_model_7)
```

The summary is as follows:

```
##
## Call:
## lm(formula = "price ~ baths * in_sacramento + beds * sqft", data =
train_set)
##
## Residuals:
##      Min       1Q   Median       3Q      Max
## -217093   -47986   -10551    33501   399965
##
```

```
## Coefficients:
##                           Estimate Std. Error t value Pr(>|t|)
## (Intercept)              -38995.37   29818.83  -1.308   0.1914
## baths                     11786.48    8049.75   1.464   0.1436
## in_sacramento1            20807.25   19003.95   1.095   0.2739
## beds                       2242.42    8047.44   0.279   0.7806
## sqft                        218.39      17.11  12.763  < 2e-16 ***
## baths:in_sacramento1     -25478.69    8895.65  -2.864   0.0043 **
## beds:sqft                   -16.83       3.92  -4.295 1.98e-05 ***
## ---
## Signif. codes:  0 '***' 0.001 '**' 0.01 '*' 0.05 '.' 0.1 ' ' 1
##
## Residual standard error: 79700 on 738 degrees of freedom
## Multiple R-squared:  0.6361, Adjusted R-squared:  0.6332
## F-statistic: 215.1 on 6 and 738 DF,  p-value: < 2.2e-16
```

Both interaction terms are significant, so we start by interpreting these. The first interaction term, **baths:in_sacramento1**, tells us that *when the house is located in Sacramento, the effect of adding a bathroom decreases by $25,478.69. It also tells us that for each additional bathroom we add, the effect of being located in Sacramento decreases by $25,478.69.*

The second interaction term, **beds:sqft**, tells us that *for each square foot by which we increase the size, the effect of adding a bedroom decreases by* **$16.431**. *It also tells us that for each bedroom we add to the house, the effect of adding one square foot to the size of the house decreases by* **$16.431**.

More formally, the **x1:x2** interaction tells us the change in the coefficient for **x1** when **x2** is increased by 1 unit, and the change in the coefficient for **x2** when **x1** is increased by 1 unit.

The intercept tells us the price when the house has 0 bathrooms, 0 bedrooms, a size of 0 square feet, and is located outside Sacramento. The coefficient for **sqft** tells us that *when we have 0 bedrooms, adding a square foot to the house affects the price by $218.39.* The coefficient for **beds** tells us that *when the size is 0 square feet, adding a bedroom affects the price by $2,242.42.* The coefficient for **in_sacramento** tells us that *when we have 0 bathrooms, being located in Sacramento adds $20,807.25 to the price.* And finally, the coefficient for **baths** tells us that *when the house is located outside Sacramento, adding a bathroom adds $11,786.48.*

If it's weird to think about a house with a size of 0 square feet and (more importantly) 0 bathrooms, this is a good time to emphasize the fact that the model does not have common sense. It does not know that such a house is not meaningful, neither does it know that the size can't be a negative number. It simply finds the coefficients that lead to the lowest prediction error in the training set. However, it is possible to make these numbers more meaningful to us. By *centering* (not scaling) the predictors, the intercept is interpreted as the price when the predictors have their mean value. In the next section, we will discuss whether we should scale our predictors as well.

Should We Standardize Predictors?

In previous chapters, we have standardized our features before training the models. By doing so, we make sure they are all on the same scale. This can be great for some types of models, especially when we mostly care about how well our model predicts something. When the goal is to interpret our coefficient estimates though, standardizing the predictors *mostly* makes our job more difficult. Now, let's standardize the numeric predictors, train our model on them, and compare it to the previous model's summary:

```
# Find scaling and centering parameters
params <- preProcess(train_set[, 3:5],
                     method = c("center", "scale"))
# Make a copy of the dataset
standardized_data <- train_set
# Transform the dataset
standardized_data[, 3:5] <- predict(params,
                                    standardized_data[, 3:5])
# Train a model on the standardized data
lin_model_7_2 <- lm(price ~ baths * in_sacramento + beds * sqft,
                    data = standardized_data)
summary(lin_model_7_2)
```

The summary of the model is as follows:

```
##
## Call:
## lm(formula = price ~ baths * in_sacramento + beds * sqft, data =
standardized_data)
##
```

```
## Residuals:
##      Min      1Q  Median      3Q     Max
## -217093  -47986  -10551   33501  399965
##
## Coefficients:
##                        Estimate Std. Error t value Pr(>|t|)
## (Intercept)              269271       4405  61.131  < 2e-16 ***
## baths                      8395       5734   1.464   0.1436
## in_sacramento1           -31843       6189  -5.145 3.43e-07 ***
## beds                     -23116       4356  -5.307 1.48e-07 ***
## sqft                     119822       5637  21.255  < 2e-16 ***
## baths:in_sacramento1     -18148       6336  -2.864   0.0043 **
## beds:sqft                -10870       2531  -4.295 1.98e-05 ***
## ---
## Signif. codes:  0 '***' 0.001 '**' 0.01 '*' 0.05 '.' 0.1 ' ' 1
##
## Residual standard error: 79700 on 738 degrees of freedom
## Multiple R-squared:  0.6361, Adjusted R-squared:  0.6332
## F-statistic: 215.1 on 6 and 738 DF,  p-value: < 2.2e-16
```

The interaction terms are still significant and the adjusted R-squared has not changed. The biggest change is in the *Estimate* column. The intercept is no longer the price when the house has 0 bathrooms, 0 bedrooms, and a size of 0 square feet, as we have centered these predictors. It is instead the price when we have the mean value of each of these predictors in our training set. Due to the scaling, the estimates for these predictors are now on the same scale. This has the benefit that they are easier to compare. On the other hand, the estimates are harder to map to our understanding of the real world. What does it mean when we say that increasing the number of square feet with one *standard deviation* increases the price by $119,822?

Hence, we might want to train the model without standardization (though possibly *with centering*) for interpretability and with standardization for the comparison of coefficient estimate sizes.

Repeated Cross-Validation

If two models are very close to one another in our cross-validation results, we need to ensure that it is not the way we created the folds that is responsible for the small difference. One way to test this is by making new folds with a different seed, and rerunning the cross-validation. We can repeat this process 100 times and average the results. Luckily, **groupdata2** and **cvms** have this functionality built in.

Exercise 52: Running Repeated Cross-Validation

In this exercise, we will use repeated cross-validation on the 8 best linear regression models from *Exercise 53, Adding Interaction Terms to Our Model*. We will only run 10 repetitions to save time:

1. Attach the **cvms** and **groupdata2** packages:

   ```
   # Attach packages
   library(cvms)
   library(groupdata2)
   library(caret)
   ```

2. Set the random seed to **2**:

   ```
   # Set seed for reproducibility and easy comparison.
   set.seed(2)
   ```

3. Load the **Sacramento** dataset:

   ```
   data(Sacramento)
   ```

4. Assign/copy the dataset to another variable name:

   ```
   full_data <- Sacramento
   ```

5. Create the **in_sacramento** variable:

   ```
   # Create one-hot encoded factor column describing
   # if the city is Sacramento or not
   full_data$in_sacramento <- factor(
       ifelse(full_data$city == "SACRAMENTO", 1, 0) )
   ```

6. Partition the dataset into a training set (80%) and a validation set (20%). Balance the ratios of the **in_sacramento** levels between the partitions and assign each partition to a variable name:

```
partitions <- partition(full_data, p = 0.8,
                         cat_col = "in_sacramento")
train_set <- partitions[[1]]
valid_set <- partitions[[2]]
```

7. Create 10 unique fold columns with **fold()**. This is done by specifying the **num_fold_cols** argument. **fold()** will then attempt to create 10 unique columns, named ".**folds_1**", ".**folds_2**", and so on:

```
# Create folds
train_set <- fold(train_set, k = 5,
                  cat_col = "in_sacramento",
                  num_fold_cols = 10)
```

8. Extract or create the fold column names. Either extract the names of the last 10 columns in the folded dataset or use **paste0()** to create the strings quickly:

```
# Create the 10 fold column names
fold_cols <- paste0(".folds_", 1:10)
# Print the names
fold_cols
##  [1] ".folds_1"   ".folds_2"   ".folds_3"
##  [4] ".folds_4"   ".folds_5"   ".folds_6"
##  [7] ".folds_7"   ".folds_8"   ".folds_9"
## [10]".folds_10"
```

9. Reconstruct the eight best formulas from the cross-validation results, using the **reconstruct_formulas()** function from **cvms**. Start by ordering the **cv_results** from *Exercise 53, Adding Interaction Terms to Our Model*, by RMSE. If you do not have access to **cv_results**, you can copy these formulas from the **model_formulas** vector in the following output and add them to a vector manually:

```
# Order cv_results by RMSE
cv_results <- cv_results[order(cv_results$RMSE),]
# Reconstruct formulas for the top 8 models
model_formulas <- reconstruct_formulas(cv_results, topn = 8)
# Print the model formulas
model_formulas
```

The output is as follows:

```
## [1] "price ~ baths * in_sacramento + beds * sqft"
## [2] "price ~ beds * in_sacramento + beds * sqft"
## [3] "price ~ baths * beds + baths * in_sacramento + sqft"
## [4] "price ~ baths * beds + baths * in_sacramento + beds * sqft"
## [5] "price ~ beds * sqft + in_sacramento * sqft"
## [6] "price ~ baths * in_sacramento + beds * sqft + in_sacramento *
sqft"
## [7] "price ~ baths + beds * in_sacramento + beds * sqft"
## [8] "price ~ baths * in_sacramento + beds * in_sacramento + beds *
sqft"
```

10. Run the repeated cross-validation with **cross_validate()**. In the **fold_cols** argument, add the list of fold column names:

```
# Cross-validate our models
# Pass the list of fold column names
# and cross_validate() will
# cross-validate with each one and
# return the average results
repeated_cv_results <- cross_validate(
    data = train_set,
    models = model_formulas,
    fold_cols = fold_cols,
    family = "gaussian")
```

11. Show the results with **kable()**:

```
# Select the metrics and model formulas
# Print with knitr::kable for fanciness
kable(select_metrics(repeated_cv_results), digits = 2)
```

The output is as follows:

RMSE	MAE	r2m	r2c	AIC	AICc	BIC	Dependent	Fixed
80027.80	57082.40	0.62	0.62	15149.23	15149.47	15184.35	price	baths*in_sacramento+beds*sqft
80160.05	56729.13	0.61	0.61	15154.74	15154.93	15185.47	price	beds*in_sacramento+beds*sqft
80469.81	57650.21	0.61	0.61	15156.24	15156.49	15191.36	price	baths*beds+bath*sin_sacramento+sqft
80299.78	57148.96	0.62	0.62	15150.29	15150.60	15189.81	price	baths*beds+baths*in_sacramen-to+beds*sqft
80297.87	56878.35	0.61	0.61	15156.65	15156.84	15187.38	price	beds*sqft+in_sacramento*sqft
80145.83	57238.52	0.62	0.62	15148.99	15149.30	15188.51	price	baths*in_sacramento+beds*sqft+in_sac-ramento*sqft
80314.02	56871.26	0.61	0.61	15154.97	15155.21	15190.09	price	baths+beds*in_sacramento+beds*sqft
80236.45	57217.04	0.62	0.62	15150.89	15151.20	15190.40	price	baths*in_sacramento+beds*in_sacra-mento+beds*sqft

Figure 5.16: Output using kable

The same model (`price ~ baths * in_sacramento + beds * sqft`) is still the best, by RMSE. The sixth model is the second best, and, in general, the rankings have changed a lot.

We could run even more cross-validation repetitions if we wanted to be sure of their rankings. If we wish to see the results of each repetition, these results are also available.

12. Show the results of the first 10 folds for the best model:

```
# Extract the fold results for the best model
fold_results_best_model <- repeated_cv_results$Results[[1]]
# Print the results of the first 10 folds
kable( head(fold_results_best_model, 10) )
```

The output is as follows:

Fold Column	Fold	RMSE	MAE	r2m	r2c	AIC	AICc	BIC
.folds_1	1	88250.99	63856.06	0.6273980	0.6273980	15118.56	15118.81	15153.68
.folds_1	2	81715.56	58278.76	0.6068757	0.6068757	15143.91	15144.15	15179.03
.folds_1	3	72816.91	52543.27	0.6075145	0.6075145	15175.44	15175.69	15210.56
.folds_1	4	67067.89	51736.86	0.6198357	0.6198357	15194.56	15194.81	15229.68
.folds_1	5	89482.97	58803.42	0.6226176	0.6226176	15113.10	15113.34	15148.22
.folds_2	1	84873.54	60769.14	0.6193009	0.6193009	15130.86	15131.10	15165.98
.folds_2	2	84161.92	61637.62	0.6291690	0.6291690	15138.87	15139.12	15173.99
.folds_2	3	82652.11	53534.44	0.6179572	0.6179572	15141.99	15142.24	15177.12
.folds_2	4	71482.51	54248.28	0.6082848	0.6082848	15180.57	15180.81	15215.69
.folds_2	5	80172.76	56857.38	0.6129375	0.6129375	15152.06	15152.30	15187.18

Figure 5.17: Results of the best model on the first 10 test folds

Figure 5.17 shows the results of the first 10 folds for the best model formula. Looking at the **RMSE** column, we see that the results vary quite a lot, depending on what fold is used as the test set. This is one of the reasons why repeated cross-validation is a good technique: we train and test the model on many combinations of the training set!

Exercise 53: Validating Models with validate()

Now that we have found the best model with **cross_validate()**, we want to train that model on the entire training set and evaluate it on the validation set. We could easily do this manually, but **cvms** has the **validate()** function that does this for us and returns the same metrics as **cross_validate()**, along with the trained model.

In this exercise, we will work with the training set from the previous exercise:

1. Validate the best model from the previous exercise:

```
# Train the model on the entire training set
# and test it on the validation set.
validation <- validate(
    train_data = train_set,
    test_data = valid_set,
    models = "price ~ baths * in_sacramento + beds * sqft",
    family = "gaussian")
```

2. The output contains the "**Results**" data frame and the trained model object. Assign these to the variable names:

```
valid_results <- validation$Results
valid_model <- validation$Models[[1]]
```

3. Print the results:

```
kable(select_metrics(valid_results), digits = 2)
```

The output is as follows:

RMSE	MAE	r2m	r2c	AIC	AICc	BIC	Dependent	Fixed
82085.62	59958.59	0.62	0.62	18935.9	18936.1	18972.81	price	baths*in_sacramento+beds*sqft

Figure 5.18: Results of the best model on the validation set

The RMSE is greater on the test set than in the cross-validation results. If we compare it to the results of the cross-validation iterations in *Figure 5.18*, it isn't higher than most of the RMSE scores, though, which indicates that the model is not overfitted.

4. Print the summary of the model:

```
summary(valid_model)
```

The summary of the model is as follows:

```
##
## Call:
## lm(formula = model_formula, data = train_set)
##
## Residuals:
##      Min       1Q   Median       3Q      Max
## -209993   -46950   -12796    33713   553773
##
## Coefficients:
##                  Estimate Std. Error t value Pr(>|t|)
## (Intercept)    -58024.456  29367.835  -1.976 0.048551 *
## baths           23083.792   7865.568   2.935 0.003441 **
## in_sacramento1  29453.042  18898.087   1.559 0.119539
## beds             6095.281   7811.066   0.780 0.435441
## sqft              209.351     17.326  12.083  < 2e-16 ***
```

```
## baths:in_sacramento1 -30085.305    8904.927  -3.379 0.000767 ***
## beds:sqft                 -17.465      3.912  -4.464 9.29e-06 ***
## ---
## Signif. codes:  0 '***' 0.001 '**' 0.01 '*' 0.05 '.' 0.1 ' ' 1
##
## Residual standard error: 79520 on 738 degrees of freedom
## Multiple R-squared:  0.6181, Adjusted R-squared:  0.615
## F-statistic: 199.1 on 6 and 738 DF,  p-value: < 2.2e-16
```

The summary differs from the one we trained in *Exercise 53, Adding Interaction Terms to Our Model*, because the different random seeds used in the exercises means that the partitions (training and validation sets) are different. The differences between the two summaries are sufficiently large that we might question which summary is most likely to be correct. Similar to how the **cross_validate()** results contain all the results of the different cross-validation iterations, it also contains the coefficient estimates of every trained model instance. We could use these to investigate what coefficient estimates are most common.

Activity 18: Implementing Linear Regression

In this activity, we will predict the price of a car in the **cars** dataset, using linear regression. Fit multiple linear regression models and compare them with cross-validation using the **cvms** package. Validate the best model on a validation set and interpret the model summary.

The dataset can be found at https://github.com/TrainingByPackt/Practical-Machine-Learning-with-R/blob/master/Data/caret_cars.csv.

The following steps should help you with the solution:

1. Attach the **groupdata2**, **cvms**, **caret**, and **knitr** packages.

2. Set the random seed to 1.

3. Load the **cars** dataset from the preceding GitHub link.

4. Partition the dataset into a training set (80%) and a validation set (20%).

5. Fit multiple linear regression models on the training set with the **lm()** function, predicting **Price**. Try different predictors.

6. View the **summary()** of each fitted model. Try to interpret the estimated coefficients. How do the interpretations change when you add or subtract predictors?

7. Create model formulas with **combine_predictors()**. Limit the number of possibilities by **a)** using only the 4 first predictors, **b)** limiting the number of fixed effects in the formulas to 3, by specifying **max_fixed_effects = 3, c)** limiting the biggest possible interaction to a two-way interaction by specifying **max_interaction_size = 2**, and **d)** limiting the number of times a predictor can be included in a formula by specifying **max_effect_frequency = 1**. These limitations will decrease the number of models to run, which you may or may not want in your own projects.

8. Create five fold columns with four folds each in the training set, using **fold()** with **k = 4** and **num_fold_cols = 5**. Feel free to choose a higher number of fold columns.

9. Perform repeated cross-validation on your model formulas with **cvms**.

10. Select the best model according to RMSE.

11. Fit the best model on the entire training set and evaluate it on the validation set. This can be done with the **validate()** function in **cvms**.

12. View and interpret the summary of the best model.

The output should be similar to the following:

```
##
## Call:
## lm(formula = Price ~ Cruise * Cylinder + Mileage, data = train_set)
##
## Residuals:
##     Min     1Q Median     3Q    Max
## -10485  -5495  -1425   3494  34693
##
## Coefficients:
##                   Estimate Std. Error t value Pr(>|t|)
## (Intercept)      8993.2446  3429.9320   2.622  0.00895 **
## Cruise          -1311.6871  3585.6289  -0.366  0.71462
## Cylinder         1809.5447   741.9185   2.439  0.01500 *
## Mileage            -0.1569     0.0367  -4.274 2.21e-05 ***
```

```
## Cruise:Cylinder   1690.0768    778.7838    2.170  0.03036 *
## ---
## Signif. codes:  0 '***' 0.001 '**' 0.01 '*' 0.05 '.' 0.1 ' ' 1
##
## Residual standard error: 7503 on 638 degrees of freedom
## Multiple R-squared:  0.424,  Adjusted R-squared:  0.4203
## F-statistic: 117.4 on 4 and 638 DF,  p-value: < 2.2e-16
```

Note

The solution for this activity can be found on page 358.

Log-Transforming Predictors

When discussing interactions, we touched upon the linearity of the relationships between our predictors and the dependent variable in the Sacramento dataset. Does it seem likely that one additional square foot affects the price of a 200 square-foot home the same as of a 3,000 square-foot home? What about 100 additional square feet, which is a 50% increase for the first home, but only a ~3.3% increase for the second?

Similarly, the difference between having one or two bedrooms in a house seems bigger than the difference between having seven and eight bedrooms.

When we have non-linear relationships, it can sometimes help to apply a non-linear transformation, such as the log transformation, to the predictor (or even the dependent variable) to try and make it more linear. There are other types of transformations as well. Note that such transformations can make the summary harder to interpret.

Besides the linearity of the variable's relation to the dependent variable, the log transformation also affects its distribution. We can plot the histogram of the **sqft** predictor before and after the log transformation:

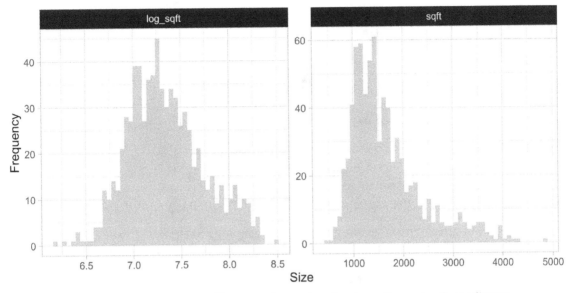

Figure 5.19: Distributions of log-transformed and untransformed sqft predictors

On the left in *Figure* 5.19, we have a histogram of the log-transformed **sqft** predictor in the training set. On the right, we have the histogram of the untransformed **sqft** predictor. Where the original version was skewed to the left, the transformed version is more normally distributed.

Exercise 54: Log-Transforming Predictors

In this exercise, we will create log-transformed versions of the three predictors – **sqft**, **beds**, and **baths**. We will create model formulas with all combinations of the transformed and non-transformed predictors, and use cross-validation to select the best model:

1. Attach **caret**, **cvms**, and **groupdata2**:

    ```
    # Attach packages
    library(caret)
    library(cvms)
    library(groupdata2)
    ```

2. Set the random seed to **3**:

```
# Set seed for reproducibility and easy comparison.
set.seed(3)
```

3. Load the **Sacramento** dataset:

```
data(Sacramento)
```

4. Assign the dataset to another variable name:

```
full_data <- Sacramento
```

5. Create the **in_sacramento** variable:

```
# Create one-hot encoded factor column describing
# if the city is Sacramento or not
full_data$in_sacramento <- factor(
    ifelse(full_data$city == "SACRAMENTO", 1, 0) )
```

6. Create log-transformed versions of **sqft**, **beds**, and **baths**:

```
# Log-transform predictors
full_data$log_sqft <- log(full_data$sqft)
full_data$log_beds <- log(full_data$beds)
full_data$log_baths <- log(full_data$baths)
```

7. Partition the dataset into a training set (80%) and validation set (20%). Balance the ratios of the **in_sacramento** levels between the partitions and assign each partition to a variable name:

```
# Partition the dataset
partitions <- partition(full_data, p = 0.8,
                        cat_col = "in_sacramento")
train_set <- partitions[[1]]
valid_set <- partitions[[2]]
```

8. Create *five* folds in the training set, using **fold()**:

```
# Create folds
train_set <- fold(train_set, k = 5,
                  cat_col = "in_sacramento")
```

9. Generate all possible model formulas with and without log transformations, using `combine_predictors()`. As we do not want both the transformed and non-transformed version of a predictor in the same formula, we supply a nested list to the **fixed_effects** argument. A sub-list should contain the various versions of a predictor that we wish to try out. Formulas with all combinations of the sub-list elements are generated. To save time, we will reduce the number of formulas generated by limiting the number of times a predictor can be included in a formula to **1**:

```
# Create all combinations of the predictors
model_formulas <- combine_predictors(
    dependent = "price",
    fixed_effects = list("in_sacramento",
                         list("sqft", "log_sqft"),
                         list("baths", "log_baths"),
                         list("beds", "log_beds")),
    max_effect_frequency = 1)
# Count the number of generated model formulas
length(model_formulas)
## [1] 255
```

10. Show the last 10 model formulas:

```
# Show the last 10 formulas
tail(model_formulas, 10)
```

The output is as follows:

```
##  [1] "price ~ log_baths + log_beds * in_sacramento * log_sqft"
##  [2] "price ~ log_baths + log_beds * in_sacramento * sqft"
##  [3] "price ~ log_baths + log_beds * in_sacramento + log_sqft"
##  [4] "price ~ log_baths + log_beds * in_sacramento + sqft"
##  [5] "price ~ log_baths + log_beds * log_sqft + in_sacramento"
##  [6] "price ~ log_baths + log_beds * sqft + in_sacramento"
##  [7] "price ~ log_baths + log_beds + in_sacramento * log_sqft"
##  [8] "price ~ log_baths + log_beds + in_sacramento * sqft"
##  [9] "price ~ log_baths + log_beds + in_sacramento + log_sqft"
## [10] "price ~ log_baths + log_beds + in_sacramento + sqft"
```

11. Run the cross-validation with **cross_validate()**:

```
# Cross-validate our models
cv_results <- cross_validate(data = train_set,
                             models = model_formulas,
                             family = "gaussian")
```

12. Order the results by RMSE and subset the best 10 models:

```
# Order by RMSE
cv_results <- cv_results[order(cv_results$RMSE),]
# Create a subset with the 10 best models
cv_results_top10 <- head(cv_results, 10)
```

13. Show the results with **kable()**:

```
# Select the metrics and model formulas
# Print with knitr::kable for fanciness
kable(select_metrics(cv_results_top10), digits = 2)
```

The output is as follows:

RMSE	MAE	r2m	r2c	AIC	AICc	BIC	Dependent	Fixed
75057.56	55273.59	0.64	0.64	15080.85	15081.09	15115.97	price	log_baths*in_sacramento+log_beds*sqft
75106.45	55267.22	0.64	0.64	15080.33	15080.57	15115.45	price	baths*in_sacramento+log_beds*sqft
75107.79	55338.85	0.64	0.64	15081.78	15082.02	15116.90	price	log_baths*in_sacramento+beds*sqft
75147.60	55370.71	0.64	0.64	15081.33	15081.58	15116.46	price	baths*in_sacramento+beds*sqft
75363.66	55475.96	0.64	0.64	15085.54	15085.74	15116.28	price	log_baths+beds*sqft+in_sacramento
75380.70	55524.71	0.64	0.64	15086.00	15086.19	15116.73	price	log_baths+log_beds*sqft+in_sacramento
75453.92	55572.53	0.64	0.64	15086.31	15086.45	15112.65	price	beds*sqft+in_sacramento
75542.26	55580.45	0.64	0.64	15086.41	15086.60	15117.14	price	baths+beds*sqft+in_sacramento
75547.26	55650.63	0.64	0.64	15087.62	15087.77	15113.97	price	log_beds*sqft+in_sacramento
75591.51	55640.01	0.64	0.64	15087.24	15087.43	15117.98	price	baths+log_beds*sqft+in_sacramento

Figure 5.20: Cross-validation output with log-transformed predictors included

The four best models are all variations of the best model from previous ones. As the improvement we gained by adding the log-transformed predictors is very small, we might prefer to leave them out, so the model is easier to interpret. In the next section, we will learn about logistic regression.

Logistic Regression

In linear regression, we modeled continuous values, such as the price of a home. In (binomial) logistic regression, we apply a logistic sigmoid function to the output, resulting in a value between 0 and 1. This value can be interpreted as the probability that the observation belongs to **class** 1. By setting a cutoff/threshold (such as 0.5), we can use it as a classifier. This is the same approach we used with the neural networks in the previous chapter. The sigmoid function is $\sigma(z) = \dfrac{1}{1 + e^{-z}}$, where z is the output from the linear regression:

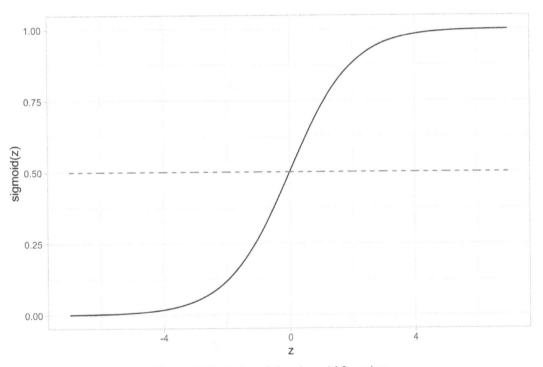

Figure 5.21: A plot of the sigmoid function

Figure 5.21 shows the sigmoid function applied to the output z. The dashed line represents our cutoff of **0.5**. If the predicted probability is above this line, the observation is predicted to be in **class** 1, otherwise, it's in **class** 0.

For logistic regression, we use the generalized version of **lm()**, called **glm()**, which can be used for multiple types of regression. As we are performing binary classification, we set the **family** argument to **binomial**.

Now, suppose we had a long list of houses from the Sacramento area and wanted to know whether they were located in a city outside of Sacramento. We could train a logistic regression classifier with the predictors in our dataset (including **price**) to classify the **in_sacramento** variable, and use that model on the list. Such a model would be useful in our context, so we will build a couple of them and discuss whether they are theoretically meaningful and how to interpret their summaries. Then, we will cross-validate the possible model formulas with **cvms**.

Exercise 55: Training Logistic Regression Models

In this exercise, we will train logistic regression models for predicting whether a home is located in Sacramento:

1. Attach the packages:

```
# Attach packages
library(caret)
library(cvms)
library(groupdata2)
library(knitr)
```

2. Set the random seed to **2**:

```
# Set seed for reproducibility and easy comparison.
set.seed(2)
```

3. Load the **Sacramento** dataset:

```
# Load the dataset
data(Sacramento)
```

4. Assign/copy the dataset to another variable name:

```
full_data <- Sacramento
```

5. Create the **in_sacramento** variable:

```
# Create one-hot encoded factor column describing
# if the city is Sacramento or not
full_data$in_sacramento <- factor(
    ifelse(full_data$city == "SACRAMENTO", 1, 0) )
```

6. Create log-transformed versions of **sqft**, **beds**, **baths**, and **price**:

```
# Log-transform predictors
full_data$log_sqft <- log(full_data$sqft)
full_data$log_beds <- log(full_data$beds)
full_data$log_baths <- log(full_data$baths)
full_data$log_price <- log(full_data$price)
```

7. Partition the dataset into a training set (80%) and a validation set (20%). Balance the ratios of the **in_sacramento** levels between the partitions and assign each partition to a variable name:

```
partitions <- partition(full_data, p = 0.8,
                         cat_col = "in_sacramento")
train_set <- partitions[[1]]
valid_set <- partitions[[2]]
```

8. Train a logistic regression model with **price** as a predictor of **in_sacramento**:

```
logistic_model_1 <- glm(in_sacramento ~ price,
                         data = train_set,
                         family = "binomial")
summary(logistic_model_1)
```

The summary of the model is as follows:

```
##
## Call:
## glm(formula = in_sacramento ~ price, family = "binomial", data = train_
set)
##
## Deviance Residuals:
##     Min      1Q   Median      3Q      Max
## -1.7461  -1.0995  -0.4591   1.0455   2.5995
##
## Coefficients:
##                 Estimate Std. Error z value Pr(>|z|)
## (Intercept)    1.486e+00  1.942e-01   7.654 1.95e-14 ***
## price         -6.910e-06  7.992e-07  -8.647  < 2e-16 ***
## ---
```

```
## Signif. codes:   0 '***' 0.001 '**' 0.01 '*' 0.05 '.'. 0.1 ' ' 1
##
## (Dispersion parameter for binomial family taken to be 1)
##
##      Null deviance: 1030.07  on 744   degrees of freedom
## Residual deviance:  930.69  on 743   degrees of freedom
## AIC: 934.69
##
## Number of Fisher Scoring iterations: 4
```

Due to the logistic output (between 0 and 1), we can't interpret the coefficient estimates the same way we did with linear regression. They now tell us whether a single unit increase in the predictor increases or decreases the *probability* that the outcome is *class 1* (though not *directly* how much it increases/decreases). As the coefficient estimate for **price** is negative, this means that the higher the price, the lower the chance that a house is located in Sacramento. Or, more accurately, the lower the chance that the model will *predict* that a house is located in Sacramento. Since changing the price of the house would not actually change the location of the house, it is not a causal relationship. In fact, the dependent variable (**in_sacramento**) is not actually dependent on any of our predictors. Hence, we shouldn't interpret the model summary as a description of *causal relationships*, but as a description of *correlations* that help the model make the best possible predictions. In general, linear and logistic models can't conclude that there are causal relationships between variables. We must instead use theoretical knowledge (and experimental design, where we intervene with the phenomenon we're trying to understand and measure the effect of the intervention) to determine whether there is *strong evidence* of a causal relationship.

Technically, the coefficient estimate is the *change* in the **log odds** of the class being 1 when the predictor is increased by one unit. Where the *odds* of something, let's call this **x**, so **odds(x)**, are defined as the probability of **x**, **p(x)**, divided by the probability against **x**, **1-p(x)**, the *log odds* are just the natural logarithm of the odds **log(p(x) / (1-p(x)))**. This function is also referred to as the **logit function**. When the log odds of **x** increase, the probability of **x** also increases.

Let's add more predictors to our model.

9. Add the number of bathrooms to the logistic model:

```
logistic_model_2 <- glm(in_sacramento ~ price + baths,
                        data = train_set,
                        family = "binomial")
summary(logistic_model_2)
```

The summary of the model is as follows:

```
##
## Call:
## glm(formula = in_sacramento ~ price + baths, family = "binomial",
##     data = train_set)
##
## Deviance Residuals:
##     Min      1Q   Median      3Q      Max
## -1.7115  -1.0913  -0.4623   1.0606   2.4275
##
## Coefficients:
##               Estimate Std. Error z value Pr(>|z|)
## (Intercept)  1.896e+00  2.678e-01   7.082 1.42e-12 ***
## price       -5.801e-06  9.150e-07  -6.340 2.30e-10 ***
## baths       -3.289e-01  1.430e-01  -2.300   0.0215 *
## ---
## Signif. codes:  0 '***' 0.001 '**' 0.01 '*' 0.05 '.' 0.1 ' ' 1
##
## (Dispersion parameter for binomial family taken to be 1)
##
##     Null deviance: 1030.07  on 744  degrees of freedom
## Residual deviance:  925.33  on 742  degrees of freedom
## AIC: 931.33
##
## Number of Fisher Scoring iterations: 4
```

For each additional bathroom, the chance that the home is located in Sacramento decreases. If we compare the **Akaike Information Criterion (AIC)** at the bottom of the summary to the AIC of the previous model, this model's AIC is lower. AIC is a common metric for comparing model architectures. The lower the AIC, the better. Like RMSE, AIC is relative to the dataset and task, so we do not compare AICs from different tasks or datasets. Given that this model has a lower AIC, we prefer it to the first model.

10. Add the **sqft** predictor:

```
logistic_model_3 <- glm(in_sacramento ~ price + baths + sqft,
                        data = train_set,
                        family = "binomial")
summary(logistic_model_3)
```

The summary of the model is as follows:

```
## 
## Call:
## glm(formula = in_sacramento ~ price + baths + sqft, family =
"binomial",
##       data = train_set)
## 
## Deviance Residuals:
##     Min      1Q   Median       3Q      Max
## -1.7353  -1.0833  -0.4555   1.0499   2.4370
## 
## Coefficients:
##               Estimate Std. Error z value Pr(>|z|)
## (Intercept)  1.897e+00  2.680e-01    7.080 1.44e-12 ***
## price       -6.401e-06  1.148e-06   -5.573 2.50e-08 ***
## baths       -4.239e-01  1.795e-01   -2.362   0.0182 *
## sqft         2.044e-04  2.308e-04    0.886   0.3758
## ---
## Signif. codes:  0 '***' 0.001 '**' 0.01 '*' 0.05 '.' 0.1 ' ' 1
## 
## (Dispersion parameter for binomial family taken to be 1)
## 
##       Null deviance: 1030.07  on 744  degrees of freedom
## Residual deviance:  924.54  on 741  degrees of freedom
## AIC: 932.54
## 
## Number of Fisher Scoring iterations: 4
```

This model has a higher AIC than the previous model, although they are so close that if we partitioned our dataset with a different random seed, it could be lower.

Now, we will generate the possible model formulas with **combine_predictors()** and cross-validate them.

11. Create five folds in the training set using **fold()**. Balance the folds by **in_sacramento**:

```
# Create folds
train_set <- fold(train_set, k = 5,
                  cat_col = "in_sacramento")
```

12. Generate model formulas with and without log transformations using **combine_predictors()**. To save time, limit the number of times a fixed effect can be included in a formula by specifying **max_effects_frequency = 1**:

```
# Create all combinations of the predictors
model_formulas <- combine_predictors(
    dependent = "in_sacramento",
    fixed_effects = list(list("price","log_price"),
                         list("sqft", "log_sqft"),
                         list("baths","log_baths"),
                         list("beds", "log_beds")),
    max_effect_frequency = 1)
# Count the number of generated model formulas
length(model_formulas)
## [1] 440
```

13. Show the last 10 model formulas:

```
# Show the last 10 formulas
tail(model_formulas, 10)
```

The last 10 model formulas are as follows:

```
##  [1] "in_sacramento ~ log_baths + log_beds * sqft + log_price"
##  [2] "in_sacramento ~ log_baths + log_beds * sqft + price"
##  [3] "in_sacramento ~ log_baths + log_beds + log_price * log_sqft"
##  [4] "in_sacramento ~ log_baths + log_beds + log_price * sqft"
##  [5] "in_sacramento ~ log_baths + log_beds + log_price + log_sqft"
##  [6] "in_sacramento ~ log_baths + log_beds + log_price + sqft"
##  [7] "in_sacramento ~ log_baths + log_beds + price * log_sqft"
##  [8] "in_sacramento ~ log_baths + log_beds + price * sqft"
##  [9] "in_sacramento ~ log_baths + log_beds + price + log_sqft"
## [10] "in_sacramento ~ log_baths + log_beds + price + sqft"
```

This generated 440 model formulas. Cross-validating all these models could take a while. Luckily, we can speed up the process by running it in *parallel*. Instead of cross-validating one model at a time, using only a single CPU core, we can utilize more cores and cross-validate multiple models at a time. To do this, we attach the **doParallel** package and register how many cores we want to use with the **registerDoParallel()** function. If we do not specify the number of cores, **registerDoParallel()** will autodetect the available cores and choose half.

14. Attach **doParallel** and register the number of cores:

```
# Attach doParallel
library(doParallel)
# Register four CPU cores
registerDoParallel(4)
```

15. Run the cross-validation with **cross_validate()**. Set **parallel** to **TRUE** and **family** to **binomial**:

```
# Cross-validate our models in parallel
cv_results <- cross_validate(data = train_set,
                             models = model_formulas,
                             family = "binomial",
                             parallel = TRUE)
```

16. Order the results by F_1 and subset the 10 best models. As we want the F_1 score to be as high as possible, we set **decreasing** to **TRUE**:

```
# Order by RMSE
cv_results <- cv_results[
    order(cv_results$F1, decreasing = TRUE),]
# Create a subset with the 10 best models
cv_results_top10 <- head(cv_results, 10)
cv_results_top10
```

The output is as follows:

```
## # A tibble: 10 x 26
##     'Balanced Accur…    F1 Sensitivity Specificity 'Pos Pred Value'
##               <dbl> <dbl>       <dbl>       <dbl>            <dbl>
##  1          0.684 0.663       0.657       0.711            0.669
##  2          0.686 0.663       0.651       0.722            0.675
##  3          0.683 0.660       0.651       0.714            0.669
##  4          0.678 0.659       0.66        0.696            0.658
##  5          0.672 0.658       0.671       0.673            0.646
##  6          0.675 0.658       0.666       0.684            0.651
##  7          0.676 0.657       0.66        0.691            0.654
##  8          0.667 0.657       0.68        0.653            0.635
##  9          0.668 0.657       0.677       0.658            0.637
## 10          0.673 0.656       0.663       0.684            0.650
```

```
## # … with 21 more variables: 'Neg Pred Value' <dbl>, AUC <dbl>, 'Lower
## #   CI' <dbl>, 'Upper CI' <dbl>, Kappa <dbl>, MCC <dbl>, 'Detection
## #   Rate' <dbl>, 'Detection Prevalence' <dbl>, Prevalence <dbl>,
## #   Predictions <list>, ROC <list>, 'Confusion Matrix' <list>,
## #   Coefficients <list>, Folds <int>, 'Fold Columns' <int>, 'Convergence
## #   Warnings' <dbl>, 'Singular Fit Messages' <int>, Family <chr>,
## #   Link <chr>, Dependent <chr>, Fixed <chr>
```

The output contains a lot of information, so we select a subset of the metrics and focus on them.

17. Select some of the metrics and show the results with **kable()**:

```
# Select the metrics and model formulas
cv_results_top10 <- select_metrics(cv_results_top10)
# Remove some of the metrics
# Note: A great alternative is dplyr::select()
# In general, the dplyr package is amazing
cv_results_top10 <- cv_results_top10[,
    !(colnames(cv_results_top10) %in%
        c("Lower CI",
          "Upper CI","Detection Rate",
          "Detection Prevalence",
          "Prevalence")), drop=FALSE]
# Print with knitr::kable for fanciness
kable(cv_results_top10, digits = 3)
```

The output is as follows:

Balanced Accuracy	F1	Sensitivity	Specificity	Pos Pred Value	Neg Pred Value	AUC	Kappa	MCC	Dependent	Fixed
0.684	0.663	0.657	0.711	0.669	0.701	0.726	0.369	0.369	in_sacramento	baths*log_price*log_sqft+log_beds
0.686	0.663	0.651	0.722	0.675	0.700	0.723	0.374	0.374	in_sacramento	log_baths*log_beds+log_price*log_sqft
0.683	0.660	0.651	0.714	0.669	0.698	0.728	0.366	0.366	in_sacramento	log_baths*log_price*log_sqft+log_beds
0.678	0.659	0.660	0.696	0.658	0.698	0.726	0.356	0.356	in_sacramento	baths*log_price*log_sqft+beds
0.672	0.658	0.671	0.673	0.646	0.698	0.715	0.344	0.344	in_sacramento	log_baths*price*sqft
0.675	0.658	0.666	0.684	0.651	0.698	0.722	0.349	0.349	in_sacramento	log_baths*log_beds*price
0.676	0.657	0.660	0.691	0.654	0.696	0.727	0.351	0.351	in_sacramento	baths*log_price*log_sqft
0.667	0.657	0.680	0.653	0.635	0.697	0.714	0.332	0.333	in_sacramento	log_baths*price+beds+sqft
0.668	0.657	0.677	0.658	0.637	0.697	0.714	0.334	0.335	in_sacramento	log_baths*price+beds
0.673	0.656	0.663	0.684	0.650	0.696	0.717	0.346	0.346	in_sacramento	baths*log_beds*price

Figure 5.22: Logistic model output

The formula **"in_sacramento ~ baths * log_price * log_sqft + log_beds"** has the highest F_1 score, although it's approximately the same as the second best model. The output contains a few metrics that we haven't covered previously. Importantly, different statistical fields have different names for the same metrics, so what we know as *Recall* is also called **Sensitivity**, and what we know as *Precision* is also called **Positive Prediction Value** (**Pos Pred Value**). We won't go into detail about the other metrics, but we do recommend learning about them. As we learned about *accuracy* in the previous chapter, we will introduce the **Balanced Accuracy** metric, which is a version of accuracy that works well with imbalanced datasets. It has the following formula:

$$\text{Balanced Accuracy} = \frac{\frac{\text{True Positives}}{\text{True Positives+False Negatives}} + \frac{\text{True Negatives}}{\text{True Negatives+False Positives}}}{2}$$

Figure 5.23: Formula for balanced accuracy

As with the regular accuracy score, we wish for balanced accuracy to be as high as possible. In the cross-validation results, it favors a different model than the F_1 score. We will learn how to choose models based on multiple metrics later.

18. Use **validate()** to train the best model on the training set and evaluate it on the validation set:

```
# Evaluate the best model on the validation set with validate()
V_results_list <- validate(
    train_data = train_set,
    test_data = valid_set,
    models = "in_sacramento ~ baths * log_price * log_sqft + log_beds",
    family = "binomial")
V_model <- V_results_list$Models[[1]]
V_results <- V_results_list$Results
# Select metrics
V_results <- select_metrics(V_results)
# Remove some of the metrics
V_results <- V_results[, !(colnames(V_results) %in% c(
    "Lower CI","Upper CI","Detection Rate",
    "Detection Prevalence", "Prevalence")), drop=FALSE]
# Print the results
kable(V_results, digits = 3)
```

The output is as follows:

Balanced Accuracy	F1	Sensitivity	Specificity	Pos Pred Value	Neg Pred Value	AUC	Kappa	MCC	Dependent	Fixed
0.69	0.65	0.602	0.778	0.707	0.688	0.769	0.383	0.387	in_sacramento	baths*log_price*log_sqft+log_beds

Figure 5.24: Validation results

The results are very similar to the cross-validation results. Now, let's view the model summary.

19. View and interpret the summary of the best model:

```
# Print the model summary and interpret it
summary(V_model)
```

The summary of the model is as follows:

```
##
## Call:
## glm(formula = model_formula, family = binomial(link = link),
##      data = train_set)
##
## Deviance Residuals:
##      Min       1Q   Median       3Q      Max
## -2.2231  -1.0373  -0.3921   1.0380   2.7434
##
## Coefficients:
##                         Estimate Std. Error z value Pr(>|z|)
## (Intercept)             101.4540   113.1667   0.897   0.3700
## baths                   -86.3490    53.1521  -1.625   0.1043
## log_price                -6.9804     9.1408  -0.764   0.4451
## log_sqft                -13.5135    16.2621  -0.831   0.4060
## log_beds                  0.6739     0.4214   1.599   0.1097
## baths:log_price           6.2569     4.2603   1.469   0.1419
## baths:log_sqft           12.8919     7.3428   1.756   0.0791 .
## log_price:log_sqft        0.9241     1.3080   0.707   0.4799
## baths:log_price:log_sqft -0.9484     0.5858  -1.619   0.1054
## ---
## Signif. codes:  0 '***' 0.001 '**' 0.01 '*' 0.05 '.' 0.1 ' ' 1
##
```

```
## (Dispersion parameter for binomial family taken to be 1)
##
##     Null deviance: 1030.07  on 744  degrees of freedom
## Residual deviance:  904.19  on 736  degrees of freedom
## AIC: 922.19
##
## Number of Fisher Scoring iterations: 5
```

Interestingly, none of the predictors or interaction terms are statistically significant. While this, in itself, would not be enough to conclude that none of the predictors affect the dependent variable, it does mean that *if there were such relationships, we would not have enough evidence (data points) to say so.* We also see that the AIC has not decreased much from the simple models we started with. With these things in mind, it would be interesting to see the *baseline evaluation*, so we know whether our model is doing better than random guessing. Normally, creating the baseline evaluation should be one of the first steps in our analysis, so we always know whether we are improving. In *Chapter 4, Introduction to neuralnet and Evaluation Methods*, we wrote the code for creating baseline evaluations ourselves. In the next two exercises, we will use the **baseline()** function from **cvms** to do it.

Recommendation: Once you feel comfortable with linear and logistic regression, the next step is to add **<u>random effects</u>** to your models. This is also known as **<u>mixed-effect modeling</u>**.

Exercise 56: Creating Binomial Baseline Evaluations with cvms

In this exercise, we will create baseline evaluations for the binary classification task from the previous exercise. The **baseline()** function will create 100 random sets of predicted probabilities and evaluate them against the dependent column, **in_sacramento**, in the validation set. It will also evaluate a set of **all 0** predictions and a set of **all 1** predictions. We will speed up the process by running the evaluations in parallel, similar to what we did in the previous exercise:

1. Set the random seed to **1**:

   ```
   # Set seed for reproducibility and easy comparison
   set.seed(1)
   ```

2. Register four cores for running the evaluations in parallel. If you have a different number of cores available, feel free to adjust the number:

```
# Attach doParallel and
# register four CPU cores
library(doParallel)
registerDoParallel(4)
```

3. Use **baseline()** to evaluate 100 random sets of probabilities against the **in_sacramento** variable in the validation set. The output is a list with two data frames. The first data frame contains the summarized results, and the second data frame contains all the evaluations of the random sets of probabilities. We will only look at the summarized results:

```
# Create baseline evaluations of the
# in_sacramento variable in the validation set
binomial_baselines <- baseline(
    test_data = valid_set,
    dependent_col = "in_sacramento",
    n = 100,
    family = "binomial",
    parallel = TRUE)
```

4. Print the summarized results:

```
# Show the summarized results
binomial_baselines$summarized_metrics
```

The output is as follows:

```
## # A tibble: 10 x 15
##      Measure 'Balanced Accur…      F1 Sensitivity Specificity
##      <chr>                <dbl>  <dbl>      <dbl>       <dbl>
##   1 Mean                 0.500  0.483      0.498       0.503
##   2 Median               0.499  0.488      0.5         0.505
##   3 SD                  0.0333 0.0389     0.0535      0.0521
##   4 IQR                 0.0420 0.0549     0.0795      0.0631
##   5 Max                  0.578  0.567      0.625       0.657
##   6 Min                  0.405  0.393      0.398       0.343
##   7 NAs                      0      0          0           0
```

```
##  8 INFs               0       0        0         0
##  9 All_0             0.5     NA        0         1
## 10 All_1             0.5    0.640      1         0
## # … with 10 more variables: 'Pos Pred Value' <dbl>, 'Neg Pred
## #   Value' <dbl>, AUC <dbl>, 'Lower CI' <dbl>, 'Upper CI' <dbl>,
## #   Kappa <dbl>, MCC <dbl>, 'Detection Rate' <dbl>, 'Detection
## #   Prevalence' <dbl>, Prevalence <dbl>
```

The left-hand column, **Measure**, tells us which statistical descriptor of the random evaluations the row describes. At the top, we have the **mean** of the various metrics. If our model was simply guessing, it would, on average, achieve an F_1 score of **0.483**. The highest F_1 score obtained by guessing was **0.567**, and the lowest was **0.393**. When always predicting **1** (that the house is located in Sacramento), the F_1 score is **0.640**, as can be seen in the row where **Measure** is **All_1**.

Our best model from the previous exercise had an F_1 score of 0.65. This is higher than even the best random guess, but only slightly higher than always predicting **1**. So, we look at the precision (here called **Pos Pred Value**) and recall (here called **Sensitivity**) to check whether it is always predicting **1**. These are both greater than .7, so that is not the case, and we conclude that our model is performing better than the baseline on the F_1 score.

In the next exercise, we will create Gaussian baseline evaluations with **cvms**.

Exercise 57: Creating Gaussian Baseline Evaluations with cvms

In this exercise, we will create baseline evaluations for the linear regression task from the first part of the chapter. The goal of the task is to predict the **price** of a house. The **baseline()** function will fit the formula "**price ~ 1**", where **1** is the intercept, on 100 random subsets of the training set, and evaluate each on the validation set. It will also fit the *intercept-only* model on the entire training set and evaluate that on the validation set as well.

The intercept-only model simply learns the average **price** in the training (sub)set and then predicts that value for everything:

1. Set the random seed to **1**:

    ```
    # Set seed for reproducibility and easy comparison
    set.seed(1)
    ```

2. Register four cores for running the evaluations in parallel. If you have a different number of cores available, feel free to adjust the number:

```
# Attach doParallel and
# register four CPU cores
library(doParallel)
registerDoParallel(4)
```

3. Use **baseline()** to fit the model formula "**price** ~ 1 " on 100 random subsets of the training set and evaluate them on the validation set. The output is a list with two data frames. The first data frame contains the summarized results, and the second data frame contains all the evaluations of the models fitted on the random subsets. We will only look at the summarized results:

```
# Create baseline evaluations of the in_sacramento variable
# in the validation set
gaussian_baselines <- baseline(
    test_data = valid_set,
    train_data = train_set,
    dependent_col = "price",
    n = 100,
    family = "gaussian",
    parallel = TRUE)
# Show the summarized results
gaussian_baselines$summarized_metrics
```

The summarized results are as follows:

```
## # A tibble: 9 x 9
##    Measure      RMSE     MAE  r2m   r2c    AIC   AICc    BIC `Training Rows`
##    <chr>        <dbl>   <dbl> <dbl> <dbl>  <dbl>  <dbl>  <dbl>          <dbl>
## 1 Mean      142928. 107071.     0     0  9637.  9637.  9644.            366.
## 2 Median    142735. 106992.     0     0  9638.  9638.  9646.            365
## 3 SD          1187.    676.     0     0  5420.  5420.  5421.            206.
## 4 IQR         1229.    557.     0     0  9664.  9664.  9666.            367.
## 5 Max       146942. 110573.     0     0 19325. 19325. 19334.            733
## 6 Min       140801. 106230.     0     0   725.   726.   728.             27
## 7 NAs            0       0      0     0     0      0      0               0
## 8 INFs           0       0      0     0     0      0      0               0
## 9 All_rows  142721. 106998.     0     0 19641. 19641. 19650.            745
```

Figure 2.25: Summarized Matrix

When always predicting the average value, our intercept-only model achieves an average RMSE of **142,928 (Min = 140,801)**, which is a lot higher than the RMSE of **75,057.56** we achieved in *Exercise 56, Log-Transforming Predictors*. Hence, we conclude that our model is better than the baseline.

Regression and Classification with Decision Trees

We can solve regression and classification tasks with a multitude of machine learning algorithms. In the previous chapter, we used *neural networks*, and, in this chapter, we have used *linear* and *logistic regression*. In the next chapter, we will learn about *decision trees* and *random forests*, which can also be used for these tasks. While linear and logistic regression models are usually easier to interpret, random forests can sometimes be better at making predictions. In this section, we will apply random forests to our dataset and compare the results to our linear and logistic regression models.

As we have seen in *Chapter 1, An Introduction to Machine Learning*, a decision tree is basically a set of *if/else* statements arranged as an upside-down tree, where the *leaf nodes* contain the possible predictions. For a specific observation, we could end up with the following paths down a tree:

- If a home is **larger than 1,500 sqft** and it has **more than 4 bedrooms**, it is predicted to be **located in Sacramento**.

- If it is **larger than 1,500 sqft** and has **4 bedrooms or fewer**, it is predicted to be **located outside Sacramento**.

- If it is **1,500 sqft or smaller** and it has **more than 2 bedrooms**, it is predicted to be **located in Sacramento**.

- If it is **1,500 sqft or smaller** and it has **2 bedrooms or fewer**, it is predicted to be **located outside Sacramento**.

In the first node, the *root node*, we ask whether the home is larger than 1,500 sqft. If so, we go to the left *child node*, which asks whether a home has more than 4 bedrooms. If not, we go to the right child node, which asks whether the home has more than 2 bedrooms. Depending on the answer in the child node, we end up in a *leaf node* (a node without child nodes) that contains the value of our prediction.

A *random forest* is an *ensemble* (a collection) of different decision trees, where the final prediction is based on the predictions from all the trees. In the next exercise, we will be training two random forest models.

Exercise 58: Training Random Forest Models

In this exercise, we will first train a random forest regression model to predict **price** in the **Sacramento** dataset, and then a random forest classification model to predict whether a home is located in Sacramento. We will not be using the log-transformed predictors for this example:

1. Attach the **randomForest** and **caret** packages:

   ```
   # Attach packages
   library(randomForest)
   library(caret)
   ```

2. Set the random seed to **1**:

   ```
   # Set seed for reproducibility and easy comparison.
   set.seed(1)
   ```

3. Fit a random forest model for predicting the price of a home:

   ```
   rf_model_regression <- randomForest(
       formula = price ~ beds + baths + sqft + in_sacramento,
       data = train_set)
   ```

4. Calculate the RMSE. First, we use the model to predict the price in the validation set. Note that we would usually start with a development set or use cross-validation until we had found the best hyperparameters for our model. Second, we calculate the RMSE with the **RMSE()** function from the **caret** package:

   ```
   # Predict prices in the validation set
   price_predictions <- predict(rf_model_regression, valid_set)
   # Calculate and print the RMSE
   RMSE(price_predictions, valid_set$price)
   ## [1] 86957.24
   ```

   While this RMSE is lower than the baseline, it is higher than the best linear regression models we trained earlier in the chapter.

5. Fit a random forest model for predicting whether the home is located in Sacramento:

   ```
   rf_model_classification <- randomForest(
       formula = in_sacramento ~ beds + baths + sqft + price,
       data = train_set)
   ```

6. Use the model to predict the **in_sacramento** variable in the validation set and create a confusion matrix with **confusionMatrix()**:

```
# Predict in_sacramento in the validation set
in_sacramento_predictions <- predict(rf_model_classification,
                                        valid_set)
# Create a confusion matrix and print it
confusionMatrix(in_sacramento_predictions,
                valid_set$in_sacramento,
                positive = "1",
                mode = "prec_recall")
```

The confusion matrix and statistics are as follows:

```
## Confusion Matrix and Statistics
##
##               Reference
## Prediction  0   1
##          0 64  28
##          1 35  60
##
##                 Accuracy : 0.6631
##                   95% CI : (0.5905, 0.7304)
##      No Information Rate : 0.5294
##      P-Value [Acc > NIR] : 0.0001434
##
##                    Kappa : 0.3268
##
##   Mcnemar's Test P-Value : 0.4496918
##
##                Precision : 0.6316
##                   Recall : 0.6818
##                       F1 : 0.6557
##               Prevalence : 0.4706
##           Detection Rate : 0.3209
##     Detection Prevalence : 0.5080
##        Balanced Accuracy : 0.6641
##
##         'Positive' Class : 1
```

Interestingly, the random forest classifier obtains very similar results to the best logistic regression model, which also obtained an F_1 score of 0.65. The balanced accuracy is 3% points lower. As we can tell from the confusion matrix, it does not predict the same class all the time, so we can conclude that it is better than the baseline.

Model Selection by Multiple Disagreeing Metrics

What happens if the metrics do not agree on the ranking of our models? In the last chapter, on classification, we learned about the precision and recall metrics, which we "merged" into the F_1 score, because it is easier to compare models on one metric than two. But what if we did not want to (or couldn't) merge two or more metrics into one (possibly arbitrary) metric?

Pareto Dominance

If a model is better than another model on one metrics, and at least as good on all other metrics, this model should be considered better overall. We say that the model dominates the other model.

If we remove all the models that are dominated by other models, we will have the nondominated models left. This set of models is referred to as the *Pareto set* (or the *Pareto front*). We will see in a moment why Pareto *front* is a fitting name.

Let's say that our Pareto set consists of two models. One has high precision, but low recall. The other has low precision, but high recall. Imagine that we don't want to use the F_1 metric or another combination of the two. Then, unless we have a preference for one of the metrics, we do not have a way to choose between the models and should instead consider including both models in our analysis or machine learning pipeline.

Exercise 59: Plotting the Pareto Front

In this exercise, we will simulate evaluation results for 20 classification models and visualize the Pareto front with the **rPref** package.

The Pareto front can be just as useful for linear regression models, where one model might have the lowest RMSE, while another has the lowest MAE. As precision and recall are slightly easier to simulate realistically, we will use these metrics for this exercise:

1. Attach the required packages **rPref**, **ggplot2** and **knitr**:

```
# Attach packages
library(rPref)
library(ggplot2)
library(knitr)
```

2. Set the random seed to **3**:

```
# Set seed for reproducibility and easier comparison
set.seed(3)
```

3. Create a data frame with 20 simulated model evaluations. The metrics are precision and recall. Use the **runif()** function to randomly sample **20** numbers between **0** and **1**:

```
# Create random set of model evaluations
# runif() samples random numbers between 0 and 1
evaluated_models <- data.frame("Model" = c(1:20),
                               "Precision" = runif(20),
                               "Recall" = runif(20))
```

4. Order the data frame by the two metrics and print it using the **kable()** function:

```
# Order the data frame by the two metrics
evaluated_models <- evaluated_models[order(evaluated_models$Precision,
                                           evaluated_models$Recall,
                                           decreasing = TRUE),]

# Inspect the simulated results
kable(evaluated_models, digits = 2)
```

The output is as follows:

Model	Precision	Recall
19	0.90	0.58
15	0.87	0.26
16	0.83	0.34
2	0.81	0.02
18	0.70	0.20
10	0.63	0.76
6	0.60	0.79
5	0.60	0.24
9	0.58	0.56
14	0.56	0.45
13	0.53	0.17
11	0.51	0.38
12	0.51	0.37
3	0.38	0.13
4	0.33	0.09
8	0.29	0.91
20	0.28	0.21
1	0.17	0.23
7	0.12	0.60
17	0.11	0.89

Figure 5.26: Model precision and recall

By simply looking at the table, we can tell that models **19** and **8** are nondominated models, as they have the highest precision and recall scores, respectively. Instead of comparing the models manually, though, we will use the **psel()** function from the **rPref** package to find the Pareto front.

5. Find the nondominated models using the **psel()** function. For the second argument, **pref**, we specify whether a metric is supposed to be as high or as low as possible:

```
# Find the Pareto front / set
front <- psel(evaluated_models,
                pref = high("Precision") * high("Recall"))
# Print the Pareto front
kable(front, digits = 2)
```

The output is as follows:

Model	Precision	Recall
19	0.90	0.58
10	0.63	0.76
6	0.60	0.79
8	0.29	0.91

Figure 5.27: Models in the Pareto front

Figure 5.26 shows the four nondominated models. Besides models **8** and **19**, we also have models **6** and **10**, which both have a *higher recall* than model **19**, but *lower precision*. While model **10** has *higher precision* than model **6**, model **6** has *higher recall* than model **10**.

6. Create a **ggplot2** object with precision on the *x-axis* and recall on the *y-axis*. Add the models as points using **geom_point()**. Increase the size of the nondominated points by adding larger points on top of the smaller points. Using the **geom_step()** function, create a line to visualize the Pareto front. Finally, add the **light** theme with **theme_light()**:

```
# Create ggplot object
# with precision on the x-axis and recall on the y-axis
ggplot(evaluated_models, aes(x = Precision, y = Recall)) +

  # Add the models as points
  geom_point(shape = 1) +

  # Add the nondominated models as larger points
```

```
geom_point(data = front, size = 3) +

# Add a line to visualize the Pareto front
geom_step(data = front, direction = "vh") +

# Add the light theme
theme_light()
```

The Pareto front plot should look as follows:

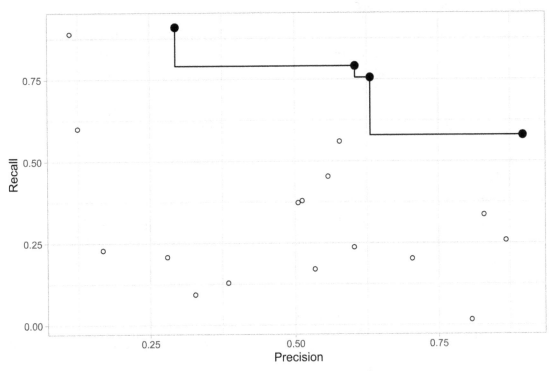

Figure 5.28: Pareto front with precision and recall

In *Figure 5.27*, the four large points are the nondominated models. That is, for each of these models, there are no other models that are better on one metric and at least as good on the other metric. What we do with this information is up to us. We might want a model with very high precision, so it rarely makes mistakes when predicting our positive class. Or we might want high recall, so it captures most of the observations in the positive class, even if it means that some of these predictions are wrong. Alternatively, the two models in the "middle" of the Pareto front might have the balance we want. It all depends on our use case.

Activity 19: Classifying Room Types

In this activity, you will classify the type of room in Airbnb listings in Amsterdam using logistic regression. You will start by creating baseline evaluations for the task. Then, you will fit and interpret multiple logistic regression models. Next, you will generate model formulas and cross-validate them with **cvms**. First, you will run a single cross-validation, and then you will use repeated cross-validation on the best 10-20 models. Finally, you will choose the nondominated models and validate them with **validate()**.

> **Note**
>
> The Amsterdam dataset has been taken from http://insideairbnb.com/get-the-data.html and modified to suit the activity. The modified dataset can be found at https://github.com/TrainingByPackt/Practical-Machine-Learning-with-R/blob/master/Data/amsterdam.listings.csv.

The following steps will help you complete the activity.

1. Attach the **groupdata2**, **cvms**, **caret**, **randomForest**, **rPref**, and **doParallel** packages.

2. Set the random seed to **3**.

3. Load the **amsterdam.listings** dataset from https://github.com/TrainingByPackt/Practical-Machine-Learning-with-R/blob/master/Data/amsterdam.listings.csv.

4. Convert the **id** and **neighbourhood** columns to factors.

5. Summarize the dataset.

6. Partition the dataset into a training set (80%) and a validation set (20%). Balance the partitions by **room_type**.

7. Prepare for running the baseline evaluations and the cross-validations in *parallel* by registering the number of cores for **doParallel**.

8. Create the baseline evaluation for the task on the validation set with the **baseline()** function from **cvms**. Run **100** evaluations in parallel. Specify the dependent column as **room_type**. Note that the default positive class is **Private room**.

9. Fit multiple logistic regression models on the training set with the **glm()** function, predicting **room_type**. Try different predictors. View the **summary()** of each fitted model and try to interpret the estimated coefficients. How do the interpretations change when you add or subtract predictors? Note that interpreting the coefficients for logarithmic predictors in logistic regression is not an easy task, so don't worry if it doesn't make sense yet.

10. Create model formulas with **combine_predictors()**. To save time, limit the interaction size to **2** by specifying **max_interaction_size = 2**, and limit the number of times an effect can be included in a formula to **1** by specifying **max_effect_frequency = 1**.

11. Create **five** fold columns with **five** folds each in the training set using **fold()** with **k = 5** and **num_fold_cols = 5**. Balance the folds by **room_type**. Feel free to choose a higher number of fold columns.

12. Perform cross-validation (**not repeated**) on your model formulas with **cvms**. Specify **fold_cols = ".folds_1"**. Order the results by F_1 and show the best 10 models.

13. Perform **repeated** cross-validation on the 10-20 best model formulas (by F_1) with **cvms**.

14. Find the Pareto front based on the F_1 and balanced accuracy scores. Use **psel()** from the **rPref** package, and specify **pref = high("F1") * high("`Balanced Accuracy`")**. Note the *ticks* around `Balanced Accuracy`.

15. Plot the Pareto front with the **ggplot2** code from *Exercise 61, Plotting the Pareto Front*. Note that you may need to add ticks around `Balanced Accuracy` when specifying **x** or **y** in **aes()** in the **ggplot** call.

16. Use **validate()** to train the *nondominated* models on the training set and evaluate them on the validation set.

17. View the summaries of the nondominated model(s).

The output should be similar to the following

```
##
## Call:
## glm(formula = model_formula, family = binomial(link = link),
##      data = train_set)
##
## Deviance Residuals:
##      Min      1Q   Median       3Q      Max
## -3.8323  -0.4836  -0.2724  -0.0919   3.9091
##
## Coefficients:
##                           Estimate Std. Error z value  Pr(>|z|)
## (Intercept)             15.3685268  0.4511978   34.062  < 2e-16 ***
## availability_365        -0.0140209  0.0030623   -4.579 4.68e-06 ***
## log_price               -3.4441520  0.0956189  -36.020  < 2e-16 ***
## log_minimum_nights      -0.7163252  0.0535452  -13.378  < 2e-16 ***
## log_number_of_reviews   -0.0823821  0.0282115   -2.920   0.0035 **
## log_reviews_per_month    0.0733808  0.0381629    1.923   0.0545 .
## availability_365:log_price  0.0042772  0.0006207    6.891 5.53e-12 ***
## log_n_o_reviews:log_r_p_month 0.3730603  0.0158122  23.593 < 2e-16 ***
## ---
## Signif. codes:  0 '***' 0.001 '**' 0.01 '*' 0.05 '.' 0.1 ' ' 1
##
## (Dispersion parameter for binomial family taken to be 1)
##
##      Null deviance: 14149.2  on 13853  degrees of freedom
## Residual deviance:  8476.7  on 13846  degrees of freedom
## AIC: 8492.7
##
## Number of Fisher Scoring iterations: 6
```

Note

The solution for this activity can be found on page 365.

Summary

In this chapter, we fitted and interpreted multiple linear and logistic regression models. We learned how to calculate the RMSE and MAE metrics, and checked their different responses to outliers. We generated model formulas and cross-validated them with the **cvms** package. To check whether our model is better than random guesses and making the same prediction every time, we created baseline evaluations for both linear regression and binary classification tasks. When multiple metrics (such as the F_1 score and balanced accuracy) disagree on the ranking of models, we learned to find the nondominated models, also known as the Pareto front. Finally, we trained two random forest models and compared them to the best performing linear and logistic regression models.

In the next chapter, you will learn about *unsupervised learning*.

Unsupervised Learning

Learning Objectives

By the end of this chapter, you will be able to:

- Distinguish between unsupervised and supervised learning
- Implement different techniques applied in clustering, such as soft and hard clustering, monothetic and polythetic clustering, and bottom-up versus top-down clustering
- Perform k-means clustering
- Compare performance using DIANA, AGNES, and k-means

In this chapter, we aim to equip you with a practical understanding of unsupervised learning.

Introduction

In this chapter, we will look at the implementation of unsupervised learning. We will explore different ways of clustering; namely, bottom-up (or **agglomerative**) and top-down (or **divisive**). We will also look at the distinction between monothetic and polythetic hierarchical clustering and delve deeper into the implementation of **k-means**, a popular clustering technique.

Before we go into the details of the chapter, let's take a brief look at an overview of machine learning. Machine learning, in general, can be divided into three distinct groups; namely, reinforcement learning, supervised learning, and unsupervised learning, as shown in *Figure 6.1*. There is also one more category, semi-supervised learning, which falls between supervised learning and unsupervised learning. Most widely used learning techniques are supervised and unsupervised learning.

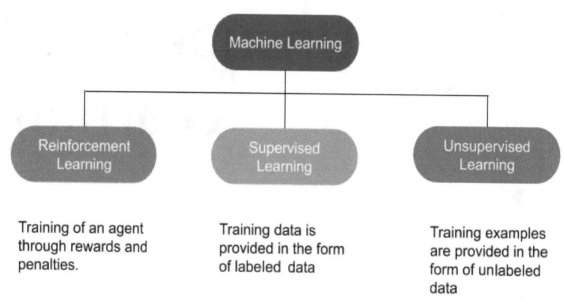

Figure 6.1: Types of machine learning

Reinforcement learning is a category of machine learning that focuses on training an agent to take actions in an environment. The agent is trained through a set of rewards and penalties. Reinforcement learning is popular in areas such as gaming and robotics.

In supervised learning, a model is provided with examples of each class. The model is trained to learn the best mapping of the input to the output in tasks such as classification and regression.

In this chapter, we will look at unsupervised learning. The main distinction vis-à-vis supervised learning is that the training examples is unlabeled. In supervised learning, we start off knowing the groups or categories that each data element belongs to. In unsupervised learning, the goal is to discover these categories. One real-life example described in *Altuncu et Al.* (2018) is the grouping of related news articles. This form of document clustering is applicable in many areas where manual categorization is impractical.

Overview of Unsupervised Learning (Clustering)

Unsupervised learning is a subcategory of machine learning that learns or trains using unlabeled data. In other words, as opposed to supervised learning, where the model is expected to predict or categorize data into a set of known classes, unsupervised learning establishes the structure within data to create the categories or groups.

Before delving into unsupervised learning and, specifically, clustering, there are a few questions you need to answer:

- Based on domain knowledge, does your dataset inherently have subgroups? If yes, how do you identify the subgroups? How many subgroups are present in the dataset?

- Are the members of each subgroup similar? Typically, clustering should only be applied to datasets that have subgroups with somewhat similar datapoints.

- Are there outliers in the dataset? Outliers can often influence the choice of which clustering algorithm to use.

Answering these questions will help us to create a better clustering model. There are different ways to perform clustering. Let's now look at three ways of classifying clustering techniques:

- Hard versus soft clusters

- Flat versus hierarchical clustering

- Monothetic versus polythetic clustering

Let's now look at these clustering techniques in detail.

Hard versus Soft Clusters

In **hard clustering**, a datapoint can only belong to one of the groups. That is, if it is a description of a dog, it can't also be a description of a horse. In **soft clustering**, members can belong to multiple subgroups with a varying degree of strength. For instance, an emoji can be judged as part sad and part angry. One soft clustering technique is the **Expected Maximization** (**EM**) algorithm. EM is a probabilistic, generative model that uses joint probability and Bayes' theorem.

The following steps, 1 to 5, explain the workings of the EM algorithm:

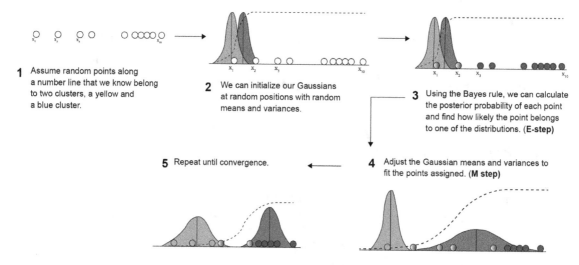

1 Assume random points along a number line that we know belong to two clusters, a yellow and a blue cluster.

2 We can initialize our Gaussians at random positions with random means and variances.

3 Using the Bayes rule, we can calculate the posterior probability of each point and find how likely the point belongs to one of the distributions. (**E-step**)

5 Repeat until convergence.

4 Adjust the Gaussian means and variances to fit the points assigned. (**M step**)

Figure 6.2: Steps of the EM algorithm

EM is regarded as a soft clustering technique since a point can belong to different clusters with different probabilities. In step 3, we establish to what extent each datapoint belongs to each distribution (for instance, x_1 belongs to the first distribution with a high probability, and the second distribution with a lower probability). In step 4, we adjust the mean and variances based on the memberships predicted in step 3. That is, the distribution mean becomes the *weighted* mean of the datapoints belonging to that distribution. Hence, the "amount" that x_1 is part of the first distribution (b_1) multiplied by its value ($b_1 x_1$) plus the amount that x_2 is part of the first distribution multiplied by its value ($b_2 x_2$), and so on, divided by the sum of the weights ($b_1 + b_2 + \dots$). Steps 3 and 4 are repeated until they stop changing (convergence).

Flat versus Hierarchical Clustering

Hierarchical clustering produces different levels of abstraction in a taxonomic fashion, unlike flat clustering, where all members are on the same level. Hierarchical clustering aims to create a dendrogram where the top cluster is a superset with all the elements. If the top level was **animal**, the second level could contain the different animal groups (**fish**, **mammal**, **birds**, and so on), and the third level could be the specific types of fish, mammals, birds, and so on:

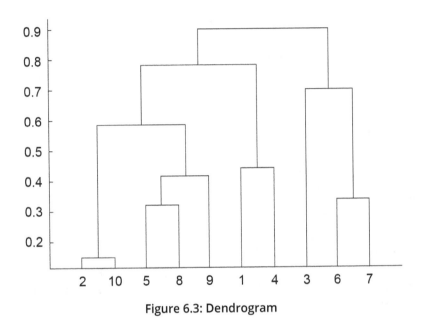

Figure 6.3: Dendrogram

In *Figure* 6.3, the vertical axis (**y**) represents dissimilarity within the cluster. As you go up, the cluster members become more dissimilar. The **x**-axis represents the objects that are recursively being grouped.

Hierarchical clustering can be executed top-down or bottom-up. As the name suggests, for top-down clustering, we subdivide bigger clusters into successively smaller clusters. Bottom-up clustering involves grouping smaller clusters into bigger ones as we move up the dendrogram. An example of top-down clustering is **recursive k-means**.

In recursive k-means, we perform several iterations. In the first iteration, we might split the data into two parts. In the second iteration, each of the two clusters is further split into other clusters. We continue iteratively splitting the clusters into smaller *sub-clusters* until the sub-clusters only contain elements of a single class, as shown in *Figure 6.4*. As you can see, by **Iteration 2**, the clusters contain similar elements out of the entire data provided:

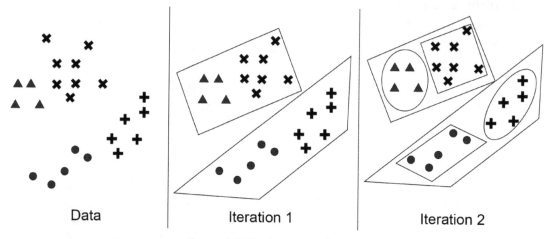

| Data | Iteration 1 | Iteration 2 |

Figure 6.4: The k-means clusters

Top-down clustering is fast but has the disadvantage of not allowing the traversal of boundaries set at higher levels. On the other hand, bottom-up clustering is slow but has the advantage of being more likely to group similar elements. In bottom-up clustering, each point is regarded as a cluster, as shown in *Figure 6.5*. In the first iteration, we find a pair of clusters that are similar and merge them into one new cluster:

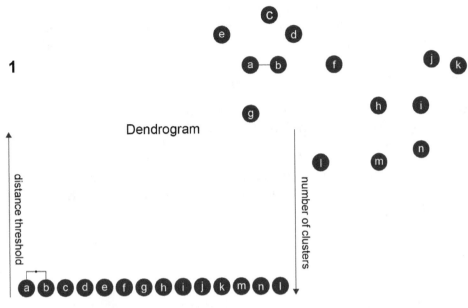

Figure 6.5: Bottom-up clustering (step 1)

Figure 6.5 shows a cluster with a pair of points, **a** and **b**. We then recursively continue the process until we have only one cluster. We can also set a threshold, where we "cut" the dendrogram at a certain threshold, as shown in *Figure* 6.6:

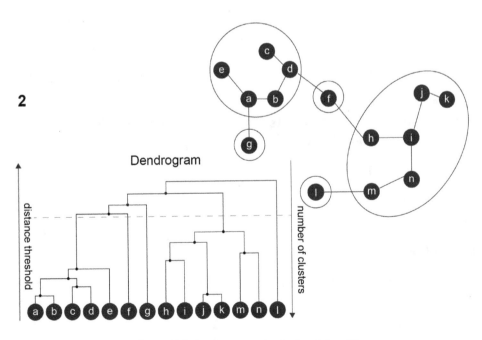

Figure 6.6: Bottom-up clustering (step 2)

An example of bottom-up clustering is **Agglomerative Clustering**. Agglomerative clustering is used to form clusters based on similarity. It is also known as AGNES. This topic will be covered in detail in *Exercise 64, Agglomerative Clustering using AGNES*.

Monothetic versus Polythetic Clustering

In monothetic clustering, the membership of a cluster is determined by the absence or presence of a single attribute. In polythetic clustering, multiple variables are used to determine the memberships.

We will use R's `mona()` function, which stands for *monothetic analysis*. It is monothetic and hierarchical. At each step, a split is made based on a single variable. `mona()` is a divisive clustering technique and requires the variables to be binary, that is, either zero or one.

> **Note**
>
> For more details of the mona algorithm, please read *Clustering in an object-oriented environment*, by Struyf et al. (1997). Struyf, Anja, Mia Hubert, and Peter Rousseeuw. "*Clustering in an object-oriented environment.*" Journal of Statistical Software 1.4 (1997): 1-30.

In the following exercise, we are going to perform clustering on a dataset that has binary values for features.

Exercise 60: Monothetic and Hierarchical Clustering on a Binary Dataset

In this exercise, we'll perform monothetic and hierarchical clustering. To start with, we will use the built-in R dataset of **animals**. This dataset contains a list of 20 animals with attributes such as *warm-blooded, can fly,* and *endangered.*

1. Attach the **cluster** package:

   ```
   library(cluster)
   ```

2. Load and view the **animals** dataset:

   ```
   data(animals)
   ```

3. View the number of observations for each column. We apply the **table** function as follows:

   ```
   apply(animals, 2, table) # simple overview
   ```

The output is as follows:

```
      war fly ver end gro hai
  1   10  16   6  12   6  11
  2   10   4  14   6  11   9
```

Figure 6.7: Summary of the attributes where 1 is "no" and 2 is "yes"

From the preceding results, of the 20 observations, 10 are warm-blooded (war) and 10 are not. 4 animals can fly and 16 cannot. 14 animals are vertebrates (ver) and 6 are not. 6 animals are endangered (end), 12 are not, and 2 are unknown (NA). 11 live on the ground (gro), 6 do not, and 3 are unknown (NA). 9 have hair (hai), while 11 do not.

4. Apply the mona() function to create clusters based on whether they are warm-blooded, can fly, are vertebrates, are endangered, live on the ground, and whether they have hair:

```
ma <- mona(animals)
ma
```

The output is as follows:

```
mona(x, ..) fit;  x of dimension 20x6
Because of NA's, revised data:
      war fly ver end gro hai
ant    0   0   0   0   1   0
bee    0   1   0   0   1   1
cat    1   0   1   0   0   1
cpl    0   0   0   0   0   1
chi    1   0   1   1   1   1
cow    1   0   1   0   1   1
duc    1   1   1   0   1   0
eag    1   1   1   1   0   0
ele    1   0   1   1   1   0
fly    0   1   0   0   0   0
fro    0   0   1   1   0   0
her    0   0   1   0   1   0
lio    1   0   1   1   1   1
liz    0   0   1   0   0   0
lob    0   0   0   0   0   0
man    1   0   1   1   1   1
rab    1   0   1   0   1   1
sal    0   0   1   0   0   0
spi    0   0   0   0   0   1
wha    1   0   1   1   1   0
```

Figure 6.8: Revised data from mona output – part 1

Figure 6.8 is the data used by **mona**, in a binary (0 or 1) form. **mona()** also outputs details of the clustering, such as the variable used at each separation step:

```
Order of objects:
 [1] ant cpl spi lob bee fly fro her liz sal cat cow rab chi lio man ele wha duc eag
Variable used:
 [1] gro  NULL hai  fly  gro  ver  end  gro  NULL war  gro  NULL end  NULL NULL hai  NULL fly  end
Separation step:
 [1] 4 0 5 3 4 2 3 4 0 1 4 0 3 0 0 4 0 2 3
```

Figure 6.9: Cluster information from mona output – part 2

5. Plot a banner:

> **Note**
>
> To read up on the banner, refer to Struyf, Anja, Mia Hubert, and Peter Rousseeuw. *"Clustering in an object-oriented environment."* Journal of Statistical Software 1.4 (1997): 1-30.

```
plot(ma)
```

The plot is as follows:

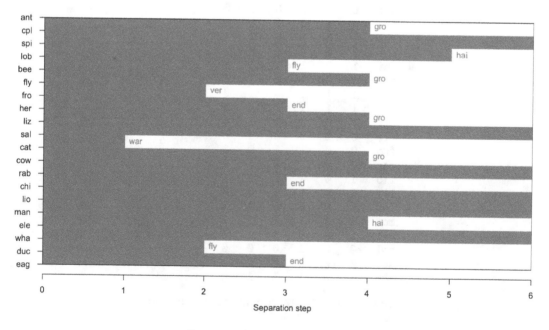

Figure 6.10: Banner using mona

To interpret the preceding graph, we start with all the elements in one group. At step one, we place all warm-blooded animals on one side (below **sal** on the **y**-axis) and all the rest on the other side (above and including **sal**). At step 2, the warm-blooded ones are split by whether they can fly, while the cold-blooded ones are split by whether they are a vertebrate. The process continues, recursively, until we can no longer affect a split.

DIANA

DIANA stands for **DI**visive **ANA**lysis clustering. It is a hierarchical clustering technique that starts with one cluster and subsequently divides the clusters until each cluster is just a single element. At each step, we select the cluster with the most dissimilar elements. The most dissimilar element within that cluster is then used as a starting point in the creation of a new cluster, consequently splitting the original cluster into two. Divisive coefficient is a unit that measures the amount of clustering structures found.

> **Note**
>
> For more information on DIANA, please refer to the work of Kaufman and Rousseeuw (1990), *Finding groups in data*. Rousseeuw, Peter J., and L. Kaufman. "*Finding groups in data.*" Hoboken: Wiley Online Library (1990).

In the next exercise, we will be covering the concepts of hierarchical clustering using DIANA.

Exercise 61: Implement Hierarchical Clustering Using DIANA

In this exercise, we will perform hierarchal clustering using DIANA. We will be using the built-in EU agricultural forces dataset. This contains the GNP (Gross National Product per capita) and the percentage of the population working in agriculture for all EU countries.

1. Attach the **cluster** package:

   ```
   library(cluster)
   ```

2. Load the **agriculture** dataset:

   ```
   data(agriculture)
   ```

3. Show the dataset:

```
agriculture
```

The output is as follows:

```
##
##          x    y
## B      16.8  2.7
## DK     21.3  5.7
## D      18.7  3.5
## GR      5.9 22.2
## E      11.4 10.9
## F      17.8  6.0
## IRL    10.9 14.0
## I      16.6  8.5
## L      21.0  3.5
## NL     16.4  4.3
## P       7.8 17.4
## UK     14.0  2.3
```

4. Apply the **diana()** function and print the output. Note that you do not need to understand the output for now, as we will plot the dendrogram to visualize the clusters in the next step. You can read the explanation of the output at **?diana**:

```
dv <- diana(agriculture, metric = "manhattan", stand = TRUE)
print(dv)
```

The output is as follows:

```
Merge:
         [,1] [,2]
[1,]      -1  -10
[2,]      -2   -9
[3,]      -3   -6
[4,]      -5   -7
[5,]       1  -12
[6,]       2    3
[7,]      -4  -11
[8,]       5   -8
[9,]       8    6
[10,]      7    4
[11,]      9   10
```

Figure 6.11: Merge information from the DIANA output – part 1

The order of objects, height, divisive coefficients, and available components are as follows:

```
Order of objects:
 [1] B   NL  UK  I   DK  L   D   F   GR  P   E   IRL
Height:
 [1] 0.4088056 0.9779013 1.8421424 2.4536949 0.5006743 1.2715233 0.7063356 7.3396907 1.3984306 3.5445277 0.7244841
Divisive coefficient:
 [1] 0.8830843

Available components:
 [1] "order"    "height"   "dc"       "merge"    "diss"     "call"     "order.lab" "data"
```

Figure 6.12: Output using diana – part 2

The **diana()** function creates clusters based on the suggested metrics, as shown in the preceding diagram.

5. Plot the banner and dendrogram:

    plot(dv)

    The banner plot will appear as follows:

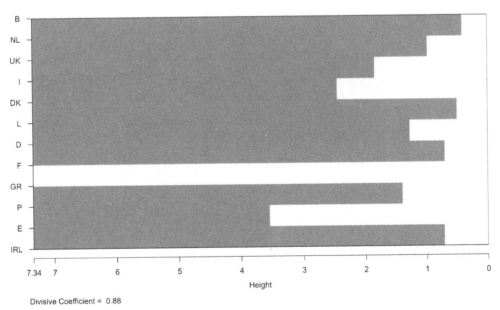

Figure 6.13: Banner using DIANA

Figure 6.13 shows the splitting banner from the **DIANA** algorithm. Imagine that you are starting off with all the countries in one group on the left, and the goal is to divide the group into smaller parts until you have the elements on the right. We split the group into two groups at a height of 7.34 (the *height* is the diameter of the cluster prior to splitting). The "**F**" group contains **F, D, L, DK, I, UK, NL**, and **B**. The "**GR**" group contains **GR, P, E**, and **IRL**. The "**GR**" group is split again at a height of ~3.5, and we now have a "**P**" group and an "**E**" group. The **P** group is split again at a height of ~1.3 into individual **P** and **GR** elements.

6. Press *Enter* to view the next plot:

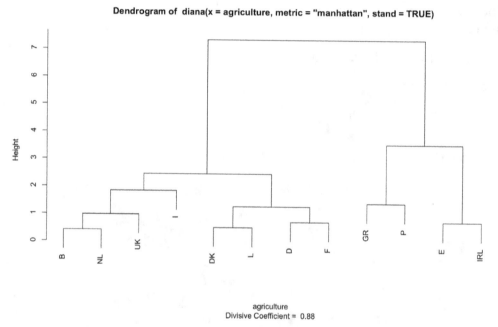

Figure 6.14: Dendrogram using DIANA

This dendrogram communicates the same information as the banner. Starting from the top, we split the cluster into two, one group with **B, NL, UK, I, DK, K, D,** and **F**, while the second group contains everything else. Each of the groups is then split into two as we go down and the elements become increasingly similar.

7. To view the dendrogram as text, use **str()**:

```
str(as.dendrogram(dv))
```

The output is as follows:

```
--[dendrogram w/ 2 branches and 12 members at h = 7.34]
  |--[dendrogram w/ 2 branches and 8 members at h = 2.45]
  |  |--[dendrogram w/ 2 branches and 4 members at h = 1.84]
  |  |  |--[dendrogram w/ 2 branches and 3 members at h = 0.978]
  |  |  |  |--[dendrogram w/ 2 branches and 2 members at h = 0.409]
  |  |  |  |  |--leaf "B"
  |  |  |  |  `--leaf "NL"
  |  |  |  `--leaf "UK"
  |  |  `--leaf "I"
  |  `--[dendrogram w/ 2 branches and 4 members at h = 1.27]
  |     |--[dendrogram w/ 2 branches and 2 members at h = 0.501]
  |     |  |--leaf "DK"
  |     |  `--leaf "L"
  |     `--[dendrogram w/ 2 branches and 2 members at h = 0.706]
  |        |--leaf "D"
  |        `--leaf "F"
  `--[dendrogram w/ 2 branches and 4 members at h = 3.54]
     |--[dendrogram w/ 2 branches and 2 members at h = 1.4]
     |  |--leaf "GR"
     |  `--leaf "P"
     `--[dendrogram w/ 2 branches and 2 members at h = 0.724]
        |--leaf "E"
        `--leaf "IRL"
```

Figure 6.15: Dendrogram using str() function

The **str()** representation of the dendrogram presents the exact splitting points. Notice, for example, the first split at height 7.34, and the next one at height 3.54.

AGNES

AGNES stands for **AG**glomerative **NES**ting and performs bottom-up or agglomerative clustering. It performs agglomerative hierarchal clustering on the given dataset. Using **agnes**, you can get the agglomerative coefficient. This coefficient denotes the amount of clustered structures found in the given dataset. Instead of *splitting* heterogeneous clusters, we now *merge* similar clusters.

Exercise 62: Agglomerative Clustering Using AGNES

For this exercise, we will use the built-in R dataset **votes.repub**, which contains the state-wise percentage of Republican votes in 31 US presidential elections.

1. Attach the **cluster** package:

   ```
   library(cluster)
   ```

2. Load the dataset:

   ```
   data(votes.repub)
   ```

3. Perform agglomerative clustering using AGNES:

   ```
   agn <- agnes(votes.repub)
   agn
   ```

   The output is as follows:

   ```
   ##
   ## Call:      agnes(x = votes.repub)
   ## Agglomerative coefficient:  0.7688431
   ## Order of objects:
   ##  [1] Alabama    Georgia    Texas    Louisiana  Arkansas   Florida
   ##  [7] Mississippi    South Carolina    Alaska    Michigan
   ##         Connecticut    New York
   ## [13] New Hampshire    Illinois    New Jersey    Pennsylvania
   ##         Indiana  Ohio
   ## [19] California    Oregon    Washington    Iowa    South Dakota
   ## [24] Kansas    Nebraska    Minnesota    North Dakota    Wisconsin
   ##         Hawaii    Maine
   ## [31] Massachusetts    Rhode Island    Arizona    Nevada    Montana
   ## [36] Colorado    Idaho    Wyoming    Utah    Oklahoma    Delaware
   ## [42] Missouri    New Mexico    West Virginia    Kentucky
   ## [46] Maryland    North Carolina    Tennessee    Virginia  Vermont
   ## Height (summary):
   ##    Min. 1st Qu.  Median    Mean 3rd Qu.    Max.
   ##   17.20   26.89   34.75   41.93   50.08  144.14
   ##
   ## Available components:
   ## [1] "order" "height" "ac" "merge" "diss" "call" "method"
   ## [8] "order.lab" "data"
   ```

From the height summary, we can tell that the first merge was made at a height of 17.20, and that the last merge was made at a height of 144.14.

4. Plot the **bannerplot** for **agnes**:

   bannerplot(agn)

   The banner plot is as follows:

Bannerplot

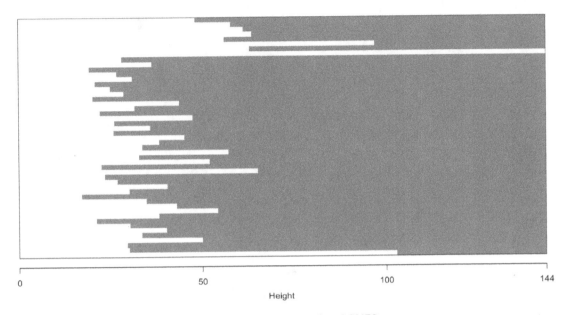

Figure 6.16: Banner using AGNES

> **Note**
>
> The white section of the banner plot represents the height.

Notice that the white section is on the left in *Figure 6.16*. We start with individual elements and group (merge) similar elements. As seen in the previous step, we make the first merge at height ~17, and successively merge up to the last merge at height ~144.

5. Plot the tree:

   pltree(agn)

The output is as follows:

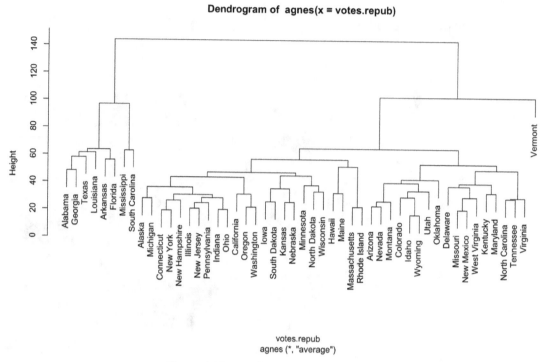

Figure 6.17: Dendrogram using AGNES

Figure 6.17 shows the dendrogram representation of the clustering. The first merge happens between Idaho and Wyoming at height ~17. We then group Connecticut and New York at height 19 and continue merging until the last grouping at height 144.

Distance Metrics in Clustering

Distance metrics, such as **Euclidean** and **Manhattan Distance** metrics, can be used to calculate **dissimilarity matrices**, containing the distances between the elements. These are useful when grouping elements or splitting clusters.

Euclidean distance uses the Pythagorean theorem to calculate the distance between two points, as shown in the following diagram:

$$d_{euc}(x, y) = \sqrt{\sum_{i=1}^{n}(x_i - y_i)^2}$$

Figure 6.18: Euclidean distance

The Manhattan distance calculates the distance that needs to be traveled to reach from one point to another:

$$d_{man}(x, y) = \sum_{i=1}^{n} |(x_i - y_i)|$$

Figure 6.19: Manhattan distance

Here, **x** and **y** are two vectors of length **n**.

The main difference is that the Euclidean distance "penalizes" outlier differences more (if, for instance, two objects are similar in most attributes but very different in one aspect) due to squaring. Note how this is similar to the discussion of the **RMSE** and **MAE** metrics from *Chapter 5, Linear and Logistic Regression Models*.

For this topic, we will see how distance metrics, such as Euclidean and Manhattan distance, can be used to calculate dissimilarity matrices.

Exercise 63: Calculate Dissimilarity Matrices Using Euclidean and Manhattan Distance

In this exercise, we will use R's **dist()** function, which computes a pairwise distance matrix, on the built-in **agriculture** dataset. We will compare the Euclidean and Manhattan distance metrics. The dataset contains the GNP (Gross National Product per capita) and the percentage of the population working in agriculture for all EU countries.

1. Attach the **cluster** package:

   ```
   library(cluster)
   ```

2. Load the dataset:

   ```
   data(agriculture)
   ```

3. Compute the Euclidean distance:

   ```
   dist(agriculture) # Euclidean distance is the default
   ```

The output is as follows:

```
              B        DK         D        GR        E        F      IRL        I        L
DK     5.408327
D      2.061553  3.405877
GR    22.339651 22.570113 22.661200
E      9.818350 11.182576 10.394710 12.567418
F      3.448188  3.512834  2.657066 20.100995  8.060397
IRL   12.747549 13.306014 13.080138  9.604166  3.140064 10.564563
I      5.803447  5.470832  5.423099 17.383325  5.727128  2.773085  7.920859
L      4.275512  2.220360  2.300000 24.035391 12.121056  4.060788 14.569145  6.660330
NL     1.649242  5.096077  2.435159 20.752349  8.280097  2.202272 11.150785  4.204759  4.669047
P     17.236299 17.864490 17.664088  5.162364  7.430343 15.164432  4.601087 12.515990 19.168985
UK     2.828427  8.052950  4.850773 21.485344  8.984431  5.303772 12.103718  6.723095  7.102112
             NL        P
DK
D
GR
E
F
IRL
I
L
NL
P     15.670673
UK     3.124100 16.323296
```

Figure 6.20: Dissimilarity matrix using the Euclidean distance

Figure 6.20 shows the dissimilarity matrix with the Euclidean distances between the countries. The greater the value, the more dissimilar the countries are. For instance, **B** is most similar to **NL**, and least similar to **GR**.

4. Compute the Manhattan distances:

```
dist(agriculture, method = "manhattan")
```

The output is as follows:

```
         B    DK    D    GR    E    F  IRL    I    L   NL    P
DK     7.5
D      2.7   4.8
GR    30.4  31.9 31.5
E     13.6  15.1 14.7 16.8
F      4.3   3.8  3.4 28.1 11.3
IRL   17.2  18.7 18.3 13.2  3.6 14.9
I      6.0   7.5  7.1 24.4  7.6  3.7 11.2
L      5.0   2.5  2.3 33.8 17.0  5.7 20.6  9.4
NL     2.0   6.3  3.1 28.4 11.6  3.1 15.2  4.4  5.4
P     23.7  25.2 24.8  6.7 10.1 21.4  6.5 17.7 27.1 21.7
UK     3.2  10.7  5.9 28.0 11.2  7.5 14.8  8.8  8.2  4.4 21.3
```

Figure 6.21: Dissimilarity matrix using the Manhattan distance

The Manhattan distance is interpreted in the same way. The greater the distance, the more dissimilar the countries are. For instance, **B** is still most similar to **NL**, and least similar to **GR**.

The **dist()** function only allows numeric values. If we had other types of variables (such as nominal, ordinal, or binary variables), we could use the **daisy()** function. In our case, the results will be the same, but let's try it anyway.

5. Use R's **daisy()** function to compute pairwise Euclidean distances:

```
daisy(agriculture, metric = "euclidean", stand = FALSE)
```

The output is as follows:

```
Dissimilarities :
           B        DK        D        GR        E        F        IRL       I        L
DK    5.408327
D     2.061553  3.405877
GR   22.339651 22.570113 22.661200
E     9.818350 11.182576 10.394710 12.567418
F     3.448188  3.512834  2.657066 20.100995  8.060397
IRL  12.747549 13.306014 13.080138  9.604166  3.140064 10.564563
I     5.803447  5.470832  5.423099 17.383325  5.727128  2.773085  7.920859
L     4.275512  2.220360  2.300000 24.035391 12.121056  4.060788 14.569145  6.660330
NL    1.649242  5.096077  2.435159 20.752349  8.280097  2.202272 11.150785  4.204759  4.669047
P    17.236299 17.864490 17.664088  5.162364  7.430343 15.164432  4.601087 12.515990 19.168985
UK    2.828427  8.052950  4.850773 21.485344  8.984431  5.303772 12.103718  6.723095  7.102112
           NL        P
DK
D
GR
E
F
IRL
I
L
NL
P    15.670673
UK    3.124100 16.323296

Metric :  euclidean
Number of objects : 12
```

Figure 6.22: Dissimilarity matrix using the Euclidean distance using daisy()

6. Use R's **daisy()** function to compute pairwise Manhattan distances:

```
daisy(agriculture, metric = "manhattan", stand = FALSE)
```

The output is as follows:

```
Dissimilarities :
      B    DK    D   GR    E    F  IRL    I    L   NL    P
DK   7.5
D    2.7   4.8
GR  30.4  31.9 31.5
E   13.6  15.1 14.7 16.8
F    4.3   3.8  3.4 28.1 11.3
IRL 17.2  18.7 18.3 13.2  3.6 14.9
I    6.0   7.5  7.1 24.4  7.6  3.7 11.2
L    5.0   2.5  2.3 33.8 17.0  5.7 20.6  9.4
NL   2.0   6.3  3.1 28.4 11.6  3.1 15.2  4.4  5.4
P   23.7  25.2 24.8  6.7 10.1 21.4  6.5 17.7 27.1 21.7
UK   3.2  10.7  5.9 28.0 11.2  7.5 14.8  8.8  8.2  4.4 21.3

Metric :  manhattan
Number of objects : 12
```

Figure 6.23: Dissimilarity matrix using the Manhattan distance and daisy()

The interpretation is the same as for step 4. In the next section, we will look at correlation-based distance metrics.

Correlation-Based Distance Metrics

The intuition behind this type of metric is that two items are considered similar if they are highly correlated. In fields such as genomics, correlation-based metrics are commonly used. Here are some common correlation-based distance metrics:

Pearson correlation distance:

Given two variables, **x** and **y**, the Pearson correlation distance is computed by:

$$d_{cor}(x, y) = 1 - \frac{\sum_{i=1}^{n}(x_i - \bar{x})(y_i - \bar{y})}{\sqrt{\sum_{i=1}^{n}(x_i - \bar{x})^2 \sum_{i=1}^{n}(y_i - \bar{y})^2}}$$

Figure 6.24: Pearson correlation distance

Pearson correlation measures the degree of a linear relationship between two profiles.

Spearman correlation distance:

Given two variables, **x** and **y**, the Spearman correlation distance is computed by:

$$d_{spear}(x, y) = 1 - \frac{\sum_{i=1}^{n}(x'_i - \bar{x}')(y'_i - \bar{y}')}{\sqrt{\sum_{i=1}^{n}(x'_i - \bar{x}')^2 \sum_{i=1}^{n}(y'_i - \bar{y}')^2}}$$

Where $x'_i = rank(x_i)$ and $y'_i = rank(y_i)$.

Figure 6.25: Spearman correlation distance

Pearson correlation is used to evaluate the linear relationship between continuous variables. Spearman and Kendall correlations are non-parametric and are used to perform rank-based correlation analysis. The rank of a vector element is its index in the sorted version of the vector. You can use the **rank()** function in R to find the rank of each element. If we ran **rank(c(0,5,3,6,7))**, the result would be **c(1,3,2,4,5)**.

Kendall correlation distance:

The Kendall correlation method is calculated from the number of concordant and discordant pairs:

$$d_{kend}(x,y) = \frac{n_c - n_d}{\frac{1}{2}n(n-1)}$$

Figure 6.26: Kendall correlation distance

Here is the definitions of the variables used in the aforementioned equation:

- n_c is the total number of concordant pairs
- n_d is the total number of discordant pairs
- **n** is the size of *x* and *y*

Given two pairs, x_1, y_1 and x_2, y_2, a concordant pair is one such that $sgn(x_1-x_2) = sgn(y_1-y_2)$, where:

$$sgn\ x = \begin{cases} -1 & : & x < 0 \\ 0 & : & x = 0 \\ 1 & : & x > 0 \end{cases}$$

Figure 6.27: sgn values of x

Similarly, a discordant pair is one such that $sgn(x_1-x_2) = -sgn(y_1-y_2)$.

In the next exercise, we will calculate the correlation-based metrics based on these formulas.

> **Note**
>
> For more information on correlation-based distance metrics, please refer the official documentation: https://www.rdocumentation.org/packages/amap/versions/0.8-17/topics/Dist

Exercise 64: Apply Correlation-Based Metrics

In this exercise, we will establish the Pearson correlation distance matrix, the Spearman correlation distance matrix, and the Kendall correlation distance matrix. We will only look at the five first rows to simplify the output.

1. Install the **factoextra** R package:

   ```
   install.packages("factoextra")
   ```

2. Attach the **factoextra** package:

   ```
   library(factoextra)
   ```

3. Load the dataset:

   ```
   df <- swiss
   ```

4. Compute the distance using the Pearson correlation:

   ```
   pearson_dist <- get_dist(df, method = "pearson")
   ```

5. Display the results as a matrix:

```
round(as.matrix(pearson_dist)[1:5, 1:5], 1)
```

The output is as follows:

```
              Courtelary Delemont Franches-Mnt Moutier Neuveville
Courtelary          0.0      0.5          0.5     0.1        0.1
Delemont            0.5      0.0          0.0     0.2        0.6
Franches-Mnt        0.5      0.0          0.0     0.2        0.6
Moutier             0.1      0.2          0.2     0.0        0.1
Neuveville          0.1      0.6          0.6     0.1        0.0
```

Figure 6.28: Pearson correlation metrics

The highest values in the (visible) correlation distance matrix are between Neuveville and Delmont, and between Neuveville and Franches-Mnt.

6. Repeat the process using the **spearman** and **kendall** correlation metrics. Compute distances using the Spearman correlation:

```
spearman_dist <- get_dist(df, method = "spearman")
```

7. Display the results as a matrix:

```
round(as.matrix(spearman_dist)[1:5, 1:5], 1)
```

The output is as follows:

```
              Courtelary Delemont Franches-Mnt Moutier Neuveville
Courtelary          0.0      1.0          0.9     0.5        0.1
Delemont            1.0      0.0          0.0     0.2        0.9
Franches-Mnt        0.9      0.0          0.0     0.2        0.9
Moutier             0.5      0.2          0.2     0.0        0.3
Neuveville          0.1      0.9          0.9     0.3        0.0
```

Figure 6.29: Spearman correlation metrics

The highest value in the (visible) correlation distance matrix is between **Courtelary** and **Delemont**.

8. Compute the distances using the **kendall** correlation metric:

```
kendall_dist <- get_dist(df, method = "kendall")
```

9. Display the results as a matrix:

```
round(as.matrix(kendall_dist)[1:5, 1:5], 1)
```

The output is as follows:

	Courtelary	Delemont	Franches-Mnt	Moutier	Neuveville
Courtelary	0.0	0.9	0.9	0.5	0.1
Delemont	0.9	0.0	0.0	0.4	0.8
Franches-Mnt	0.9	0.0	0.0	0.3	0.7
Moutier	0.5	0.4	0.3	0.0	0.4
Neuveville	0.1	0.8	0.7	0.4	0.0

Figure 6.30: Kendall correlation metrics

The highest values in the (visible) correlation distance matrix are between **Courtelary** and **Delemont**, and between **Courtelary** and **Frances-Mnt**.

As we can tell from the varying results, the type of correlation-based distance metric chosen would affect the algorithms relying on the correlation distances matrix.

Applications of Clustering

Clustering is useful in a variety of fields. We will look at two of them in detail:

- **Market segmentation**: Segmentation is the process of splitting a heterogeneous group of consumers or customers into smaller homogeneous groups. These smaller groups can be targeted differently based on their characteristics and behavior. Segmentation is important to businesses because it shapes both marketing efforts and product development. Businesses designing products must decide which product is targeted to which segment of consumers or customers. They must consequently decide what features to include, how to price the product, and how to take it to market. All these actions are heavily influenced by the characteristics of the different segments.

  Most businesses start off not knowing how to group their customers. Clustering is useful in helping these businesses to identify segments in their data.

- **Document clustering and information retrieval**: In the information and knowledge age, we have seen unprecedented growth in the amount of digital information. This information is often in documents that include raw text in different formats. Tweets, news articles, blogs, research papers, and publications can all be considered documents. In order to be able to group news articles that are related, search engine companies often employ text and document clustering techniques.

Additionally, in order to pick out high-level topics, document clustering can be applied together with topic modeling to perform some form of information retrieval.

k-means Clustering

The k-means clustering algorithm is one of the most popular clustering techniques. It produces hard (an element can only be a member of one cluster), flat, and polythetic (membership is determined by similarity based on multiple attributes) clusters. The k-means algorithm has no training or testing data *per se*. It works by creating clusters around **centroids**. A centroid is an average cluster member; that is, the center of a cluster. k-means requires us to specify the number of clusters (*k*). It is important to note that the number of clusters specified greatly affects the performance of the k-means algorithm. Deciding on the number of clusters can be informed by domain knowledge. For example, knowing about the features of a given dataset will help to set parameters for clusters. In situations where this information is not available, there are two techniques we can use to help us decide on the correct number of clusters.

Exploratory Data Analysis Using Scatter Plots

In situations where data can be plotted in two dimensions, we can use scatter plots to perform exploratory data analysis:

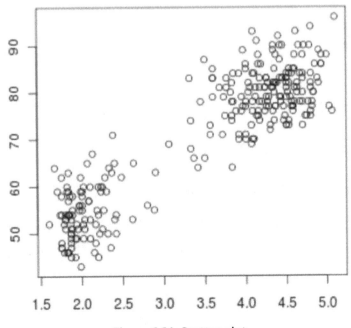

Figure 6.31: Scatter plot

Just by eyeballing how the data is grouped, we can come up with an estimate of the number of clusters that exist within the data. In *Figure 6.31*, we can identify two clusters within the data.

The Elbow Method

The **elbow** method works by running k-means successively with different values of **k** each time, computing an average score for all of the clusters. This score is usually the **distortion score**, which is calculated as the **sum of squared distances** from each point to its centroid. Other scores that might be used include the **CH score** (Calinski and Harabasz) and the **Silhouette Coefficient**. The CH score is calculated as the ratio of dispersion between, and within, the clusters. The Silhouette Coefficient is a score ranging from –1 to +1 that signifies how similar a sample is to its own cluster compared to other clusters.

The optimal number of clusters is selected as the point where the line graph makes an **elbow**, as shown in *Figure 6.32*:

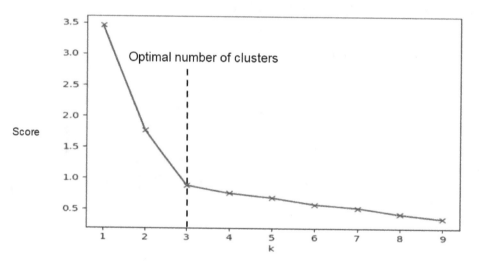

Figure 6.32: The elbow method

Here are the basic steps of the k-means clustering algorithm:

1. Start by specifying the number of clusters (**k**).

2. Initialize **k** random centroids based on datapoints in the data.

3. Repeat the following steps:

Cluster assignment: For each point, find the nearest centroid and assign it to that cluster. To find the nearest centroid, use one of the distance metrics discussed previously, such as the Euclidean distance.

Move the centroid: Adjust each centroid so that it minimizes the distance within the cluster variance.

Stop after a predetermined number of iterations, or once cluster assignment stops making any changes.

We will implement k-means in the next exercise.

Exercise 65: Implementation of k-means Clustering in R

For this exercise, we will use a publicly available dataset that looks at the arrests per state within the US in 1973. The data has 4 columns and 50 rows and appears as follows in an Excel sheet:

> **Note**
>
> The dataset has been modified and can be found at https://github.com/ TrainingByPackt/Practical-Machine-Learning-with-R/blob/master/Data/USArrests. csv. The USArrests dataset is derived from real crime data. However, due to sensitivity and the violent and extreme nature of some of the crimes, we have taken the editorial decision to leave out descriptions. Readers should use their own discretion as to whether they wish to research any further details about the USArrests dataset.

1. Attach the required packages:

```
library(cluster)
library(factoextra) # used for visualization
# unlike earlier where we used it for correlation
```

2. Load the data:

```
df <- read.csv("USArrests.csv")
```

3. Set the row names to the values of the **X** column (the state names). Remove the **X** column afterward:

```
rownames(df) <- df$X
df$X <- NULL
```

> **Note**
>
> The row names (states) become a column, **X**, when you save it as a CSV file. So, we need to change it back, since the row names are used in the plot in step 7.

4. Scale and standardize the data using the **scale()** function:

```
df <- scale(df)
```

5. Find three clusters in the data. Note that the **kmeans()** function only accepts numeric columns. In case of categorical columns, we would need to convert those columns to numeric using methods such as one hot encoding, label encoding and so on.

```
k3 <- kmeans(df, centers = 3, nstart = 20)
str(k3)
```

The output is as follows:

```
List of 9
 $ cluster      : Named int [1:50] 3 3 3 3 3 3 1 1 3 3 ...
 ..- attr(*, "names")= chr [1:50] "1" "2" "3" "4" ...
 $ centers      : num [1:3, 1:5] 0.304 0.282 -0.407 -0.489 -0.962 ...
 ..- attr(*, "dimnames")=List of 2
 .. ..$ : chr [1:3] "1" "2" "3"
 .. ..$ : chr [1:5] "X" "Crime1" "Crime2" "Crime3" ...
 $ totss        : num 245
 $ withinss     : num [1:3] 31.8 21.2 68.7
 $ tot.withinss: num 122
 $ betweenss    : num 123
 $ size         : int [1:3] 16 13 21
 $ iter         : int 3
 $ ifault       : int 0
 - attr(*, "class")= chr "kmeans"
```

Figure 6.33: Cluster information

Printing out the **kmeans** object as in the preceding example returns the following elements:

1.	cluster	A vector of integers (from 1:k) indicating the cluster to which each point is allocated.
2.	centers	A matrix of cluster centers.
3.	totss	Total sum of squares.
4.	withinss	Vector of within-cluster sum of squares, one component per cluster.
5.	tot.withinss	Total within-cluster sum of squares, i.e. sum(withinss).
6.	betweenss	The between-cluster sum of squares, i.e. totss-tot.withinss.
7.	size	The number of points in each cluster.
8.	iter	The number of (outer) iterations.
9	ifault	integer: indicator of a possible algorithm problem – for experts.

Figure 6.34: k-means object

6. View **k3**:

```
k3
```

The output of k-means clustering is as follows:

```
##
## K-means clustering with 3 clusters of sizes 17, 13, 20
##
## Cluster means:
##       Crime1      Crime2      Crime3      Crime4
## 1 -0.4469795 -0.3465138   0.4788049 -0.2571398
## 2 -0.9615407 -1.1066010 -0.9301069 -0.9667633
```

```
## 3  1.0049340  1.0138274  0.1975853  0.8469650
##
## Clustering vector:
##   Alabama Alaska Arizona Arkansas California Colorado
##      3      3      3       1        3         3
##   Connecticut Delaware Florida Georgia Hawaii Idaho
##        1          1        3        3       1     2
##   Illinois Indiana Iowa Kansas Kentucky Louisiana
##      3        1      2     1       2         3
##   Maine Maryland Massachusetts Michigan Minnesota Mississippi
##     2       3          1           3         2          3
##   Missouri Montana Nebraska Nevada  New Hampshire New Jersey
##      3        2        2       3          2            1
##   New Mexico New York North Carolina North Dakota Ohio Oklahoma
##       3          3          3              2        1      1
##   Oregon Pennsylvania Rhode Island South Carolina South Dakota
##     1         1            1              3              2
##   Tennessee Texas Utah Vermont Virginia Washington
##      3        3     1     2        1         1
##   West Virginia Wisconsin Wyoming
##        2            2         1
##
## Within cluster sum of squares by cluster:
## [1] 19.62285 11.95246 46.74796
##  (between_SS / total_SS =  60.0 %)
##
## Available components:
##
## [1] "cluster"      "centers"       "totss"         "withinss"      "tot.
withinss" "betweenss"
## [7] "size"         "iter"          "ifault"
```

7. Use the **fviz_cluster()** function:

```
fviz_cluster(k3, data = df)
```

The output will be as follows:

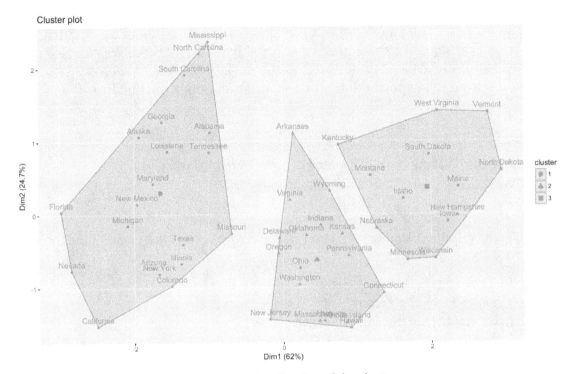

Figure 6.35: Visualization of the clusters

We used three clusters in the previous example. How do we determine the optimal number of clusters?

8. To apply the **elbow** method described earlier, we need to install the **NbClust** package:

```
install.packages("NbClust")
```

9. Thereafter, we can attach the package:

    ```
    library(NbClust)
    ```

    The **fviz_nbclust()** function plots the score against the number of clusters, k, as shown in the following diagram. In this example, we use "**wss**", which stands for **within cluster sums of squares**. This measures the variability within a cluster. The smaller it is, the more compact the clusters are. The silhouette coefficient described earlier can also be used by specifying it as a method. We can also use the **gap statistic**, which is calculated as the deviation of the observed intracluster variation from the expected intracluster variation under the null hypothesis.

    > **Note**
    >
    > To learn more about the null hypothesis, refer to the following link:
    > https://en.wikipedia.org/wiki/Null_hypothesis

10. Use the **wss** method to measure the variation within the cluster and plot the **elbow** graph:

    ```
    fviz_nbclust(df, kmeans, method = "wss") +
        geom_vline(xintercept = 4, linetype = 2) +
        labs(subtitle = "Elbow method")
    ```

The output is as follows:

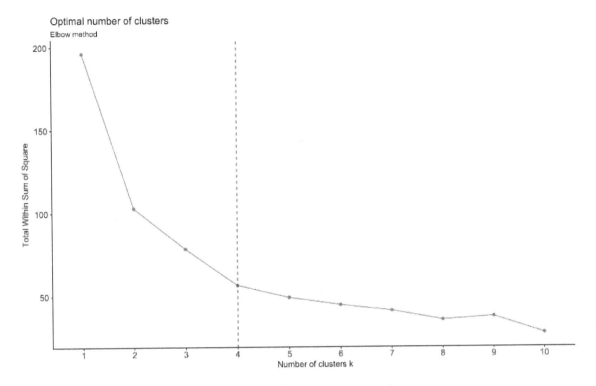

Figure 6.36: Elbow graph using wss

Observing *Figure* 6.36, we can determine that the optimal number of clusters is four. Running the k-means code from earlier, but with **k** set as **4**, yields a slightly different visualization:

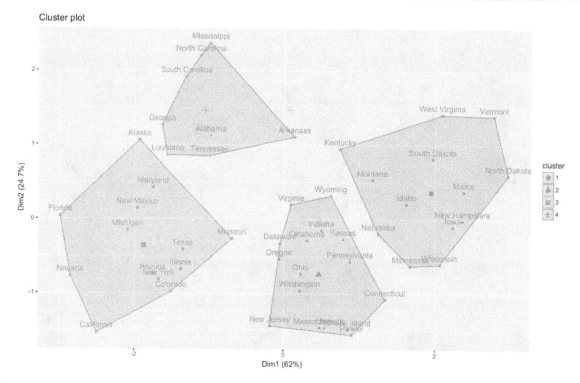

Figure 6.37: Visualization after performing wss

These clusters are better as the points are closer to their centroid, as seen in *Figure* 6.37.

Activity 20: Perform DIANA, AGNES, and k-means on the Built-In Motor Car Dataset

This activity builds upon earlier exercises that implemented DIANA, AGNES, and k-means clustering on different datasets. The aim of this activity is to implement different clustering techniques as well as to compare the results of each method and find the best clusters. We want to implement three clustering techniques using the **cars** dataset.

The dataset can be found at https://github.com/TrainingByPackt/Practical-Machine-Learning-with-R/blob/master/Data/mtcars.csv.

Here are the steps to complete the activity:

1. Attach the **cluster** and **factoextra** packages.

2. Load the dataset.

3. Prepare the data as demonstrated in the preceding implementation. Set the row names to the values of the **X** column and remove it, remove rows with missing data, and standardize the dataset.

4. Implement divisive hierarchical clustering using DIANA. This is similar to *Exercise 63, Implement Hierarchical Clustering Using DIANA*. For easy comparison, save the dendrogram output.

5. Implement bottom-up hierarchical clustering using AGNES. This is similar to *Exercise 64, Agglomerative Clustering Using AGNES*. Take note of the dendrogram created for comparison purposes later on.

6. Implement k-means clustering. Use the **elbow** method to determine the optimal number of clusters.

7. For easy comparison, consider the elements in the smaller clusters for each method.

Expected output:

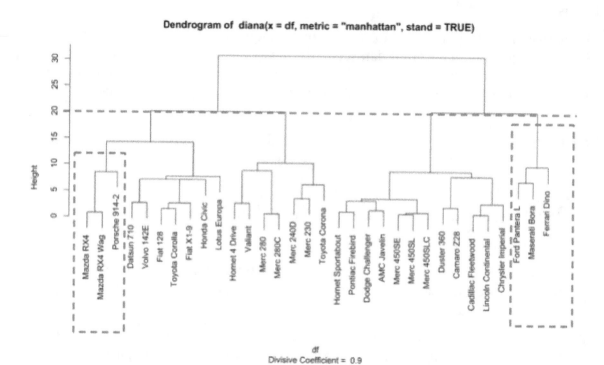

Figure 6.38: Dendrogram for DIANA with a cut at 20

The dendrogram for AGNES with a cut at 4 will look as follows:

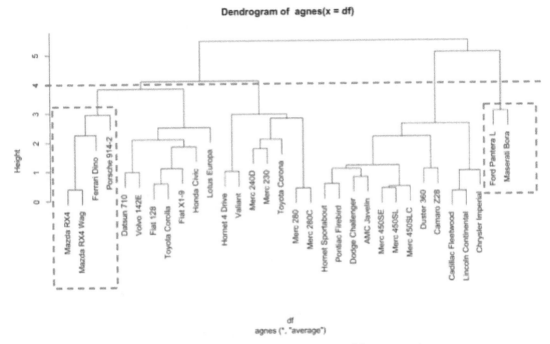

Figure 6.39: Dendrogram for AGENS with a cut at 4

The following output is obtained after k-means clustering is performed:

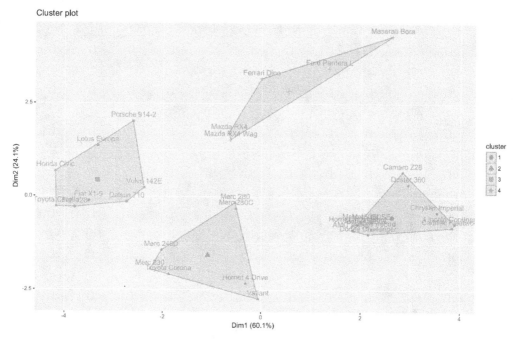

Figure 6.40: K-means clustering

> **Note**
>
> The solution for this activity can be found on page 379.

Summary

In this chapter, we have learned to differentiate between supervised and unsupervised learning. We also performed and compared the DIANA, AGNES, and k-means clustering techniques, and discussed the applications of clustering.

We have thus covered the basics of identifying machine learning-related business problems, preparing datasets for analysis, and selecting and training suitable model architectures and evaluating their performance. We covered the basics of a commonly used set of machine learning methods and used different R packages, such as **rpart**, **randomForest**, **MICE**, **groupdata2**, and **cvms**. Having worked with tasks such as classification, regression, and clustering, you now possess the tools required to tackle many of your data-related business problems.

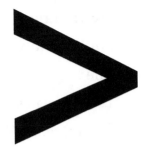

Appendix

About

This section is included to assist the students to perform the activities present in the book. It includes detailed steps that are to be performed by the students to complete and achieve the objectives of the book.

Chapter 1: An Introduction to Machine Learning

Activity 1: Finding the Distribution of Diabetic Patients in the PimaIndiansDiabetes Dataset

Solution:

1. Load the dataset.

   ```
   PimaIndiansDiabetes<-read.csv("PimaIndiansDiabetes.csv")
   ```

2. Create a variable **PimaIndiansDiabetesData** for further use.

   ```
   #Assign it to a local variable for further use
   PimaIndiansDiabetesData<- PimaIndiansDiabetes
   ```

3. Use the **head()** function to view the first five rows of the dataset.

   ```
   #Display the first five rows
   head(PimaIndiansDiabetesData)
   ```

   The output is as follows:

	pregnant	glucose	pressure	triceps	insulin	mass	pedigree	age	diabetes
1	6	148	72	35	0	33.6	0.627	50	pos
2	1	85	66	29	0	26.6	0.351	31	neg
3	8	183	64	0	0	23.3	0.672	32	pos
4	1	89	66	23	94	28.1	0.167	21	neg
5	0	137	40	35	168	43.1	2.288	33	pos
6	5	116	74	0	0	25.6	0.201	30	neg

   From the preceding data, identify the input features and find the column that is the predictor variable. The output variable is diabetes.

4. Display the different categories of the output variable:

   ```
   levels(PimaIndiansDiabetesData$diabetes)
   ```

   The output is as follows:

   ```
   [1] "neg" "pos"
   ```

5. Load the required library for plotting graphs.

   ```
   library(ggplot2)
   ```

6. Create a bar plot to view the output variables.

```
barplot <- ggplot(data= PimaIndiansDiabetesData, aes(x=age))
barplot + geom_histogram(binwidth=0.2, color="black",
aes(fill=diabetes))  + ggtitle("Bar plot of Age")
```

The output is as follows:

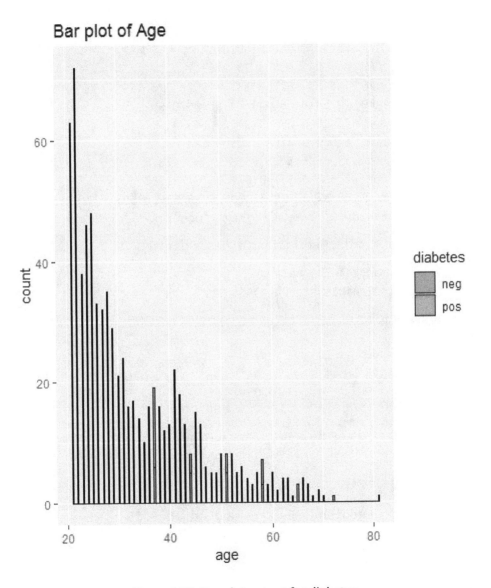

Figure 1.36: Bar plot output for diabetes

We can conclude that we have the most data for the age group of 20-30. Graphical representation thus allows us to understand the data.

Activity 2: Grouping the PimaIndiansDiabetes Data

Solution :

1. View the structure of the **PimaIndiansDiabetes** dataset.

```
#View the structure of the data
str(PimaIndiansDiabetesData)
```

The output is as follows:

```
'data.frame':768 obs. of  9 variables:
 $ pregnant: num  6 1 8 1 0 5 3 10 2 8 ...
 $ glucose : num  148 85 183 89 137 116 78 115 197 125 ...
 $ pressure: num  72 66 64 66 40 74 50 0 70 96 ...
 $ triceps : num  35 29 0 23 35 0 32 0 45 0 ...
 $ insulin : num  0 0 0 94 168 0 88 0 543 0 ...
 $ mass    : num  33.6 26.6 23.3 28.1 43.1 25.6 31 35.3 30.5 0 ...
 $ pedigree: num  0.627 0.351 0.672 0.167 2.288 ...
 $ age     : num  50 31 32 21 33 30 26 29 53 54 ...
 $ diabetes: Factor w/ 2 levels "neg","pos": 2 1 2 1 2 1 2 1 2 2 ...
```

2. View the summary of the **PimaIndiansDiabetes** dataset.

```
#View the Summary of the data
summary(PimaIndiansDiabetesData)
```

The output is as follows:

```
    pregnant          glucose          pressure          triceps
 Min.   : 0.000   Min.   :  0.0   Min.   :  0.00   Min.   : 0.00
 1st Qu.: 1.000   1st Qu.: 99.0   1st Qu.: 62.00   1st Qu.: 0.00
 Median : 3.000   Median :117.0   Median : 72.00   Median :23.00
 Mean   : 3.845   Mean   :120.9   Mean   : 69.11   Mean   :20.54
 3rd Qu.: 6.000   3rd Qu.:140.2   3rd Qu.: 80.00   3rd Qu.:32.00
 Max.   :17.000   Max.   :199.0   Max.   :122.00   Max.   :99.00
    insulin           mass           pedigree            age
 Min.   :  0.0   Min.   : 0.00   Min.   :0.0780   Min.   :21.00
 1st Qu.:  0.0   1st Qu.:27.30   1st Qu.:0.2437   1st Qu.:24.00
 Median : 30.5   Median :32.00   Median :0.3725   Median :29.00
 Mean   : 79.8   Mean   :31.99   Mean   :0.4719   Mean   :33.24
 3rd Qu.:127.2   3rd Qu.:36.60   3rd Qu.:0.6262   3rd Qu.:41.00
 Max.   :846.0   Max.   :67.10   Max.   :2.4200   Max.   :81.00
 diabetes
 neg:500
 pos:268
```

Figure 1.37: Summary of PimaIndiansDiabetes data

3. View the statistics of the columns of `PimaIndiansDiabetes` dataset grouped by the **diabetes** column.

```
#Perform Group by and view statistics for the columns
#Install the package
install.packages("psych")

library(psych) #Load package psych to use function describeBy
Use describeby with pregnancy and diabetes columns.
describeBy(PimaIndiansDiabetesData$pregnant,
PimaIndiansDiabetesData$diabetes)
```

The output is as follows:

```
Descriptive statistics by group
group: neg
    vars   n mean    sd median trimmed  mad min max range skew kurtosis    se
X1     1 500  3.3 3.02      2    2.88 2.97   0  13    13 1.11     0.65 0.13
------------------------------------------------------------------------------

--------------------

group: pos
    vars   n mean    sd median trimmed  mad min max range skew kurtosis    se
X1     1 268 4.87 3.74      4     4.6 4.45   0  17    17  0.5    -0.47 0.23
```

We can view the mean, median, min, and max of the number of times pregnant attribute in the group of people who have diabetes (pos) and who do not have diabetes (neg).

4. Use **describeby** with pressure and diabetes.

```
describeBy(PimaIndiansDiabetesData$pressure,
PimaIndiansDiabetesData$diabetes)
```

The output is as follows:

```
 Descriptive statistics by group
group: neg
    vars   n  mean    sd median trimmed   mad min max range skew
kurtosis   se
X1     1 500 68.18 18.06     70   69.97 11.86   0 122   122 -1.8     5.58
0.81
------------------------------------------------------------------------------

--------------------
```

```
group: pos
   vars   n  mean    sd median trimmed    mad min max range  skew
kurtosis   se
X1     1 268 70.82 21.49     74   73.99 11.86   0 114   114 -1.92      4.53
1.31
```

We can view the **mean**, **median**, **min**, and **max** of the pressure in the group of people who have diabetes (**pos**) and who do not have diabetes (**neg**).

We have learned how to view the structure of any dataset and print the statistics about the range of every column using **summary()**.

Activity 3: Performing EDA on the PimaIndiansDiabetes Dataset

Solution:

1. Load the **PimaIndiansDaibetes** dataset.

   ```
   PimaIndiansDiabetes<-read.csv("PimaIndiansDiabetes.csv")
   ```

2. View the correlation among the features of the PimaIndiansDiabetes dataset.

   ```
   #Calculate correlations
   correlation <- cor(PimaIndiansDiabetesData[,1:4])
   ```

3. Round it to the second nearest digit.

   ```
   #Round the values to the nearest 2 digit
   round(correlation,2)
   ```

   The output is as follows:

   ```
             pregnant glucose pressure triceps
   pregnant     1.00    0.13     0.14   -0.08
   glucose      0.13    1.00     0.15    0.06
   pressure     0.14    0.15     1.00    0.21
   triceps     -0.08    0.06     0.21    1.00
   ```

4. Pair them on a plot.

   ```
   #Plot the pairs on a plot
   pairs(PimaIndiansDiabetesData[,1:4])
   ```

The output is as follows:

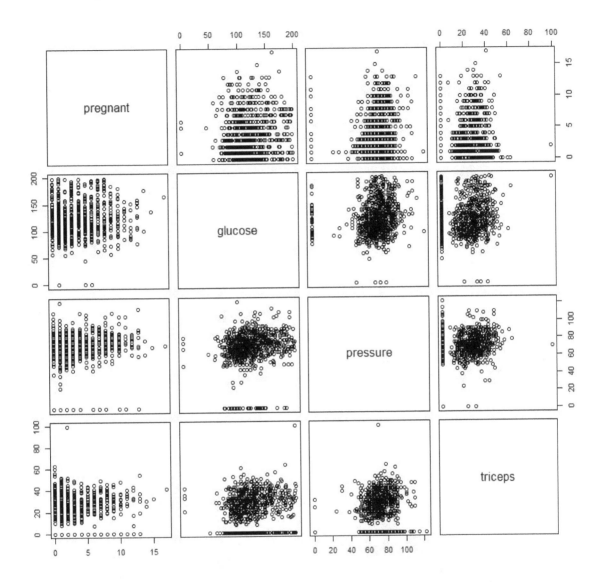

Figure 1.38: A pair plot for the diabetes data

5. Create a box plot to view the data distribution for the pregnant column and color by diabetes.

```
# Load library
library(ggplot2)
boxplot <- ggplot(data=PimaIndiansDiabetesData, aes(x=diabetes,
y=pregnant))
boxplot + geom_boxplot(aes(fill=diabetes)) +
  ylab("Pregnant") + ggtitle("Diabetes Data Boxplot") +
  stat_summary(fun.y=mean, geom="point", shape=5, size=4)
```

The output is as follows:

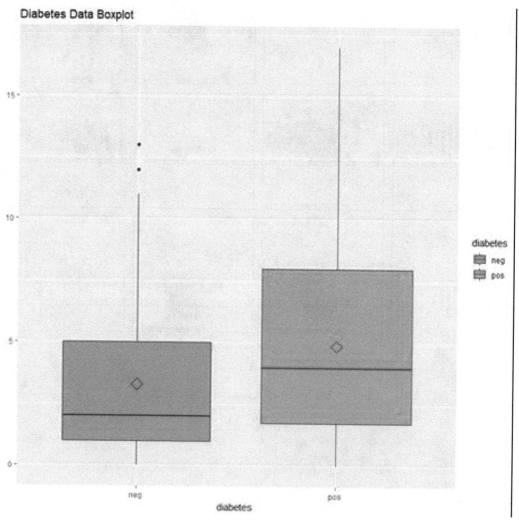

Figure 1.39: The box plot output using ggplot

In the preceding graph, we can see the distribution of "number of times pregnant" in people who do not have diabetes (neg) and in people who have diabetes (pos).

Activity 4: Building Linear Models for the GermanCredit Dataset

Solution:

These are the steps that will help you solve the activity:

1. Load the data.

    ```
    GermanCredit <-read.csv("GermanCredit.csv")
    ```

2. Subset the data.

    ```
    GermanCredit_Subset=GermanCredit[,1:10]
    ```

3. Fit a linear model using **lm()**.

    ```
    # fit model
    fit <- lm(Duration~., GermanCredit_Subset)
    ```

4. Summarize the results using the **summary()** function.

    ```
    # summarize the fit
    summary(fit)
    ```

    The output is as follows:

    ```
    Call:
    lm(formula = Duration ~ ., data = GermanCredit_Subset)

    Residuals:
        Min      1Q  Median      3Q     Max
    -44.722  -5.524  -1.187   4.431  44.287
    ```

    Coefficients:

	Estimate	Std. Error	t value	Pr(>|t|)	
(Intercept)	2.0325685	2.3612128	0.861	0.38955	
Amount	0.0029344	0.0001093	26.845	< 2e-16	***
InstallmentRatePercentage	2.7171134	0.2640590	10.290	< 2e-16	***
ResidenceDuration	0.2068781	0.2625670	0.788	0.43094	
Age	-0.0689299	0.0260365	-2.647	0.00824	**
NumberExistingCredits	-0.3810765	0.4903225	-0.777	0.43723	
NumberPeopleMaintenance	-0.0999072	0.7815578	-0.128	0.89831	
Telephone	0.6354927	0.6035906	1.053	0.29266	
ForeignWorker	4.9141998	1.4969592	3.283	0.00106	**

```
ClassGood                  -2.0068114  0.6260298  -3.206  0.00139 **
---
Signif. codes:  0 '***' 0.001 '**' 0.01 '*' 0.05 '.' 0.1 ' ' 1

Residual standard error: 8.784 on 990 degrees of freedom
Multiple R-squared:  0.4742,    Adjusted R-squared:  0.4694
F-statistic:  99.2 on 9 and 990 DF,  p-value: < 2.2e-16
```

5. Use **predict()** to make the predictions.

```
# make predictions
predictions <- predict(fit, GermanCredit_Subset)
```

6. Calculate the RMSE for the predictions.

```
# summarize accuracy
rmse <- sqrt(mean((GermanCredit_Subset$Duration - predictions)^2))
print(rmse)
```

The output is as follows:

```
[1] 76.3849
```

In this activity, we have learned to build a linear model, make predictions on new data, and evaluate performance using RMSE.

Activity 5: Using Multiple Variables for a Regression Model for the Boston Housing Dataset

Solution:

These are the steps that will help you solve the activity:

1. Load the dataset.

```
BostonHousing <-read.csv("BostonHousing.csv")
```

2. Build a regression model using multiple variables.

```
#Build multi variable regression
regression <- lm(medv~crim + indus+rad , data = BostonHousing)
```

3. View the summary of the built regression model.

```
#View the summary
summary(regression)
```

The output is as follows:

```
Call:
lm(formula = medv ~ crim + indus + rad, data = BostonHousing)

Residuals:
    Min      1Q  Median      3Q     Max
-12.047  -4.860  -1.736   3.081  32.596

Coefficients:
             Estimate Std. Error t value Pr(>|t|)
(Intercept) 29.27515    0.68220  42.913  < 2e-16 ***
crim        -0.23952    0.05205  -4.602 5.31e-06 ***
indus       -0.51671    0.06336  -8.155 2.81e-15 ***
rad         -0.01281    0.05845  -0.219   0.827
---
Signif. codes:  0 '***' 0.001 '**' 0.01 '*' 0.05 '.' 0.1 ' ' 1

Residual standard error: 7.838 on 502 degrees of freedom
Multiple R-squared:  0.2781,    Adjusted R-squared:  0.2737
F-statistic: 64.45 on 3 and 502 DF,  p-value: < 2.2e-16
```

4. Plot the regression model using the **plot()** function.

```
#Plot the fit
plot(regression)
```

The output is as follows:

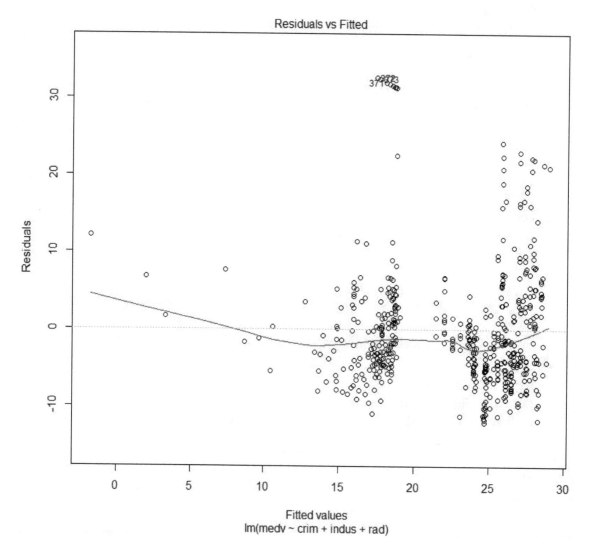

Figure 1.40: Residual versus fitted values

The preceding plot compares the predicted values and the residual values.

Hit \<Return\> to see the next plot:

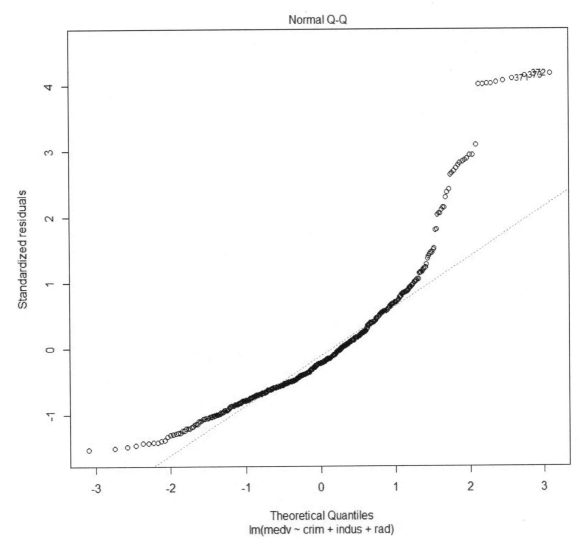

Figure 1.41: Normal QQ

The preceding plot shows the distribution of error. It is a normal probability plot. A normal distribution of error will display a straight line.

Hit \<Return\> to see the next plot:

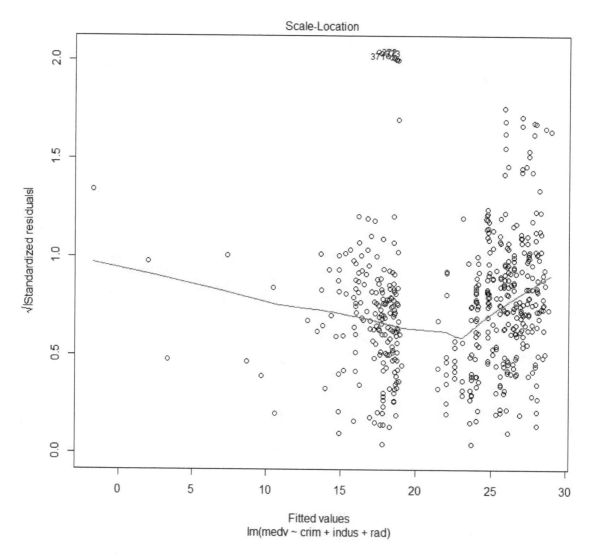

Figure 1.42: Scale location plot

The preceding plot compares the spread and the predicted values. We can see how the spread is with respect to the predicted values.

Hit <Return> to see the next plot:

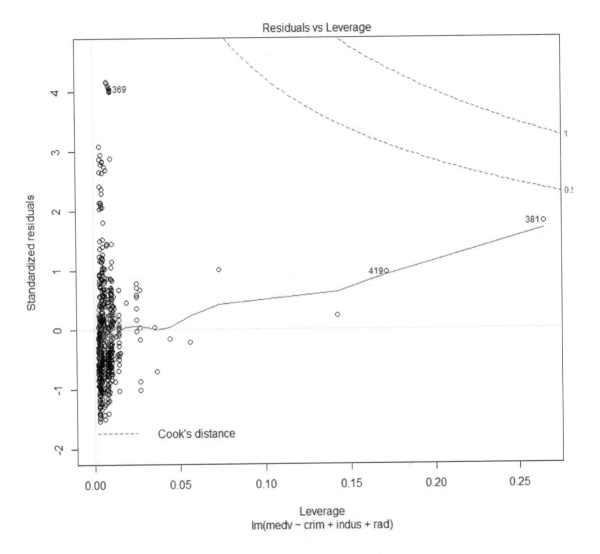

Figure 1.43: Cook's distance plot

This plot helps to identify which data points are influential to the regression model, that is, which of our model results would be affected if we included or excluded them.

We have now explored the datasets with one or more variables.

Chapter 2: Data Cleaning and Pre-processing

Activity 6: Pre-processing using Center and Scale

Solution:

In this exercise, we will perform the *center* and *scale* pre-processing operations.

1. Load the `mlbench` library and the `PimaIndiansDiabetes` dataset:

   ```
   # Load Library caret
   library(caret)
   library(mlbench)


   # load the dataset PimaIndiansDiabetes
   data(PimaIndiansDiabetes)
   ```

   View the summary:

   ```
   # view the data
   summary(PimaIndiansDiabetes [,1:2])
   ```

   The output is as follows:

   ```
         pregnant              glucose
    Min.    : 0.000    Min.    :  0.0
    1st Qu.: 1.000    1st Qu.: 99.0
    Median : 3.000    Median :117.0
    Mean    : 3.845    Mean    :120.9
    3rd Qu.: 6.000    3rd Qu.:140.2
    Max.    :17.000    Max.    :199.0
   ```

2. User **prePocess()** to pre-process the data to **center** and **scale**:

   ```
   # to standardise we will scale and center
   params <- preProcess(PimaIndiansDiabetes [,1:2], method=c("center",
   "scale"))
   ```

3. Transform the dataset using **predict()**:

   ```
   # transform the dataset
   new_dataset <- predict(params, PimaIndiansDiabetes [,1:2])
   ```

4. Print the summary of the new dataset:

   ```
   # summarize the transformed dataset
   summary(new_dataset)
   ```

The output is as follows:

```
      pregnant              glucose
Min.    :-1.1411    Min.    :-3.7812
1st Qu.:-0.8443    1st Qu.:-0.6848
Median :-0.2508    Median :-0.1218
Mean    : 0.0000    Mean    : 0.0000
3rd Qu.: 0.6395    3rd Qu.: 0.6054
Max.    : 3.9040    Max.    : 2.4429
```

We will notice that the values are now mean centering values.

Activity 7: Identifying Outliers

Solution:

1. Load the dataset:

```
mtcars = read.csv("mtcars.csv")
```

2. Load the outlier package and use the outlier function to display the outliers:

```
#Load the outlier library
library(outliers)
```

3. Detect outliers in the dataset using the **outlier()** function:

```
#Detect outliers
outlier(mtcars)
```

The output is as follows:

```
    mpg      cyl     disp      hp     drat      wt     qsec      vs       am
   gear     carb
 33.900    4.000 472.000 335.000    4.930    5.424   22.900
  1.000    1.000    5.000    8.000
```

4. Display the other side of the outlier values:

```
#This detects outliers from the other side
outlier(mtcars,opposite=TRUE)
```

The output is as follows:

```
   mpg    cyl   disp     hp   drat     wt   qsec    vs    am
  gear   carb
10.400  8.000 71.100 52.000  2.760  1.513 14.500 0.000 0.000
 3.000  1.000
```

5. Plot a box plot:

```
#View the outliers
boxplot(Mushroom)
```

The output is as follows:

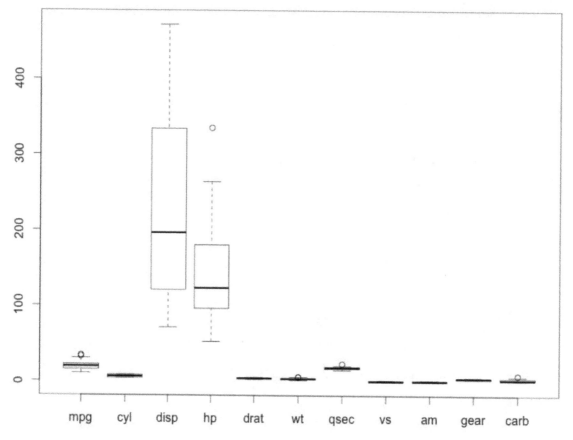

Figure 2.36: Outliers in the mtcars dataset.

The circle marks are the outliers.

Activity 8: Oversampling and Undersampling

Solution:

The detailed solution is as follows:

1. Read the mushroom CSV file:

```
ms<-read.csv('mushrooms.csv')
summary(ms$bruises)
```

The output is as follows:

```
   f    t
4748 3376
```

2. Perform downsampling:

```
set.seed(9560)
undersampling <- downSample(x = ms[, -ncol(ms)], y = ms$bruises)
table(undersampling$bruises)
```

The output is as follows:

```
   f    t
3376 3376
```

3. Perform oversampling:

```
set.seed(9560)
oversampling <- upSample(x = ms[, -ncol(ms)],y = ms$bruises)
table(oversampling$bruises)
```

The output is as follows:

```
   f    t
4748 4748
```

In this activity, we learned to use **downSample()** and **upSample()** from the **caret** package to perform downsampling and oversampling.

Activity 9: Sampling and OverSampling using ROSE

Solution:

The detailed solution is as follows:

1. Load the German credit dataset:

   ```
   #load the dataset
   library(caret)
   library(ROSE)
   data(GermanCredit)
   ```

2. View the samples in the German credit dataset:

   ```
   #View samples
   head(GermanCredit)
   str(GermanCredit)
   ```

3. Check the number of unbalanced data in the German credit dataset using the **summary()** method:

   ```
   #View the imbalanced data
   summary(GermanCredit$Class)
   ```

   The output is as follows:

   ```
   Bad Good
   300  700
   ```

4. Use **ROSE** to balance the numbers:

   ```
   balanced_data <- ROSE(Class ~ ., data  = stagec,seed=3)$data
   table(balanced_data$Class)
   ```

   The output is as follows:

   ```
   Good  Bad
   480   520
   ```

   Using the preceding example, we learned how to increase and decrease the class count using **ROSE**.

Chapter 3: Feature Engineering

Activity 10: Calculating Time series Feature – Binning

Solution:

1. Load the **caret** library:

   ```
   #Time series features
   library(caret)

   #Install caret if not installed
   #install.packages('caret')
   ```

2. Load the **GermanCredit** dataset:

   ```
   GermanCredit = read.csv("GermanCredit.csv")
   duration<- GermanCredit$Duration #take the duration column
   ```

3. Check the data summary as follows:

   ```
   summary(duration)
   ```

   The output is as follows:

   ```
   Min. 1st Qu.  Median   Mean 3rd Qu.    Max.
   4.0    12.0    18.0    20.9    24.0    72.0
   ```

   Figure 3.27: The summary of the Duration values of German Credit dataset

4. Load the **ggplot2** library:

   ```
   library(ggplot2)
   ```

5. Plot using the command:

   ```
   ggplot(data=GermanCredit, aes(x=GermanCredit$Duration)) +
     geom_density(fill='lightblue') +
     geom_rug() +
     labs(x='mean Duration')
   ```

The output is as follows:

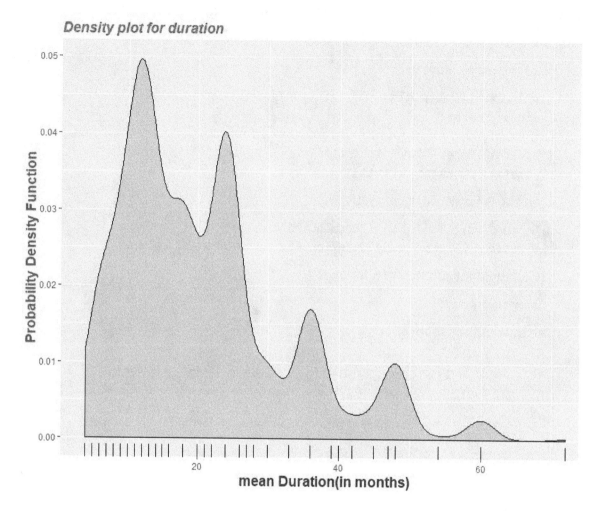

Figure 3.28: Plot of the duration vs density

6. Create bins:

```
#Creating Bins
# set up boundaries for intervals/bins
breaks <- c(0,10,20,30,40,50,60,70,80)
```

7. Create labels:

```
# specify interval/bin labels
labels <- c("<10", "10-20", "20-30", "30-40", "40-50", "50-60", "60-70",
"70-80")
```

8. Bucket the datapoints into the bins.

```
# bucketing data points into bins
bins <- cut(duration, breaks, include.lowest = T, right=FALSE,
labels=labels)
```

9. Find the number of elements in each bin:

```
# inspect bins
summary(bins)
```

The output is as follows:

```
summary(bins)
   <10 10-20 20-30 30-40 40-50 50-60 60-70 70-80
   143   403   241   131    66     2    13     1
```

10. Plot the bins:

```
#Ploting the bins
plot(bins, main="Frequency of Duration", ylab="Duration Count",
xlab="Duration Bins",col="bisque")
```

The output is as follows:

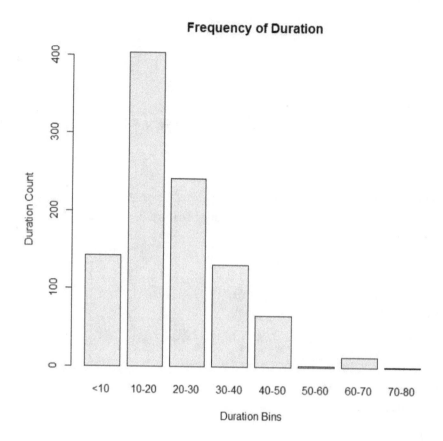

Figure 3.29: Plot of duration in bins

We can conclude that the maximum number of customers are within the range of 10 to 20.

Activity 11: Identifying Skewness

Solution:

1. Load the library **mlbench.**

```
#Skewness
library(mlbench)
library(e1071)
```

2. Load the **PimaIndainsDiabetes** data.

```
PimaIndiansDiabetes = read.csv("PimaIndiansDiabetes.csv")
```

3. Print the skewness of the glucose column, using the **skewness()** function.

```
#Printing the skewness of the columns
#Not skewed
skewness(PimaIndiansDiabetes$glucose)
```

The output is as follows:

```
[1] 0.1730754
```

4. Plot the histogram using the **histogram()** function.

```
histogram(PimaIndiansDiabetes$glucose)
```

The output is as follows:

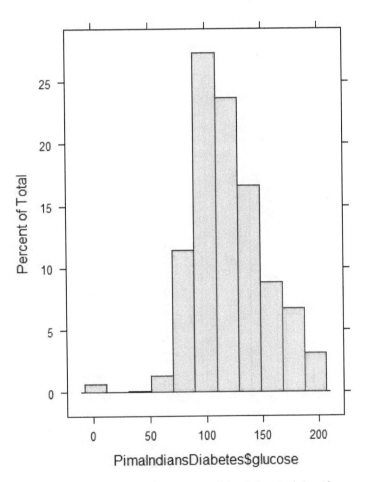

Figure 3.30: Histogram of the glucose values of the PrimaIndainsGlucose dataset

A negative skewness value means that the data is skewed to the left and a positive skewness value means that the data is skewed to the right. Since the value here is 0.17, the data is neither completely left or right skewed. Therefore, it is not skewed.

5. Find the skewness of the age column using the **skewness()** function.

```
#Highly skewed
skewness(PimaIndiansDiabetes$age)
```

The output is as follows:

```
[1] 1.125188
```

6. Plot the histogram using the **histogram()** function.

```
histogram(PimaIndiansDiabetes$age)
```

The output is as follows:

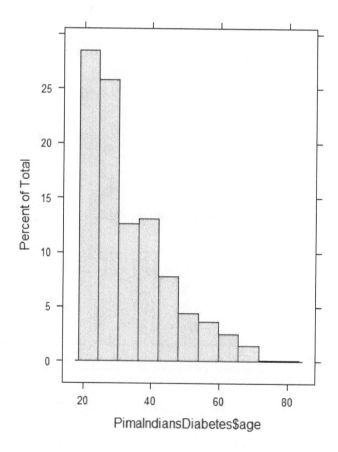

Figure 3.31: Histogram of the age values of the PrimaIndiansDiabetes dataset

The positive skewness value means that it is skewed to the right as we can see above.

Activity 12: Generating PCA

Solution:

1. Load the **GermanCredit** data.

    ```
    #PCA Analysis
    data(GermanCredit)
    ```

2. Create a subset of first 9 columns into another variable names **GermanCredit_subset**

    ```
    #Use the German Credit Data
    GermanCredit_subset <- GermanCredit[,1:9]
    ```

3. Find the principal components:

    ```
    #Find out the Principal components
    principal_components <- prcomp(x = GermanCredit_subset, scale. = T)
    ```

4. Print the principal components:

    ```
    #Print the principal components
    print(principal_components)
    ```

    The output is as follows:

    ```
    Standard deviations (1, .., p=9):
    [1] 1.3505916 1.2008442 1.1084157 0.9721503 0.9459586
    0.9317018 0.9106746 0.8345178 0.5211137


    Rotation (n x k) = (9 x 9):
    ```

```
Standard deviations (1, .., p=9):
[1] 1.3505916 1.2008442 1.1084157 0.9721503 0.9459586 0.9317018 0.9106746 0.8345178 0.5211137

Rotation (n x k) = (9 x 9):
                                 PC1         PC2         PC3         PC4         PC5         PC6         PC7         PC8         PC9
Duration                  0.58346016 -0.20189333  0.12607255 -0.21394820 -0.36935166  0.007214856 -0.18401918 -0.07228018 -0.61772568
Amount                    0.63752012 -0.19597234 -0.20145979  0.01877283 -0.06099068  0.031119661 -0.10715380 -0.09832788  0.69884609
InstallmentRatePercentage -0.11091325  0.21017115  0.63060195 -0.35109100 -0.49102817  0.231088890  0.14106768  0.04384568  0.32598981
ResidenceDuration          0.15008720  0.50427875  0.08265692  0.43069132 -0.18654202 -0.221281544 -0.42182623  0.51846212  0.01859594
Age                        0.12965396  0.59827665 -0.05602464  0.24438107 -0.08053172  0.038094595  0.11150502 -0.73307644 -0.06799295
NumberExistingCredits      0.08144692  0.40299991 -0.14933373 -0.59017205  0.42288252  0.339609189 -0.40121515  0.06984228 -0.01839272
NumberPeopleMaintenance    0.01856789  0.26671893 -0.48949217 -0.42738113 -0.29772936 -0.473379812  0.39954279  0.18380489  0.01044675
Telephone                 -0.39964528 -0.17281706 -0.11414936 -0.16231291 -0.30734854 -0.337741629 -0.65030093 -0.35155164  0.12660953
ForeignWorker              0.18657318  0.03188044  0.51083921 -0.16759647  0.46425426 -0.664581419  0.02974633 -0.12136714  0.04809892
```

Figure 3.32: Histogram of the age values of the PrimaIndiansDiabetes dataset

Therefore, by using principal component analysis we can identify the top nine principal components in the dataset. These components are calculated from multiple fields and they can be used as features on their own.

Activity 13: Implementing the Random Forest Approach

Solution:

1. Load the **GermanCredit** data:

   ```
   data(GermanCredit)
   ```

2. Create a subset to load the first ten columns into **GermanCredit_subset**.

   ```
   GermanCredit_subset <- GermanCredit[,1:10]
   ```

3. Attach the **randomForest** package:

   ```
   library(randomForest)
   ```

4. Train a random forest model using **random_forest =randomForest(Class~., data=GermanCredit_subset)**:

   ```
   random_forest = randomForest(Class~., data=GermanCredit_subset)
   ```

5. Invoke **importance()** for the trained **random_forest**:

   ```
   # Create an importance based on mean decreasing gini
   importance(random_forest)
   ```

   The output is as follows:

   ```
   importance(random_forest)
                              MeanDecreaseGini
   Duration                          70.380265
   Amount                           121.458790
   InstallmentRatePercentage         27.048517
   ResidenceDuration                 30.409254
   Age                               86.476017
   NumberExistingCredits             18.746057
   NumberPeopleMaintenance           12.026969
   Telephone                         15.581802
   ForeignWorker                      2.888387
   ```

6. Use the `varImp()` function to view the list of important variables.

```
varImp(random_forest)
```

The output is as follows:

```
                              Overall
Duration                     70.380265
Amount                      121.458790
InstallmentRatePercentage    27.048517
ResidenceDuration            30.409254
Age                          86.476017
NumberExistingCredits        18.746057
NumberPeopleMaintenance      12.026969
Telephone                    15.581802
ForeignWorker                 2.888387
```

In this activity, we built a random forest model and used it to see the importance of each variable in a dataset. The variables with higher scores are considered more important. Having done this, we can sort by importance and choose the top 5 or top 10 for the model or set a threshold for importance and choose all the variables that meet the threshold.

Activity 14: Selecting Features Using Variable Importance

Solution:

1. Install the following packages:

```
install.packages("rpart")
library(rpart)
library(caret)
set.seed(10)
```

2. Load the **GermanCredit** dataset:

```
data(GermanCredit)
```

3. Create a subset to load the first ten columns into **GermanCredit_subset**:

```
GermanCredit_subset <- GermanCredit[,1:10]
```

4. Train an **rpart** model using **rPartMod <- train(Class ~ ., data=GermanCredit_ subset, method="rpart")**:

```
#Train a rpart model
rPartMod <- train(Class ~ ., data=GermanCredit_subset, method="rpart")
```

5. Invoke the **varImp()** function, as in **rpartImp <- varImp(rPartMod)**.

```
#Find variable importance
rpartImp <- varImp(rPartMod)
```

6. Print **rpartImp.**

```
#Print variable importance
print(rpartImp)
```

The output is as follows:

```
rpart variable importance
```

	Overall
Amount	100.000
Duration	89.670
Age	75.229
ForeignWorker	22.055
InstallmentRatePercentage	17.288
Telephone	7.813
ResidenceDuration	4.471
NumberExistingCredits	0.000
NumberPeopleMaintenance	0.000

7. Plot **rpartImp** using **plot()**.

```
#Plot top 5 variable importance
plot(rpartImp, top = 5, main='Variable Importance')
```

The output is as follows:

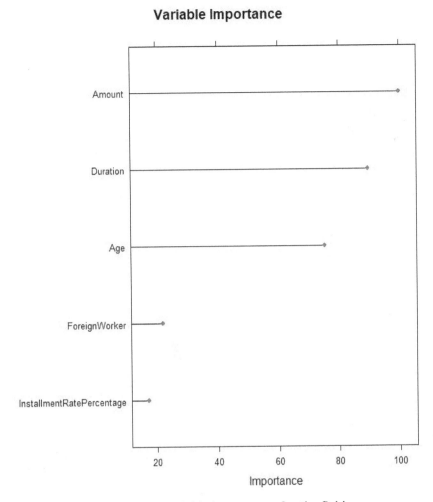

Figure 3.33: Variable importance for the fields

From the preceding plot, we can observe that **Amount**, **Duration**, and **Age** have high importance values.

Chapter 4: Introduction to neuralnet and Evaluation Methods

Activity 15: Training a Neural Network

Solution:

1. Attach the packages:

```
# Attach the packages
library(caret)
library(groupdata2)
library(neuralnet)
library(NeuralNetTools)
```

2. Set the seed value for reproducibility and easier comparison:

```
# Set seed for reproducibility and easier comparison
set.seed(1)
```

3. Load the **GermanCredit** dataset:

```
# Load the German Credit dataset
GermanCredit <- read.csv("GermanCredit.csv")
```

4. Remove the **Age** column:

```
# Remove the Age column
GermanCredit$Age <- NULL
```

5. Create balanced partitions such that all three partitions have the same ratio of each class:

```
# Partition with same ratio of each class in all three partitions
partitions <- partition(GermanCredit, p = c(0.6, 0.2),
                        cat_col = "Class")
train_set <- partitions[[1]]
dev_set <- partitions[[2]]
valid_set <- partitions[[3]]
```

6. Find the preprocessing parameters for scaling and centering from the training set:

```
# Find scaling and centering parameters
params <- preProcess(train_set[, 1:6], method=c("center", "scale"))
```

7. Apply standardization to the first six predictors in all three partitions, using the preProcess parameters from the previous step:

```
# Transform the training set
train_set[, 1:6] <- predict(params, train_set[, 1:6])

# Transform the development set
dev_set[, 1:6] <- predict(params, dev_set[, 1:6])

# Transform the validation set
valid_set[, 1:6] <- predict(params, valid_set[, 1:6])
```

8. Train the neural network classifier:

```
# Train the neural network classifier
nn <- neuralnet(Class == "Good" ~ InstallmentRatePercentage +
                ResidenceDuration + NumberExistingCredits,
                train_set, linear.output = FALSE)
```

9. Plot the network with its weights:

```
# Plot the network
plotnet(nn, var_labs=FALSE)
```

The output is as follows:

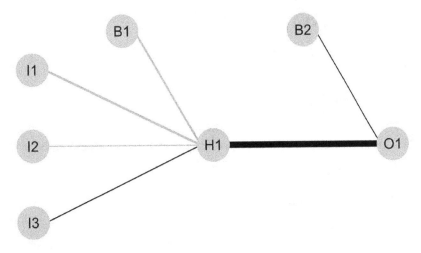

Figure 4.18: Neural network architecture using three predictors

10. Print the error:

```
train_error <- nn$result.matrix[1]
train_error
```

The output is as follows:

```
## [1] 62.15447
```

The random initialization of the neural network weights can lead to slightly different results from one training to another. To avoid this, we use the **set.seed()** function at the beginning of the script, which helps when comparing models. We could also train the same model architecture with five different seeds to get a better sense of its performance.

Activity 16: Training and Comparing Neural Network Architectures

Solution:

1. Attach the packages:

```
# Attach the packages
library(groupdata2)
library(caret)
library(neuralnet)
library(mlbench)
```

2. Set the random seed to 1:

```
# Set seed for reproducibility and easier comparison
set.seed(1)
```

3. Load the **PimaIndiansDiabetes2** dataset:

```
# Load the PimaIndiansDiabetes2 dataset
PimaIndiansDiabetes2 <- read.csv("PimaIndiansDiabetes2.csv")
```

4. Summarize the dataset.

```
summary(PimaIndiansDiabetes2)
```

The summary is as follows:

```
##      pregnant            glucose           pressure           triceps
##   Min.   : 0.000    Min.   : 44.0    Min.   : 24.00    Min.   : 7.00
##   1st Qu.: 1.000    1st Qu.: 99.0    1st Qu.: 64.00    1st Qu.:22.00
##   Median : 3.000    Median :117.0    Median : 72.00    Median :29.00
##   Mean   : 3.845    Mean   :121.7    Mean   : 72.41    Mean   :29.15
##   3rd Qu.: 6.000    3rd Qu.:141.0    3rd Qu.: 80.00    3rd Qu.:36.00
##   Max.   :17.000    Max.   :199.0    Max.   :122.00    Max.   :99.00
##                     NA's   :5        NA's   :35        NA's   :227
##
##      insulin             mass             pedigree            age
##   Min.   : 14.00    Min.   :18.20    Min.   :0.0780    Min.   :21.00
##   1st Qu.: 76.25    1st Qu.:27.50    1st Qu.:0.2437    1st Qu.:24.00
##   Median :125.00    Median :32.30    Median :0.3725    Median :29.00
##   Mean   :155.55    Mean   :32.46    Mean   :0.4719    Mean   :33.24
##   3rd Qu.:190.00    3rd Qu.:36.60    3rd Qu.:0.6262    3rd Qu.:41.00
##   Max.   :846.00    Max.   :67.10    Max.   :2.4200    Max.   :81.00
##   NA's   :374       NA's   :11
##
##   diabetes
##   neg:500
##   pos:268
```

5. Handle missing data (quick solution). Start by assigning the dataset to a new name:

```
# Assign/copy dataset to a new name
diabetes_data <- PimaIndiansDiabetes2
```

6. Remove the **triceps** and **insulin** columns:

```
# Remove the triceps and insulin columns
diabetes_data$triceps <- NULL
diabetes_data$insulin <- NULL
```

7. Remove all rows containing missing data (NAs):

```
# Remove all rows with NAs (missing data)
diabetes_data <- na.omit(diabetes_data)
```

8. Partition the dataset into a training set (60%), a development set (20%), and a validation set (20%). Use **cat_col="diabetes"** to balance the ratios of each class between the partitions:

```
# Partition with same ratio of each class in all three partitions
partitions <- partition(diabetes_data, p = c(0.6, 0.2),
                        cat_col = "diabetes")
train_set <- partitions[[1]]
dev_set <- partitions[[2]]
valid_set <- partitions[[3]]
```

9. Find the **preProcess** parameters for scaling and centering the first six features:

```
# Find scaling and centering parameters
params <- preProcess(train_set[, 1:6], method = c("center", "scale"))
```

10. Apply the scaling and centering to each partition:

```
# Transform the training set
train_set[, 1:6] <- predict(params, train_set[, 1:6])

# Transform the development set
dev_set[, 1:6] <- predict(params, dev_set[, 1:6])

# Transform the validation set
valid_set[, 1:6] <- predict(params, valid_set[, 1:6])
```

11. Train multiple neural network architectures. Adjust them by changing the number of nodes and/or layers. In the model formula, use **diabetes == "pos"**:

```
# Training multiple neural nets
nn4 <- neuralnet(diabetes == "pos" ~ ., train_set,
                 linear.output = FALSE, hidden = c(3))
nn5 <- neuralnet(diabetes == "pos" ~ ., train_set,
                 linear.output = FALSE, hidden = c(2,1))
nn6 <- neuralnet(diabetes == "pos" ~ ., train_set,
                 linear.output = FALSE, hidden = c(3,2))
```

12. Put the model objects into a list:

```
# Put the model objects into a list
models <- list("nn4"=nn4,"nn5"=nn5,"nn6"=nn6)
```

13. Create one-hot encoding of the **diabetes** variable:

```
# Evaluating each model on the dev_set


# Create one-hot encoding of diabetes variable
dev_true_labels <- ifelse(dev_set$diabetes == "pos", 1, 0)
```

14. Create a for loop for evaluating the models. By running the evaluations in a for loop, we avoid repeating the code:

```
# Evaluate one model at a time in a loop, to avoid repeating the code
for (i in 1:length(models)){

    # Predict the classes in the development set
    dev_predicted_probabilities <- predict(models[[i]], dev_set)
    dev_predictions <- ifelse(dev_predicted_probabilities > 0.5, 1, 0)


    # Create confusion Matrix
    confusion_matrix <- confusionMatrix(as.factor(dev_predictions),
                                        as.factor(dev_true_labels),
                                        mode="prec_recall",
                                        positive = "1")


    # Print the results for this model
    # Note: paste0() concatenates the strings
    # to (name of model + " on the dev...")
    print( paste0( names(models)[[i]], " on the development set: "))
    print(confusion_matrix)


}
```

The output is as follows:

```
## [1] "nn4 on the development set: "
## Confusion Matrix and Statistics
##
##              Reference
## Prediction   0   1
##          0  79  19
##          1  16  30
##
##                     Accuracy : 0.7569
##                       95% CI : (0.6785, 0.8245)
##          No Information Rate : 0.6597
```

```
##      P-Value [Acc > NIR] : 0.007584
##
##                   Kappa : 0.4505
##  Mcnemar's Test P-Value : 0.735317
##
##               Precision : 0.6522
##                  Recall : 0.6122
##                      F1 : 0.6316
##              Prevalence : 0.3403
##          Detection Rate : 0.2083
##    Detection Prevalence : 0.3194
##       Balanced Accuracy : 0.7219
##
##        'Positive' Class : 1
##
## [1] "nn5 on the development set: "
## Confusion Matrix and Statistics
##
##           Reference
## Prediction  0  1
##          0 77 16
##          1 18 33
##
##                Accuracy : 0.7639
##                  95% CI : (0.686, 0.8306)
##     No Information Rate : 0.6597
##     P-Value [Acc > NIR] : 0.004457
##
##                   Kappa : 0.4793
##  Mcnemar's Test P-Value : 0.863832
##
##               Precision : 0.6471
##                  Recall : 0.6735
##                      F1 : 0.6600
##              Prevalence : 0.3403
##          Detection Rate : 0.2292
##    Detection Prevalence : 0.3542
##       Balanced Accuracy : 0.7420
##
```

```
##            'Positive' Class : 1
##
## [1] "nn6 on the development set: "
## Confusion Matrix and Statistics
##
##              Reference
## Prediction   0   1
##           0 76 14
##           1 19 35
##
##                Accuracy : 0.7708
##                  95% CI : (0.6935, 0.8367)
##     No Information Rate : 0.6597
##     P-Value [Acc > NIR] : 0.002528
##
##                   Kappa : 0.5019
##   Mcnemar's Test P-Value : 0.486234
##
##               Precision : 0.6481
##                  Recall : 0.7143
##                      F1 : 0.6796
##              Prevalence : 0.3403
##          Detection Rate : 0.2431
##    Detection Prevalence : 0.3750
##       Balanced Accuracy : 0.7571
##
##            'Positive' Class : 1
```

15. As the **nn6** model has the highest accuracy and F1 score, it is the best model.

16. Evaluate the best model on the validation set. Start by creating the one-hot encoding of the **diabetes** variable in the validation set:

```
# Create one-hot encoding of Class variable
valid_true_labels <- ifelse(valid_set$diabetes == "pos", 1, 0)
```

17. Use the best model to predict the **diabetes** variable in the validation set:

```
# Predict the classes in the validation set
predicted_probabilities <- predict(nn6, valid_set)
predictions <- ifelse(predicted_probabilities > 0.5, 1, 0)
```

18. Create a confusion matrix:

```
# Create confusion Matrix
confusion_matrix <- confusionMatrix(as.factor(predictions),
                               as.factor(valid_true_labels),
                               mode="prec_recall", positive = "1")
```

19. Print the results:

```
# Print the results for this model
# Note that by separating two function calls by ";"
# we can have multiple calls per line
print("nn6 on the validation set:"); print(confusion_matrix)
```

The output is as follows:

```
## [1] "nn6 on the validation set:"
## Confusion Matrix and Statistics
##
##              Reference
## Prediction  0   1
##          0 70  16
##          1 25  35
##
##                 Accuracy : 0.7192
##                   95% CI : (0.6389, 0.7903)
##      No Information Rate : 0.6507
##      P-Value [Acc > NIR] : 0.04779
##
##                    Kappa : 0.4065
##   Mcnemar's Test P-Value : 0.21152
##
##                Precision : 0.5833
##                   Recall : 0.6863
##                       F1 : 0.6306
##               Prevalence : 0.3493
##           Detection Rate : 0.2397
##     Detection Prevalence : 0.4110
##        Balanced Accuracy : 0.7116
##
##         'Positive' Class : 1
```

20. Plot the best model:

```
plotnet(nn6, var_labs=FALSE)
```

The output will look as follows:

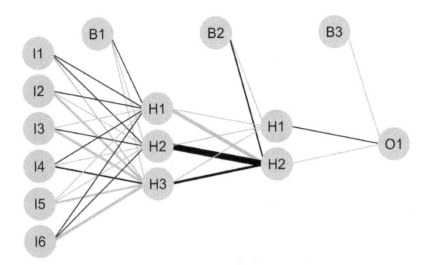

Figure 4.19: The best neural network architecture without cross-validation.

In this activity, we have trained multiple neural network architectures and evaluated the best model on the validation set.

Activity 17: Training and Comparing Neural Network Architectures with Cross-Validation

Solution:

1. Attach the packages.

```
# Attach the packages
library(groupdata2)
library(caret)
library(neuralnet)
library(mlbench)
```

2. Set the random seed to 1.

```
# Set seed for reproducibility and easier comparison
set.seed(1)
```

3. Load the **PimaIndiansDiabetes2** dataset.

```
# Load the PimaIndiansDiabetes2 dataset
data(PimaIndiansDiabetes2)
```

4. Handle missing data (quick solution).

   Start by assigning the dataset to a new name.

```
# Handling missing data (quick solution)

# Assign/copy dataset to a new name
diabetes_data <- PimaIndiansDiabetes2
```

5. Remove the **triceps** and **insulin** columns.

```
# Remove the triceps and insulin columns
diabetes_data$triceps <- NULL
diabetes_data$insulin <- NULL
```

6. Remove all rows with **NAs**.

```
# Remove all rows with Nas (missing data)
diabetes_data <- na.omit(diabetes_data)
```

7. Partition the dataset into a training set (80%) and validation set (20%). Use **cat_col="diabetes"** to balance the ratios of each class between the partitions.

```
# Partition into a training set and a validation set
partitions <- partition(diabetes_data, p = 0.8, cat_col = "diabetes")
train_set <- partitions[[1]]
valid_set <- partitions[[2]]
```

8. Find the **preProcess** parameters for scaling and centering the first six features.

```
# Find scaling and centering parameters
# Note: We could also decide to do this inside the training loop!
params <- preProcess(train_set[, 1:6], method=c("center", "scale"))
```

9. Apply the scaling and centering to both partitions.

```
# Transform the training set
train_set[, 1:6] <- predict(params, train_set[, 1:6])

# Transform the validation set
valid_set[, 1:6] <- predict(params, valid_set[, 1:6])
```

10. Create 4 folds in the training set, using the **fold()** function. Use **cat_col="diabe-tes"** to balance the ratios of each class between the folds.

```
# Create folds for cross-validation
# Balance on the Class variable
train_set <- fold(train_set, k=4, cat_col = "diabetes")
# Note: This creates a factor in the dataset called ".folds"
# Take care not to use this as a predictor.
```

11. Write the cross-validation training section.
    Start by initializing the vectors for collecting errors and accuracies.

```
## Cross-validation loop


# Change the model formula in the loop and run the below
# for each model architecture you're testing


# Initialize vectors for collecting errors and accuracies
errors <- c()
accuracies <- c()
```
Start the training for loop. We have 4 folds, so we need 4 iterations.
```
# Training loop
for (part in 1:4){
```

12. Assign the chosen fold as test set and the rest of the folds as train set. Be aware of the indentation.

```
# Assign the chosen fold as test set
# and the rest of the folds as train set
cv_test_set <- train_set[train_set$.folds == part,]
cv_train_set <- train_set[train_set$.folds != part,]
```

13. Train the neural network with your chosen predictors.

```
# Train neural network classifier
# Make sure not to include the .folds column as a predictor!
nn <- neuralnet(diabetes == "pos" ~ .,
                cv_train_set[, 1:7],
                linear.output = FALSE,
                hidden=c(2,2))
```

14. Append the error to the **errors** vector.

```
# Append error to errors vector
errors <- append(errors, nn$result.matrix[1])
```

15. Create one-hot encoding of the target variable in the CV test set.

```
# Create one-hot encoding of Class variable
true_labels <- ifelse(cv_test_set$diabetes == "pos", 1, 0)
```

16. Use the trained neural network to predict the target variable in the CV test set.

```
# Predict the class in the test set
# It returns probabilities that the observations are "pos"
predicted_probabilities <- predict(nn, cv_test_set)
predictions <- ifelse(predicted_probabilities > 0.5, 1, 0)
```

17. Calculate accuracy. We could also use **confusionMatrix()** here, if we wanted other metrics.

```
# Calculate accuracy manually
# Note: TRUE == 1, FALSE == 0
cv_accuracy <- sum(true_labels == predictions) / length(true_labels)
```

18. Append the calculated accuracy to the **accuracies** vector.

```
# Append the accuracy to the accuracies vector
accuracies <- append(accuracies, cv_accuracy)
```

19. Close the for loop.

```
}
```

20. Calculate **average_error** and print it.

```
# Calculate average error and accuracy
# Note that we could also have gathered the predictions from all the
# folds and calculated the accuracy only once. This could lead to slightly
# different results, e.g. if the folds are not exactly the same size.

average_error <- mean(errors)
average_error
```

The output is as follows:

```
## [1] 28.38503
```

21. Calculate **average_accuracy** and print it. Note that we could also have gathered the predictions from all the folds and calculated the accuracy only once.

```
average_accuracy <- mean(accuracies)
average_accuracy
```

The output is as follows:

```
## [1] 0.7529813
```

22. Evaluate the best model architecture on the validation set. Start by training an instance of the model architecture on the entire training set.

```
# Once you have chosen the best model, train it on the entire training set
# and evaluate on the validation set

# Note that we set the stepmax, to make sure
# it has enough training steps to converge
nn_best <- neuralnet(diabetes == "pos" ~ .,
                     train_set[, 1:7],
                     linear.output = FALSE,
                     hidden=c(2,2),
                     stepmax = 2e+05)
```

23. Create an one-hot encoding of the diabetes variable in the validation set.

```
# Find the true labels in the validation set
valid_true_labels <- ifelse(valid_set$diabetes == "pos", 1, 0)
```

24. Use the model to predict the diabetes variable in the validation set.

```
# Predict the classes in the validation set
predicted_probabilities <- predict(nn_best, valid_set)
predictions <- ifelse(predicted_probabilities > 0.5, 1, 0)
```

25. Create a confusion matrix.

```
# Create confusion matrix
confusion_matrix <- confusionMatrix(as.factor(predictions),
                                    as.factor(valid_true_labels),
                                    mode="prec_recall", positive = "1")
```

26. Print the results.

```
# Print the results for this model
print("nn_best on the validation set:")
## [1] "nn_best on the validation set:"

print(confusion_matrix)
## Confusion Matrix and Statistics
##
##           Reference
## Prediction  0  1
```

```
##            0 78 20
##            1 17 30
##
##                  Accuracy : 0.7448
##                    95% CI : (0.6658, 0.8135)
##      No Information Rate : 0.6552
##      P-Value [Acc > NIR] : 0.01302
##
##                     Kappa : 0.4271
##  Mcnemar's Test P-Value : 0.74231
##
##                 Precision : 0.6383
##                    Recall : 0.6000
##                        F1 : 0.6186
##               Prevalence : 0.3448
##            Detection Rate : 0.2069
##      Detection Prevalence : 0.3241
##         Balanced Accuracy : 0.7105
##
##           'Positive' Class : 1
##
```

27. Plot the neural network.

```
plotnet(nn_best, var_labs=FALSE)
```

The output will be as follows:

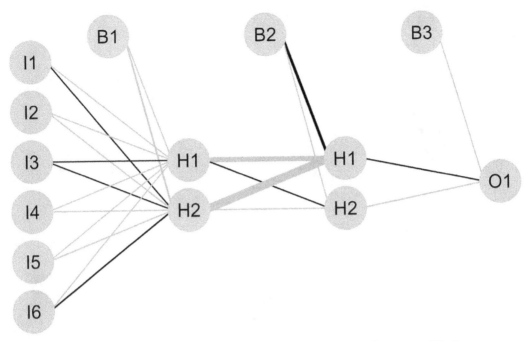

Figure 4.20: Best neural network architecture found with cross-validation.

Chapter 5: Linear and Logistic Regression Models

Activity 18: Implementing Linear Regression

Solution:

1. Attach the packages:

```
# Attach packages
library(groupdata2)
library(cvms)
library(caret)
library(knitr)
```

2. Set the random seed to 1:

```
# Set seed for reproducibility and easy comparison
set.seed(1)
```

3. Load the **cars** dataset from **caret**:

```
# Load the cars dataset
data(cars)
```

4. Partition the dataset into a training set (80%) and a validation set (20%):

```
# Partition the dataset
partitions <- partition(cars, p = 0.8)
train_set <- partitions[[1]]
valid_set <- partitions[[2]]
```

5. Fit multiple linear regression models on the training set with the **lm()** function, predicting Price. Try different predictors. View and interpret the **summary()** of each fitted model. How do the interpretations change when you add or subtract predictors?

```
# Fit a couple of linear models and interpret them
# Model 1 - Predicting price by mileage
model_1 <- lm(Price ~ Mileage, data = train_set)
summary(model_1)
```

The summary of the model is as follows:

```
##
## Call:
## lm(formula = Price ~ Mileage, data = train_set)
##
## Residuals:
```

```
##    Min     1Q Median     3Q     Max
## -12977   -7400  -3453   6009   45540
##
## Coefficients:
##                Estimate Std. Error t value Pr(>|t|)
## (Intercept)   2.496e+04  1.019e+03  24.488  < 2e-16 ***
## Mileage      -1.736e-01  4.765e-02  -3.644 0.000291 ***
## ---
## Signif. codes:  0 '***' 0.001 '**' 0.01 '*' 0.05 '.' 0.1 ' ' 1
##
## Residual standard error: 9762 on 641 degrees of freedom
## Multiple R-squared:  0.02029,    Adjusted R-squared:  0.01876
## F-statistic: 13.28 on 1 and 641 DF,  p-value: 0.0002906
# Model 2 - Predicting price by number of doors
model_2 <- lm(Price ~ Doors, data = train_set)
summary(model_2)
```

The summary of the model is as follows:

```
##
## Call:
## lm(formula = Price ~ Doors, data = train_set)
##
## Residuals:
##    Min     1Q Median     3Q     Max
## -12540   -7179  -2934   5814   45805
##
## Coefficients:
##                Estimate Std. Error t value Pr(>|t|)
## (Intercept)    25682.2     1662.1  15.452   <2e-16 ***
## Doors          -1176.6      457.5  -2.572   0.0103 *
## ---
## Signif. codes:  0 '***' 0.001 '**' 0.01 '*' 0.05 '.' 0.1 ' ' 1
##
## Residual standard error: 9812 on 641 degrees of freedom
## Multiple R-squared:  0.01021,    Adjusted R-squared:  0.008671
## F-statistic: 6.615 on 1 and 641 DF,  p-value: 0.01034
# Model 3 - Predicting price by mileage and number of doors
model_3 <- lm(Price ~ Mileage + Doors, data = train_set)
summary(model_3)
```

The summary of the model is as follows:

```
## 
## Call:
## lm(formula = Price ~ Mileage + Doors, data = train_set)
## 
## Residuals:
##     Min      1Q Median     3Q    Max
## -12642   -7503  -3000   5595  43576
## 
## Coefficients:
##                Estimate Std. Error t value Pr(>|t|)
## (Intercept)  2.945e+04  1.926e+03  15.292  < 2e-16 ***
## Mileage     -1.786e-01  4.744e-02  -3.764 0.000182 ***
## Doors       -1.242e+03  4.532e+02  -2.740 0.006308 **
## ---
## Signif. codes:  0 '***' 0.001 '**' 0.01 '*' 0.05 '.' 0.1 ' ' 1
## 
## Residual standard error: 9713 on 640 degrees of freedom
## Multiple R-squared:  0.03165,    Adjusted R-squared:  0.02863
## F-statistic: 10.46 on 2 and 640 DF,  p-value: 3.388e-05
```

6. Create model formulas with **combine_predictors()**. Limit the number of possibilities by a) using only the first four predictors, b) limiting the number of fixed effects in the formulas to three by specifying **max_fixed_effects = 3**, c) limiting the biggest possible interaction to a two-way interaction by specifying **max_interaction_size = 2**, and d) limiting the number of times a predictor can be included in a formula by specifying **max_effect_frequency = 1**. These limitations will decrease the number of models to run, which you may or may not want in your own projects:

```
# Create list of model formulas with combine_predictors()
# Use only the 4 first predictors (to save time)
# Limit the number of fixed effects (predictors) to 3,
# Limit the biggest possible interaction to a 2-way interaction
# Limit the number of times a fixed effect is included to 1
model_formulas <- combine_predictors(
    dependent = "Price",
    fixed_effects = c("Mileage", "Cylinder",
                      "Doors", "Cruise"),
    max_fixed_effects = 3,
```

```
        max_interaction_size = 2,
        max_effect_frequency = 1)
   # Output model formulas
   model_formulas
```

The output is as follows:

```
##  [1] "Price ~ Cruise"
##  [2] "Price ~ Cylinder"
##  [3] "Price ~ Doors"
##  [4] "Price ~ Mileage"
##  [5] "Price ~ Cruise * Cylinder"
##  [6] "Price ~ Cruise * Doors"
##  [7] "Price ~ Cruise * Mileage"
##  [8] "Price ~ Cruise + Cylinder"
##  [9] "Price ~ Cruise + Doors"
## [10] "Price ~ Cruise + Mileage"
## [11] "Price ~ Cylinder * Doors"
## [12] "Price ~ Cylinder * Mileage"
## [13] "Price ~ Cylinder + Doors"
## [14] "Price ~ Cylinder + Mileage"
## [15] "Price ~ Doors * Mileage"
## [16] "Price ~ Doors + Mileage"
## [17] "Price ~ Cruise * Cylinder + Doors"
## [18] "Price ~ Cruise * Cylinder + Mileage"
## [19] "Price ~ Cruise * Doors + Cylinder"
## [20] "Price ~ Cruise * Doors + Mileage"
## [21] "Price ~ Cruise * Mileage + Cylinder"
## [22] "Price ~ Cruise * Mileage + Doors"
## [23] "Price ~ Cruise + Cylinder * Doors"
## [24] "Price ~ Cruise + Cylinder * Mileage"
## [25] "Price ~ Cruise + Cylinder + Doors"
## [26] "Price ~ Cruise + Cylinder + Mileage"
## [27] "Price ~ Cruise + Doors * Mileage"
## [28] "Price ~ Cruise + Doors + Mileage"
## [29] "Price ~ Cylinder * Doors + Mileage"
## [30] "Price ~ Cylinder * Mileage + Doors"
## [31] "Price ~ Cylinder + Doors * Mileage"
## [32] "Price ~ Cylinder + Doors + Mileage"
```

7. Create fivefold columns with four folds each in the training set, using **fold()** with **k = 4** and **num_fold_cols = 5**. Feel free to choose a higher number of fold columns:

```
# Create 5 fold columns with 4 folds each in the training set
train_set <- fold(train_set, k = 4,
                  num_fold_cols = 5)
```

8. Create the fold column names with **paste0()**:

```
# Create list of fold column names
fold_cols <- paste0(".folds_", 1:5)
```

9. Perform repeated cross-validation on your model formulas with **cvms**:

```
# Cross-validate the models with cvms
CV_results <- cross_validate(train_set,
                             models = model_formulas,
                             fold_cols = fold_cols,
                             family = "gaussian")
```

10. Print the top 10 performing models according to **RMSE**. Select the best model:

```
# Select the best model by RMSE
# Order by RMSE
CV_results <- CV_results[order(CV_results$RMSE),]
# Select the 10 best performing models for printing
# (Feel free to view all the models)
CV_results_top10 <- head(CV_results, 10)
# Show metrics and model definition columns
# Use kable for a prettier output
kable(select_metrics(CV_results_top10), digits = 2)
```

The output is as follows:

RMSE	MAE	r2m	r2c	AIC	AICc	BIC	Dependent	Fixed
7525.02	5886.01	0.42	0.42	9981.42	9981.60	10006.49	Price	Cruise*Cylinder+Mileage
7539.53	6000.60	0.42	0.42	9979.88	9980.05	10004.95	Price	Cruise+Cylinder*Doors
7547.48	5989.54	0.42	0.42	9984.31	9984.49	10009.38	Price	Cruise*Mileage+Cylinder
7550.46	6002.03	0.42	0.42	9982.99	9983.11	10003.88	Price	Cruise+Cylinder+Mileage
7556.99	5980.23	0.42	0.42	9980.49	9980.67	10005.56	Price	Cruise+Cylinder*Mileage
7582.88	6005.76	0.41	0.41	9988.05	9988.23	10013.12	Price	Cruise*Cylinder+Doors
7593.05	6048.19	0.41	0.41	9989.18	9989.36	10014.25	Price	Cruise*Doors+Cylinder
7602.91	6070.76	0.41	0.41	9989.15	9989.27	10010.04	Price	Cruise+Cylinder+Doors
7619.15	5955.93	0.41	0.41	9993.25	9993.37	10014.14	Price	Cruise*Cylinder
7638.78	6037.54	0.40	0.40	9994.22	9994.30	10010.93	Price	Cruise+Cylinder

Figure 5.29: Top 10 performing models using RMSE

11. Fit the best model on the entire training set and evaluate it on the validation set. This can be done with the **validate()** function in **cvms**:

```
# Evaluate the best model on the validation set with validate()
V_results <- validate(
    train_data = train_set,
    test_data = valid_set,
    models = "Price ~ Cruise * Cylinder + Mileage",
    family = "gaussian")
```

12. The output contains the results data frame and the trained model. Assign these to variable names:

```
valid_results <- V_results$Results
valid_model <- V_results$Models[[1]]
```

13. Print the results:

```
# Print the results
kable(select_metrics(valid_results), digits = 2)
```

The output is as follows:

RMSE	MAE	r2m	r2c	AIC	AICc	BIC	Dependent	Fixed
8145.83	6152.31	0.42	0.42	13306.76	13306.89	13333.55	Price	Cruise*Cylinder+Mileage

Figure 5.30: Results of the validated model

14. View and interpret the summary of the best model:

```
# Print the model summary and interpret it
summary(valid_model)
```

The summary is as follows:

```
##
## Call:
## lm(formula = model_formula, data = train_set)
##
## Residuals:
##     Min      1Q  Median      3Q     Max
## -10485   -5495   -1425    3494   34693
##
## Coefficients:
##                    Estimate Std. Error t value Pr(>|t|)
## (Intercept)      8993.2446  3429.9320   2.622  0.00895 **
## Cruise          -1311.6871  3585.6289  -0.366  0.71462
## Cylinder         1809.5447   741.9185   2.439  0.01500 *
## Mileage            -0.1569     0.0367  -4.274 2.21e-05 ***
## Cruise:Cylinder  1690.0768   778.7838   2.170  0.03036 *
## ---
## Signif. codes:  0 '***' 0.001 '**' 0.01 '*' 0.05 '.' 0.1 ' ' 1
##
## Residual standard error: 7503 on 638 degrees of freedom
## Multiple R-squared:  0.424,  Adjusted R-squared:  0.4203
## F-statistic: 117.4 on 4 and 638 DF,  p-value: < 2.2e-16
```

Activity 19: Classifying Room Types

Solution:

1. Attach the **groupdata2**, **cvms**, **caret**, **randomForest**, **rPref**, and **doParallel** packages:

```
library(groupdata2)
library(cvms)
library(caret)
library(randomForest)
library(rPref)
library(doParallel)
```

2. Set the random seed to 3:

```
set.seed(3)
```

3. Load the **amsterdam.listings** dataset from https://github.com/TrainingByPackt/Practical-Machine-Learning-with-R/blob/master/Data/amsterdam.listings.csv:

```
# Load the amsterdam.listings dataset
full_data <- read.csv("amsterdam.listings.csv")
```

4. Convert the **id** and **neighbourhood** columns to factors:

```
full_data$id <- factor(full_data$id)
full_data$neighbourhood <- factor(full_data$neighbourhood)
```

5. Summarize the dataset:

```
summary(full_data)
```

The summary of data is as follows:

```
##        id                         neighbourhood          room_type
##   2818    :    1    De Baarsjes - Oud-West :3052    Entire home/apt:13724
##   20168   :    1    De Pijp - Rivierenbuurt:2166    Private room    : 3594
##   25428   :    1    Centrum-West           :2019
##   27886   :    1    Centrum-Oost           :1498
##   28658   :    1    Westerpark             :1315
##   28871   :    1    Zuid                   :1187
##   (Other):17312    (Other)                 :6081
##   availability_365    log_price      log_minimum_nights log_number_of_
reviews
##   Min.   :  0.00    Min.   :2.079    Min.   :0.0000      Min.   :0.000
##   1st Qu.:  0.00    1st Qu.:4.595    1st Qu.:0.6931      1st Qu.:1.386
##   Median :  0.00    Median :4.852    Median :0.6931      Median :2.398
##   Mean   : 48.33    Mean   :4.883    Mean   :0.8867      Mean   :2.370
```

```
## 3rd Qu.: 49.00    3rd Qu.:5.165    3rd Qu.:1.0986    3rd Qu.:3.219
## Max.    :365.00    Max.    :7.237   Max.    :4.7875   Max.    :6.196
##
## log_reviews_per_month
## Min.    :-4.60517
## 1st Qu.:-1.42712
## Median :-0.61619
## Mean    :-0.67858
## 3rd Qu.: 0.07696
## Max.    : 2.48907
##
```

6. Partition the dataset into a training set (80%) and a validation set (20%). Balance the partitions by **room_type**:

```
partitions <- partition(full_data, p = 0.8,
                         cat_col = "room_type")
train_set <- partitions[[1]]
valid_set <- partitions[[2]]
```

7. Prepare for running the baseline evaluations and the cross-validations in parallel by registering the number of cores for **doParallel**:

```
# Register four CPU cores
registerDoParallel(4)
```

8. Create the baseline evaluation for the task on the validation set with the baseline() function from **cvms**. Run 100 evaluations in parallel. Specify the dependent column as **room_type**. Note that the default positive class is Private room:

```
room_type_baselines <- baseline(test_data = valid_set,
                                dependent_col = "room_type",
                                n = 100,
                                family = "binomial",
                                parallel = TRUE)
# Inspect summarized metrics
room_type_baselines$summarized_metrics
```

The output is as follows:

```
## # A tibble: 10 x 15
##     Measure 'Balanced Accur…      F1 Sensitivity Specificity
##     <chr>           <dbl>    <dbl>      <dbl>        <dbl>
## 1 Mean            0.502   0.295      0.503        0.500
## 2 Median          0.502   0.294      0.502        0.500
## 3 SD              0.0101  0.00954    0.0184       0.00924
## 4 IQR             0.0154  0.0131     0.0226       0.0122
## 5 Max             0.525   0.317      0.551        0.522
## 6 Min             0.480   0.275      0.463        0.480
## 7 NAs             0       0          0            0
## 8 INFs            0       0          0            0
## 9 All_0           0.5     NA         0            1
## 10 All_1          0.5     0.344      1            0
## # … with 10 more variables: 'Pos Pred Value' <dbl>, 'Neg Pred
## #   Value' <dbl>, AUC <dbl>, 'Lower CI' <dbl>, 'Upper CI' <dbl>,
## #   Kappa <dbl>, MCC <dbl>, 'Detection Rate' <dbl>, 'Detection
## #   Prevalence' <dbl>, Prevalence <dbl>
```

9. Fit multiple logistic regression models on the training set with the **glm()** function, predicting **room_type**. Try different predictors. View the **summary()** of each fitted model and try to interpret the estimated coefficients. Observe how the interpretations change when you add or subtract predictors:

```
logit_model_1 <- glm("room_type ~ log_number_of_reviews",
                data = train_set, family="binomial")
summary(logit_model_1)
```

The summary of the model is as follows:

```
## ## Call:
## glm(formula = "room_type ~ log_number_of_reviews", family = "binomial",
##      data = train_set)
##
## ## Deviance Residuals:
##      Min       1Q   Median       3Q      Max
## -1.3030  -0.7171  -0.5668  -0.3708   2.3288
##
## ## Coefficients:
##                          Estimate Std. Error z value Pr(>|z|)
## (Intercept)              -2.64285    0.05374  -49.18   <2e-16 ***
## log_number_of_reviews     0.49976    0.01745   28.64   <2e-16 ***
## ---
```

```
## Signif. codes:  0 '***' 0.001 '**' 0.01 '*' 0.05 '.' 0.1 ' ' 1
##
## (Dispersion parameter for binomial family taken to be 1)
##
##       Null deviance: 14149  on 13853  degrees of freedom
## Residual deviance: 13249  on 13852  degrees of freedom
## AIC: 13253
##
## Number of Fisher Scoring iterations: 4
```

10. Add **availability_365** as a predictor:

```
logit_model_2 <- glm(
    "room_type ~ availability_365 + log_number_of_reviews",
    data = train_set, family = "binomial")
summary(logit_model_2)
```

The summary of the model is as follows:

```
##
## Call:
## glm(formula = "room_type ~ availability_365 + log_number_of_reviews",
##      family = "binomial", data = train_set)
##
## Deviance Residuals:
##     Min      1Q  Median      3Q     Max
## -1.5277  -0.6735  -0.5535  -0.3688  2.3365
##
## Coefficients:
##                         Estimate Std. Error z value Pr(>|z|)
## (Intercept)           -2.6622105  0.0533345  -49.91   <2e-16 ***
## availability_365       0.0039866  0.0002196   18.16   <2e-16 ***
## log_number_of_reviews  0.4172148  0.0178015   23.44   <2e-16 ***
## ---
## Signif. codes:  0 '***' 0.001 '**' 0.01 '*' 0.05 '.' 0.1 ' ' 1
##
## (Dispersion parameter for binomial family taken to be 1)
##
##       Null deviance: 14149  on 13853  degrees of freedom
## Residual deviance: 12935  on 13851  degrees of freedom
## AIC: 12941
##
## Number of Fisher Scoring iterations: 4
```

11. Add **log_price** as a predictor:

```
logit_model_3 <- glm(
    "room_type ~ availability_365 + log_number_of_reviews + log_price",
    data = train_set, family = "binomial")
summary(logit_model_3)
```

The summary of the model is as follows:

```
##
## Call:
## glm(formula = "room_type ~ availability_365 + log_number_of_reviews +
log_price",
##      family = "binomial", data = train_set)
##
## Deviance Residuals:
##     Min      1Q   Median      3Q      Max
## -3.7678  -0.5805  -0.3395  -0.1208   3.9864
##
## Coefficients:
##                          Estimate Std. Error z value Pr(>|z|)
## (Intercept)             12.6730455  0.3419771   37.06   <2e-16 ***
## availability_365         0.0081215  0.0002865   28.34   <2e-16 ***
## log_number_of_reviews    0.3613055  0.0199845   18.08   <2e-16 ***
## log_price               -3.2539506  0.0745417  -43.65   <2e-16 ***
## ---
## Signif. codes:  0 '***' 0.001 '**' 0.01 '*' 0.05 '.' 0.1 ' ' 1
##
## (Dispersion parameter for binomial family taken to be 1)
##
##     Null deviance: 14149.2  on 13853  degrees of freedom
## Residual deviance:  9984.7  on 13850  degrees of freedom
## AIC: 9992.7
##
## Number of Fisher Scoring iterations: 6
```

12. Add **log_minimum_nights** as a predictor:

```
logit_model_4 <- glm(
    "room_type ~ availability_365 + log_number_of_reviews + log_price +
log_minimum_nights",
        data = train_set, family = "binomial")
summary(logit_model_4)
```

The summary of the model is as follows:

```
##
## Call:
## glm(formula = "room_type ~ availability_365 + log_number_of_reviews +
log_price + log_minimum_nights",
##      family = "binomial", data = train_set)
##
## Deviance Residuals:
##     Min       1Q    Median       3Q      Max
## -3.6268  -0.5520  -0.3142  -0.1055   4.6062
##
## Coefficients:
##                        Estimate Std. Error z value Pr(>|z|)
## (Intercept)            13.470868   0.354695   37.98   <2e-16 ***
## availability_365        0.008310   0.000295   28.17   <2e-16 ***
## log_number_of_reviews   0.360133   0.020422   17.64   <2e-16 ***
## log_price              -3.252957   0.076343  -42.61   <2e-16 ***
## log_minimum_nights     -1.007354   0.051131  -19.70   <2e-16 ***
## ---
## Signif. codes:  0 '***' 0.001 '**' 0.01 '*' 0.05 '.' 0.1 ' ' 1
##
## (Dispersion parameter for binomial family taken to be 1)
##
##     Null deviance: 14149.2  on 13853  degrees of freedom
## Residual deviance:  9543.9  on 13849  degrees of freedom
## AIC: 9553.9
##
## Number of Fisher Scoring iterations: 6
```

13. Replace **log_number_of_reviews** with **log_reviews_per_month**:

```
logit_model_5 <- glm(
    "room_type ~ availability_365 + log_reviews_per_month + log_price +
log_minimum_nights",
    data = train_set, family = "binomial")
summary(logit_model_5)
```

The summary of the model is as follows:

```
## 
## Call:
## glm(formula = "room_type ~ availability_365 + log_reviews_per_month +
## log_price + log_minimum_nights",
##       family = "binomial", data = train_set)
## 
## Deviance Residuals:
##     Min      1Q   Median      3Q      Max
## -3.7351  -0.5229  -0.2934  -0.0968   4.7252
## 
## Coefficients:
##                          Estimate Std. Error z value Pr(>|z|)
## (Intercept)             14.7495851  0.3652303   40.38   <2e-16 ***
## availability_365         0.0074308  0.0003019   24.61   <2e-16 ***
## log_reviews_per_month    0.6364218  0.0246423   25.83   <2e-16 ***
## log_price               -3.2850702  0.0781567  -42.03   <2e-16 ***
## log_minimum_nights      -0.8504701  0.0526379  -16.16   <2e-16 ***
## ---
## Signif. codes:  0 '***' 0.001 '**' 0.01 '*' 0.05 '.' 0.1 ' ' 1
## 
## (Dispersion parameter for binomial family taken to be 1)
## 
##     Null deviance: 14149  on 13853  degrees of freedom
## Residual deviance:  9103  on 13849  degrees of freedom
## AIC: 9113
## 
## Number of Fisher Scoring iterations: 6
```

14. Create model formulas with **combine_predictors()**. To save time, limit the interaction size to 2 by specifying **max_interaction_size = 2**, and limit the number of times an effect can be included in a formula to 1 by specifying **max_effect_frequency = 1**:

```
model_formulas <- combine_predictors(
    dependent = "room_type",
    fixed_effects = c("log_minimum_nights",
                      "log_number_of_reviews",
                      "log_price",
```

```
                    "availability_365",
                    "log_reviews_per_month"),
        max_interaction_size = 2,
        max_effect_frequency = 1)
  head(model_formulas, 10)
```

The output is as follows:

```
##  [1] "room_type ~ availability_365"
##  [2] "room_type ~ log_minimum_nights"
##  [3] "room_type ~ log_number_of_reviews"
##  [4] "room_type ~ log_price"
##  [5] "room_type ~ log_reviews_per_month"
##  [6] "room_type ~ availability_365 * log_minimum_nights"
##  [7] "room_type ~ availability_365 * log_number_of_reviews"
##  [8] "room_type ~ availability_365 * log_price"
##  [9] "room_type ~ availability_365 * log_reviews_per_month"
## [10] "room_type ~ availability_365 + log_minimum_nights"
```

15. Create fivefold columns with five folds each in the training set, using **fold()** with **k = 5** and **num_fold_cols = 5**. Balance the folds by **room_type**. Feel free to choose a higher number of fold columns:

```
train_set <- fold(train_set, k = 5,
                  num_fold_cols = 5,
                  cat_col = "room_type")
```

16. Perform cross-validation (not repeated) on your model formulas with **cvms**. Specify **fold_cols = ".folds_1"**. Order the results by **F1** and show the best 10 models:

```
initial_cv_results <- cross_validate(
    train_set,
    models = model_formulas,
    fold_cols = ".folds_1",
    family = "binomial",
    parallel = TRUE)
initial_cv_results <- initial_cv_results[
    order(initial_cv_results$F1, decreasing = TRUE),]
head(initial_cv_results, 10)
```

The output is as follows:

```
## # A tibble: 10 x 26
##    'Balanced Accur…    F1 Sensitivity Specificity 'Pos Pred Value'
##              <dbl> <dbl>     <dbl>       <dbl>           <dbl>
## 1          0.764 0.662     0.567       0.962           0.797
## 2          0.764 0.662     0.565       0.963           0.798
## 3          0.763 0.662     0.563       0.963           0.801
## 4          0.763 0.661     0.563       0.963           0.800
## 5          0.761 0.654     0.564       0.958           0.778
## 6          0.757 0.653     0.549       0.966           0.807
## 7          0.757 0.652     0.549       0.965           0.804
## 8          0.758 0.649     0.560       0.957           0.774
## 9          0.756 0.649     0.550       0.962           0.792
## 10         0.758 0.649     0.559       0.957           0.775
## # … with 21 more variables: 'Neg Pred Value' <dbl>, AUC <dbl>, 'Lower
## #   CI' <dbl>, 'Upper CI' <dbl>, Kappa <dbl>, MCC <dbl>, 'Detection
## #   Rate' <dbl>, 'Detection Prevalence' <dbl>, Prevalence <dbl>,
## #   Predictions <list>, ROC <list>, 'Confusion Matrix' <list>,
## #   Coefficients <list>, Folds <int>, 'Fold Columns' <int>, 'Convergence
## #   Warnings' <dbl>, 'Singular Fit Messages' <int>, Family <chr>,
## #   Link <chr>, Dependent <chr>, Fixed <chr>
```

17. Perform repeated cross-validation on the 10-20 best model formulas (by F1) with **cvms**:

```
# Reconstruct the best 20 models' formulas
reconstructed_formulas <- reconstruct_formulas(
    initial_cv_results,
    topn = 20)

# Create fold_cols
fold_cols <- paste0(".folds_", 1:5)

# Perform repeated cross-validation
repeated_cv_results <- cross_validate(
    train_set,
    models = model_formulas,
    fold_cols = fold_cols,
    family = "binomial",
    parallel = TRUE)
```

```
# Order by F1
repeated_cv_results <- repeated_cv_results[
    order(repeated_cv_results$F1, decreasing = TRUE),]

# Inspect the 10 best modelsresults
head(repeated_cv_results)
```

The output is as follows:

```
## # A tibble: 6 x 27
##    'Balanced Accur…    F1 Sensitivity Specificity 'Pos Pred Value'
##              <dbl> <dbl>       <dbl>       <dbl>            <dbl>
## 1            0.764 0.662       0.566       0.962            0.796
## 2            0.763 0.661       0.564       0.963            0.798
## 3            0.763 0.660       0.562       0.963            0.800
## 4            0.762 0.659       0.561       0.963            0.800
## 5            0.761 0.654       0.563       0.958            0.780
## 6            0.758 0.654       0.551       0.965            0.805
## # … with 22 more variables: 'Neg Pred Value' <dbl>, AUC <dbl>, 'Lower
## #   CI' <dbl>, 'Upper CI' <dbl>, Kappa <dbl>, MCC <dbl>, 'Detection
## #   Rate' <dbl>, 'Detection Prevalence' <dbl>, Prevalence <dbl>,
## #   Predictions <list>, ROC <list>, 'Confusion Matrix' <list>,
## #   Coefficients <list>, Results <list>, Folds <int>, 'Fold
## #   Columns' <int>, 'Convergence Warnings' <dbl>, 'Singular Fit
## #   Messages' <int>, Family <chr>, Link <chr>, Dependent <chr>,
## #   Fixed <chr>
```

18. Find the Pareto front based on the F1 and balanced accuracy scores. Use **psel()** from the **rPref** package and specify **pref = high("F1") * high("`Balanced Accuracy`")**. Note the ticks around `Balanced Accuracy`:

```
# Find the Pareto front
front <- psel(repeated_cv_results,
              pref = high("F1") * high("`Balanced Accuracy`"))
# Remove rows with NA in F1 or Balanced Accuracy
front <- front[complete.cases(front[1:2]), ]
# Inspect front
front
```

The output is as follows:

```
## # A tibble: 1 x 27
##    'Balanced Accur…    F1 Sensitivity Specificity 'Pos Pred Value'
##               <dbl> <dbl>      <dbl>       <dbl>             <dbl>
## 1         0.764 0.662      0.566       0.962             0.796
## # … with 22 more variables: 'Neg Pred Value' <dbl>, AUC <dbl>, 'Lower
## #   CI' <dbl>, 'Upper CI' <dbl>, Kappa <dbl>, MCC <dbl>, 'Detection
## #   Rate' <dbl>, 'Detection Prevalence' <dbl>, Prevalence <dbl>,
## #   Predictions <list>, ROC <list>, 'Confusion Matrix' <list>,
## #   Coefficients <list>, Results <list>, Folds <int>, 'Fold
## #   Columns' <int>, 'Convergence Warnings' <dbl>, 'Singular Fit
## #   Messages' <int>, Family <chr>, Link <chr>, Dependent <chr>,
## #   Fixed <chr>
```

The best model according to F_1 is also the best model by balanced accuracy, so the Pareto front only contains one model.

19. Plot the Pareto front with the **ggplot2** code from *Exercise 61, Plotting the Pareto Front*. Note that you may need to add ticks around 'Balanced Accuracy' when specifying **x** or **y** in **aes()** in the **ggplot** call:

```
# Create ggplot object
# with precision on the x-axis and precision on the y-axis
ggplot(repeated_cv_results, aes(x = F1, y = 'Balanced Accuracy')) +

  # Add the models as points
  geom_point(shape = 1, size = 0.5) +

  # Add the nondominated models as larger points
  geom_point(data = front, size = 3) +

  # Add a line to visualize the pareto front
  geom_step(data = front, direction = "vh") +

  # Add the light theme
  theme_light()
```

The output is similar to the following:

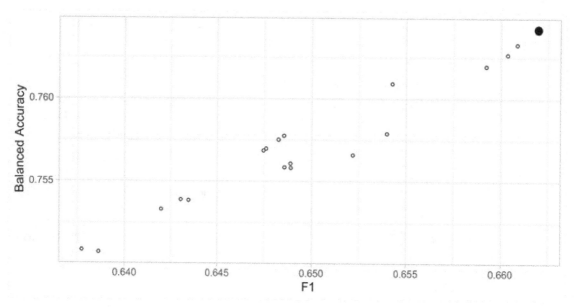

Figure 5.31: Pareto front with the F1 and balanced accuracy scores

20. Use **validate()** to train the nondominated models on the training set and evaluate them on the validation set:

```
# Reconstruct the formulas for the front models
reconstructed_formulas <- reconstruct_formulas(front)
# Validate the models in the Pareto front
v_results_list <- validate(train_data = train_set,
                           test_data = valid_set,
                           models = reconstructed_formulas,
                           family = "binomial")
# Assign the results and model(s) to variable names
v_results <- v_results_list$Results
v_model <- v_results_list$Models[[1]]
v_results
```

The output is as follows:

```
## # A tibble: 1 x 24
##    'Balanced Accur…    F1 Sensitivity Specificity 'Pos Pred Value'
##                 <dbl> <dbl>      <dbl>       <dbl>          <dbl>
## 1             0.758 0.652      0.554       0.962          0.794
## # … with 19 more variables: 'Neg Pred Value' <dbl>, AUC <dbl>, 'Lower
## #   CI' <dbl>, 'Upper CI' <dbl>, Kappa <dbl>, MCC <dbl>, 'Detection
## #   Rate' <dbl>, 'Detection Prevalence' <dbl>, Prevalence <dbl>,
## #   Predictions <list>, ROC <list>, 'Confusion Matrix' <list>,
## #   Coefficients <list>, 'Convergence Warnings' <dbl>, 'Singular Fit
## #   Messages' <dbl>, Family <chr>, Link <chr>, Dependent <chr>,
## #   Fixed <chr>
```

These results are a lot better than the baseline on both F1 and balanced accuracy.

21. View the summaries of the nondominated model(s):

```
summary(v_model)
```

The summary of the model is as follows:

```
##
## Call:
## glm(formula = model_formula, family = binomial(link = link),
##     data = train_set)
##
## Deviance Residuals:
##     Min       1Q   Median       3Q      Max
## -3.8323  -0.4836  -0.2724  -0.0919   3.9091
##
## Coefficients:
##                    Estimate Std. Error z value  Pr(>|z|)
## (Intercept)      15.3685268  0.4511978  34.062   < 2e-16 ***
## availability_365 -0.0140209  0.0030623  -4.579  4.68e-06 ***
## log_price        -3.4441520  0.0956189 -36.020   < 2e-16 ***
## log_minimum_nights -0.7163252 0.0535452 -13.378   < 2e-16 ***
```

```
## log_number_of_reviews        -0.0823821  0.0282115  -2.920   0.0035 **
## log_reviews_per_month         0.0733808  0.0381629   1.923   0.0545 .
## availability_365:log_price    0.0042772  0.0006207   6.891 5.53e-12 ***
## log_n_o_reviews:log_r_p_month 0.3730603  0.0158122  23.593 < 2e-16 ***
## ---
## Signif. codes:  0 '***' 0.001 '**' 0.01 '*' 0.05 '.' 0.1 ' ' 1
##
## (Dispersion parameter for binomial family taken to be 1)
##
##      Null deviance: 14149.2  on 13853  degrees of freedom
## Residual deviance:  8476.7  on 13846  degrees of freedom
## AIC: 8492.7
##
## Number of Fisher Scoring iterations: 6
```

Note, that we have shortened `log_number_of_reviews` and `log_reviews_per_month` in the interaction term, `log_n_o_reviews:log_r_p_month`. The coefficients for the two interaction terms are both statistically significant. The interaction term `log_n_o_reviews:log_r_p_month` tells us that when `log_number_of_reviews` increases by one unit, the coefficient for `log_reviews_per_month` increases by 0.37, and vice versa. We might question the meaningfulness of including both these predictors in the model, as they have some of the same information. If we also had the number of months the listing had been listed, we should be able to recreate `log_number_of_reviews` from `log_reviews_per_month` and the number of months, which would probably be easier to interpret as well.

The second interaction term, `availability_365:log_price`, tells us that when `availability_365` increases by a single unit, the coefficient for `log_price` increases by 0.004, and vice versa. The coefficient estimate for `log_price` is -3.44, meaning that when `availability_365` is low, a higher `log_price` decreases the probability that the listing is a private room. This fits with the intuition that a private room is usually cheaper than an entire home/apartment.

The coefficient for `log_minimum_nights` tells us that when there is a higher minimum requirement for the number of nights when we book the listing, there's a lower probability that the listing is a private room.

Chapter 6: Unsupervised Learning

Activity 20: Perform DIANA, AGNES, and k-means on the Built-In Motor Car Dataset

Solution:

1. Attach the cluster and factoextra packages:

   ```
   library(cluster)
   library(factoextra)
   ```

2. Load the dataset:

   ```
   df <- read.csv("mtcars.csv")
   ```

3. Set the row names to the values of the X column (the state names). Remove the X column afterward:

   ```
   rownames(df) <- df$X
   df$X <- NULL
   ```

   > **Note**
   >
   > The row names (states) become a column, X, when you save it as a CSV file. So, we need to change it back, as the row names are used in the plot in step 7.

4. Remove those rows with missing data and standardize the dataset:

   ```
   df <- na.omit(df)
   df <- scale(df)
   ```

5. Implement divisive hierarchical clustering using DIANA. For easy comparison, document the dendrogram output. Feel free to experiment with different distance metrics:

   ```
   dv <- diana(df,metric = "manhattan", stand = TRUE)
   plot(dv)
   ```

The output is as follows:

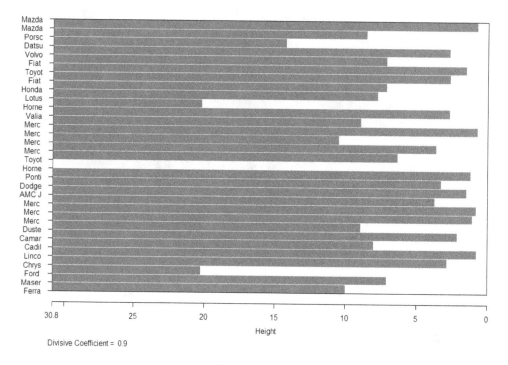

Figure 6.41: Banner from diana()

The next plot is as follows:

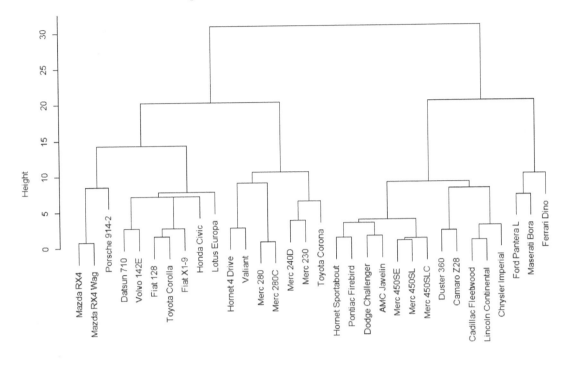

Figure 6.42: Dendrogram from diana()

6. Implement bottom-up hierarchical clustering using AGNES. Take note of the dendrogram created for comparison purposes later on:

```
agn <- agnes(df)
pltree(agn)
```

The output is as follows:

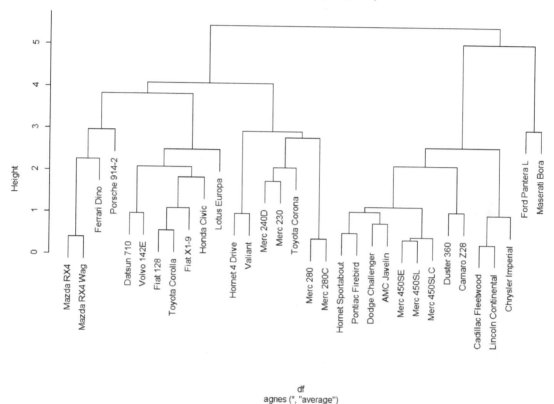

Figure 6.43: Dendrogram from agnes()

7. Implement k-means clustering. Use the elbow method to determine the optimal number of clusters:

```
fviz_nbclust(mtcars, kmeans, method = "wss") +
    geom_vline(xintercept = 4, linetype = 2) +
    labs(subtitle = "Elbow method")
```

The output is as follows:

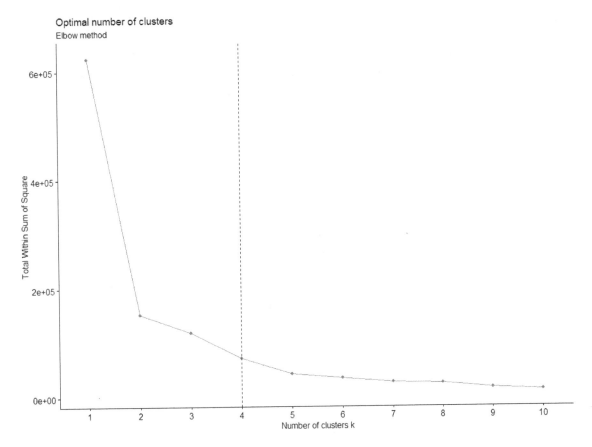

Figure 6.44: Optimal clusters using the elbow method

8. Perform k-means clustering with four clusters:

```
k4 <- kmeans(df, centers = 4, nstart = 20)
fviz_cluster(k4, data = df)
```

The output is as follows:

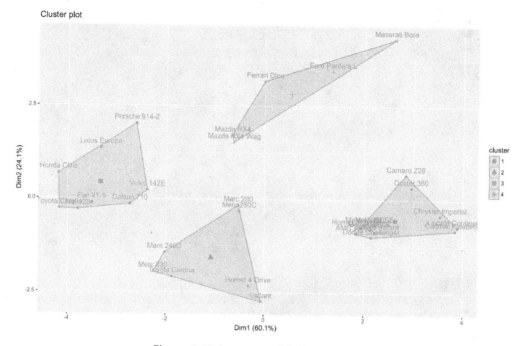

Figure 6.45: k-means with four clusters

9. Compare the clusters, starting with the smallest one. The following are your expected results for DIANA, AGNES, and k-means, respectively:

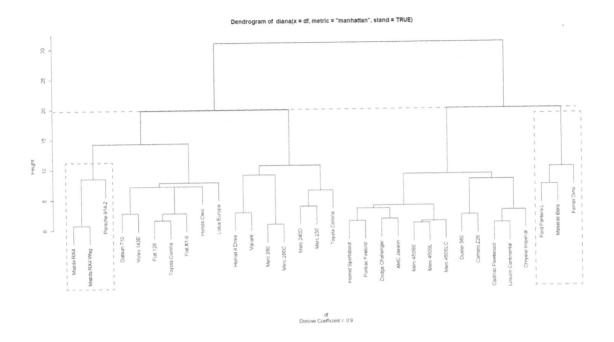

Figure 6.46: Dendrogram from running DIANA, cut at 20

If we consider cutting the DIANA tree at height 20, the Ferrari is clustered together with the Ford and the Maserati (the smallest cluster):

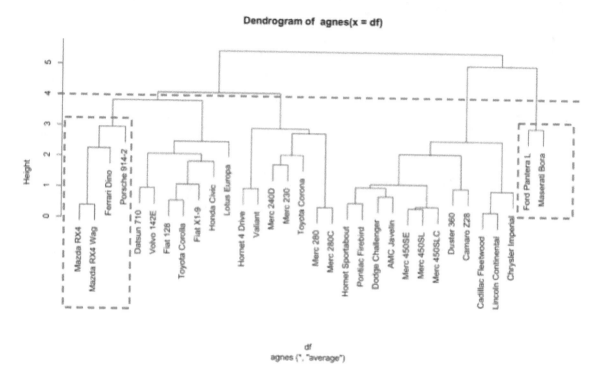

Figure 6.47: Dendrogram from agnes, cut at 4

Meanwhile, cutting the AGNES dendrogram at height 4 results in the Ferrari being clustered with the Mazda RX4, the Mazda RX4 Wag, and the Porsche. k-means clusters the Ferrari with the Mazdas, the Ford, and the Maserati.

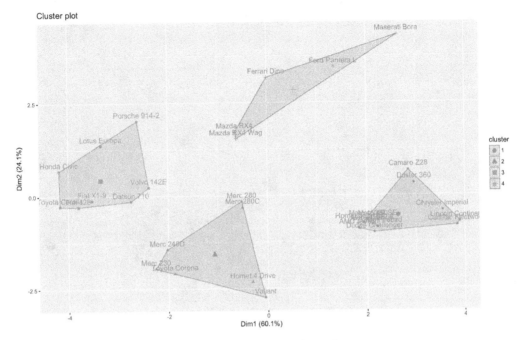

Figure 6.48: kmeans clustering

Clearly, the choice of clustering technique and algorithms results in different clusters being created. It is important to apply some domain knowledge to determine the most valuable end results.

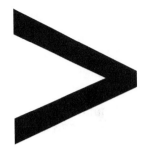

Index

About

All major keywords used in this book are captured alphabetically in this section. Each one is accompanied by the page number of where they appear.

CPSIA information can be obtained
at www.ICGtesting.com
Printed in the USA
FSHW020245130920
73586FS